To Tom&
Towards one
...

A GLOBAL PARLIAMENT

Principles of World Federation

CHRISTOPHER HAMER

Published and distributed by
Oyster Bay Books
PO Box 64
Oyster Bay NSW 2225
Australia
http://www.ozemail.com.au/~obbooks

Cover illustration: view of the Clock Tower of the Palce of Westminster
from *The Houses of Parliament*, by Sir Bryan Fell and K.R. Mackenzie,
14th ed (Her Majesty's Stationery Office, London, 1988)

ISBN 0 646 35530 9

Printed in Australia by Fast Books
(a division of Wild & Woolley Pty Ltd)
16 Darghan Street
Glebe NSW 2037
http://www.fastbooks.com.au

For Phillip and Rowena

Contents

Preface

World federation is a large and fascinating topic: but how does a theoretical physicist come to be writing about it?

Physicists are quite used to discussing large and hypothetical concepts, as a matter of fact. They will happily speculate on what happened during the first three minutes of the Universe, for instance. More to the point, many of them have felt a special sense of responsibility for the problem of nuclear weapons, ever since the Trinity test at Alamogordo and the dropping of atomic bombs on Hiroshima and Nagasaki. This was vividly expressed in a famous statement by Robert Oppenheimer: "In some sort of crude sense which no vulgarity, no humour, no over-statement can quite extinguish, the physicists have known sin; and this is a knowledge which they cannot lose."

After the Second World War had ended, many physicists threw themselves wholeheartedly into the search for peace and disarmament, and for control of the atomic weapons which they had created. World federation was seen as the ultimate answer to this problem, as it still is today. Albert Einstein himself was among the leaders of the movement, and campaigned energetically on these issues until his death. He was supported by other distinguished members of the Emergency Committee of Atomic Scientists, such as Harold Urey, Hans Bethe, Philip Morse, Linus Pauling, Leo Szilard and Victor Weisskopf. The scientists' campaign against nuclear weapons was continued in later years through the Pugwash Committee, whose work was recognized by the award of the 1995 Nobel Peace Prize to Joseph Rotblat. Other physicists to write on the issues of peace and world federation have included the 'father of the Soviet H-bomb', Andrei Sakharov, and the great theoretical physicist Freeman Dyson.

These issues form the basis of an interdisciplinary general studies course which I have convened at the University of New South Wales for the last ten years, which is entitled *Nuclear Arms and the New World Order*. The course is taken by students from all disciplines, and is taught jointly by the Schools of Physics and Political Science. This book is an outgrowth of that course, and my hope is that it will make a worthwhile contribution to the debate on these great themes.

Our generation has been lucky enough, or clever enough, to avoid the twin catastrophes of world war and nuclear holocaust. Our responsibility is all the greater, I believe, to continue the struggle towards a better and a safer world, so that our children and our grandchildren will no longer have a nuclear sword of Damocles hanging over their heads, or be slaughtered by millions for the sake of some dubious political cause. The path to this end is clear: it lies in the direction of greater international trust and understanding, more co-operation between nations, and ultimately, in a process which may take decades or centuries to complete, their integration into some sort of loose world federation. The threat of nuclear war has receded somewhat in recent years, but this only means that we should redouble our efforts to eliminate the threat entirely. There are plenty of other global problems looming over us which also demand a co-ordinated global response.

The book is pitched at about the level of our general studies course, and is aimed at the interested man (or woman) in the street, rather than an expert political scientist. It is particularly aimed at members of the peace, social justice, and church-based social movements. It should be useful as a reference in courses on peace studies, or civics courses in schools. It may also be useful as a reference in political science courses on federalism, international relations, or international security, although of course I am not a professional political scientist. There is a considerable amount of background material in Chapters 2 to 4, covering the history of the world federalist movement, the nuclear arms race, the United Nations, and the European Union. Some readers may not be interested in these details, and may feel inclined to skip to the conclusions of these chapters. Others, I hope, may find the material interesting and informative.

I would like to thank those members of the University who have helped in teaching our Nuclear Arms course over the years: Tony Palfreeman, Richard Lucy, David Neilson, Michael Box, John Smith, Joe Wolfe, Gail Box, Michael Burton and Mary Cawte. The comments and discussions of the many students who have taken the course have been very useful. A surprisingly large number of them seem to accept that a world federation is likely, even within their own lifetimes, but only about a third of them seem convinced that this is a good thing! Much of the book was written while I was on study leave in the pleasant surroundings of the Peace Research Centre at the University of Sydney: I would like to thank Prof. Jaan Oitmaa and the University of NSW for granting me this opportunity, and Dr. Keith Suter and Prof. Stuart Rees for their hospitality at the Centre. I am very grateful to Lynda-ann Blanchard, Wendy Lambourne, Michael Morison, Jeanne Leppard and other members of the Centre for their help and companionship during my stay. Most especially, I owe especial thanks to Stuart Rees and Tony Palfreeman for their invaluable help and advice, and for reading and commenting on the manuscript. Stuart did his best to improve my stuttering English, while Tony Palfreeman added the perspective of a political scientist, and demanded clearer definitions of terms like "federation'" and "integration". For the most part, I have preferred the philosophy of the Red Queen. Last but not least, I would like to thank my wife and family for their patience and forbearance while the book was being written.

A GLOBAL PARLIAMENT

Principles of World Federation

Introduction

Everybody knows that the world has become a "global village", in the famous phrase of Marshall McLuhan. We all have to live together and work together on one small planet Earth, which seems to grow smaller and more fragile with every passing year. What we need now is a properly constituted 'village council', to deal with the global problems that confront all of us in common, and to move us towards a safer and more prosperous future. That is the argument for world federation in a nutshell, and the basic premise of this book. The present United Nations is clearly inadequate for the task.

The book begins with an outline of some of the reasons why we need such a village council. First is the problem of nuclear weapons. In order to abolish them, we must be able to guarantee the security of each nation without them. We need to construct a universal system of common security based upon international law, which can settle international disputes without recourse to weapons:- or again, a world federation. William Penn recognized the principle in 1692: *"Peace is maintained by Justice, which is a Fruit of Government as Government is from Society, and Society from Consent"*. The greenhouse effect and other massive environmental problems also require a global approach. A world federation would help to promote free trade and economic development around the world. It would act to combat starvation, poverty and disease in Third World regions. It would co-ordinate global programs of research and development in areas of science and technology such as space exploration and astronomy, particle physics, and the human genome. As H.G. Wells once foretold, it would open a whole new era of hope and progress for humanity.

The next three chapters provide some background material, which is important for a thorough understanding of the topic. Chapter 2 consists of some brief historical excerpts. The concept of world citizenship or the global village goes back at least to Ancient Greece: *"I am not an Athenian, or a Greek, but a citizen of the world"*, said Socrates. Schemes for European or world federation are traced from Pierre Dubois in 1306 through the Duc de Sully, William Penn, the Abbé de St. Pierre, Rousseau, Kant and others. The growth of international organizations from Waterloo up to the League of Nations is briefly described. We recall the astonishing rise of the world federalist movement after World War II, driven by the fear of atomic weapons; and its equally sudden collapse in the anti-Communist hysteria of the Korean War. The nuclear arms race that followed, and the long siege of the Cold War which ended so suddenly after the advent of Mikhail Gorbachev, are summarized. Chapter 2 closes with a brief account of some specific proposals for world federation since the Second World War.

Chapter 3 is a discussion of the world security organization we have at present, in the United Nations. Its foundation at the end of World War II is recalled, and its structure is outlined very briefly: in essence it is an alliance of the Great Powers to keep the peace, following the pattern of the Concert of Europe and the League of Nations. The UN can pride itself on some remarkable achievements over the years, but it is basically far too weak to be effective. Its shortcomings are analyzed, and a brief description is given of the many attempts to reform it. So far, no significant constitutional reform has ever been achieved.

We turn in chapter 4 to the remarkable example provided by the European Union. Whereas the movement for world federation has failed up till now, the European federalists have had remarkable success in their efforts. The initiatives of Jean Monnet, Paul-Henri Spaak and others are described, which led successively to the foundation of the European Coal and Steel Community, the Common Market, and finally the European Union. The integration of Europe still has a long way to go, but already some sort of federation has emerged, making another war between the nations of Western Europe virtually inconceivable. Some important lessons can be extracted from the European experience.

Many people have given detailed structural blueprints of a possible world federation; but such details can really be settled only by the delegates who are eventually gathered at the founding convention. A more useful exercise, it seems to me, is to try and formulate some broad general principles which could form the basis for such a federation. For the most part, these have already been recognized and adopted by the European Union, and to a lesser extent by the United Nations. Democracy and the rule of law would be automatic selections as guiding principles along with a basic conception of human rights; and the evolution of the European Union has thrown up some further important ideas such as 'subsidiarity', 'solidarity' and 'flexibility', which should also be widely acceptable. Taken together, these principles give an overall guide to the division of rights and responsibilities between the federation, the member states, and the individual citizens. The rights and freedoms of the citizen would be protected by the principles of democracy and human rights, while the domestic sovereignty of the member nations would be protected by the principle of subsidiarity.

A vital objective of world federation, almost by definition, would be the achievement of 'universality': that is, the federation should include all of the nations upon earth. At the present time, however, the principles of democracy and universality are not mutually compatible, for the simple reason that not all the nations upon earth are democratic. This is a dilemma that has long bedevilled the world federalist movement. Some arguments are given why any prospective world federation should be restricted, in the first instance, to democratic states alone. While universality may be taken as the ultimate aim, it should not be taken as a *sine qua non* right from the outset.

Chapter 6 examines some of the classic problems and objections faced by proponents of world federalism. These include the reluctance of nation-states to surrender their sovereignty, and the lack of common values between different nations. There is the problem of how international law is to be enforced; and the fear that diverse national cultures will be submerged and lost. Finally, there is the widespread fear (which we shall argue has little rational justification) that a world government would lead to world tyranny. These are the great obstacles to world federation, which have hitherto proved insuperable. Some momentous political changes have occurred over recent years, however, which allow a whole new perspective on the issue. The Soviet Union has collapsed and the Cold War has ended, thus removing the deep divide between East and West which was the single largest barrier to world federation. Another vital development has been the creation of the European Union, which demonstrates that integration between sovereign nations is possible.

The last chapter discusses the question of how a world federation can be established, assuming that we agree it is a good idea. This is called the 'transition' problem. Various options are discussed, such as reform of the United Nations, expansion of the European Union, or the growth of other regional organizations. It seems inevitable that the process will have to be a gradual and evolutionary one, following the European example. The crucial question then is, how do we make a start? One possible avenue could be the formation of a World Peace-Keeping

Association, complementary to the United Nations, made up of the democratic nations of the world. The Association could maintain a standing peace-keeping force to carry out the peace-keeping obligations of its members under the aegis of the UN, and to preserve their individual security; and it should also include a democratic Assembly representative of the member states. It would thus repair two of the most glaring deficiencies of the present United Nations; and it would form a natural basis for wider and deeper integration in the future. A reformed NATO organization could fulfil this role. These possibilities are explored in some detail.

Whether by this avenue or another, there is no reason why the first small steps towards world federation could not be taken quite soon. The dawning of a new millennium would provide the perfect symbolic opportunity: it depends on the vision and foresight of the world's statesmen whether that opportunity is taken or not. In the long run, at any rate, I believe that the formation of some sort of global federation is virtually inevitable.

Chapter 1

The Need for World Federation

For I dipt into the future, far as human eye could see,
Saw a Vision of the world, and all the wonder that would be;

...

Till the war-drum throbb'd no longer, and
the battle-flags were furled
In the Parliament of man, the Federation of the world.
There the common sense of most shall hold
a fretful realm in awe,
And the kindly earth shall slumber, lapt in universal law.

Alfred, Lord Tennyson,
Locksley Hall, 1842

Advancing technology has been the crucial factor in drawing together the global village. Two centuries ago, a traveller might have covered fifty miles in a day in a horse-drawn carriage. Nowadays, he or she can travel half way around the world in the same time by air. Two centuries ago, letters carried by sailing-ship might take a month to get from Europe to America; but now, messages travel at the speed of thought anywhere around the globe, by telephone, fax, or email - provided that the line isn't busy.

The result has been a staggering increase in the volume of international travel and trade. The number of international visitors to France each year is now about the same as the total population. People in the affluent modern world think nothing of going to Bali or Hawaii or the Bermudas for a holiday, or visiting Los Angeles to take their children to Disneyland, or popping over the Channel to do a bit of shopping in London. A man may have his breakfast in New York, and his dinner in Los Angeles, while his luggage sails serenely on, perhaps, to Osaka, Japan. A businessman will routinely fly off to a trade fair in Hamburg or Tokyo, and an academic will attend an international conference in Sicily or Singapore.

At any of these professional conferences or conventions, people from all over the globe meet on an equal footing. Outstanding talent may emerge in men and women of any race or creed. In the field of theoretical physics, for example, the Nobel-Prize winning leaders of the field have included a Jewish-American, Richard Feynman, and a Chinese-American, Chen-Ning Yang, as well as a Pakistani, Abdus Salam, and an Italian, Enrico Fermi. All are united in a single great enterprise, the advancement of human knowledge. All accept the same basic set of principles, and all speak the same jargon, expressed in the universal language called 'broken English'. The same situation holds in other academic or professional fields: medicine, or architecture, or even law.

The increasing speed of travel and communication is drawing people ever closer together into a single worldwide community, the aforesaid global village. At the same time, however, many difficult issues and problems are emerging which affect all of the villagers in common, and which really demand a common approach if they are to be tackled effectively. Hence the need for a 'village council'. Let us examine some of these issues more closely.

Peace and Security

As civilized nations have advanced in knowledge, the weapons of war have progressively become more powerful and more deadly. From bows and arrows to cannons and missiles, and from gunpowder to nuclear warheads, the destructive power available to the military machine has increased to almost unimaginable levels. At the height of the Cold War, the USA and the Soviet Union between them possessed some 50,000 nuclear warheads of various types, with a total explosive capacity equivalent to about four tons of TNT for every person on earth.[1] Considering that on average it took about one ton of TNT to kill somebody in World War II, it became at least a mathematical possibility that a full-scale nuclear war, with the consequent radioactive fallout and nuclear winter, might destroy all human life on earth. It would certainly have been the greatest single disaster ever to befall human civilization. We were faced with the grotesque possibility that a single technician at the touch of a button could literally destroy a city, and incinerate hundreds of thousands of other human beings. The joke has been carried a little too far, and for most reasonable people the idea of war between the superpowers has become unthinkable. As both Mikhail Gorbachev and Ronald Reagan agreed, "nuclear war cannot be won, and must never be fought". The world would be a very much safer place if we could eliminate nuclear weapons entirely.

When Mikhail Gorbachev came to power in the Soviet Union, a new and hopeful era in international relations was begun. The Cold War was ended, and for the first time some nuclear weapons were actually removed or destroyed. Intermediate range missiles have been removed from Europe under the INF Treaty, and under the START Treaties the strategic nuclear forces of the US and the former USSR are due to be cut by a factor of two-thirds by the year 2003. The popular demands for nuclear disarmament have finally had some success.

It must be recognized, however, that this is not the end of the business. We cannot rid ourselves permanently of these weapons simply by throwing them away. As many people have pointed out, the atom bomb cannot be uninvented, and a nation can always build new ones if it wants to. At the present time, there is a continued danger of 'horizontal proliferation'. India and Pakistan have just recently declared themselves openly as possessors of nuclear weapons, and Iraq, Iran and Libya have also attempted to acquire them. There have even been warnings that terrorist organizations might try to get hold of them. To guard against these possibilities, and to ensure their own security, each of the superpowers will feel obliged to keep a 'minimum deterrent' of a few hundred or a few thousand warheads. Even when the START Treaties are fully implemented, the remaining nuclear stockpiles will still amount to one ton of TNT equivalent for every human being on earth; and in times of renewed international tension, these stockpiles could well begin to grow again.

An example of this process was seen between the two World Wars. People were so sickened by the slaughter in the trenches of the First World War that they determined to "end war forever". Some major disarmament agreements were signed, including the Washington Naval Agreement of 1922, which actually provided for the destruction of new battleships being completed on the slipways. Yet when Hitler rose to power in Germany, and the nations of Europe felt themselves under threat, they rushed to rearm once more. Thus disarmament is not by itself the answer to our problem, although it is a step in the right direction.

So how *can* we rid ourselves, once and for all, of the menace of nuclear arms? The answer to this question is the same for nuclear weapons as it is for any other sort of weapon, and has been known for centuries. The argument runs as follows.

First one must ask, why do nations feel a *need* for these weapons? Why do they spend something approaching one trillion dollars annually on armaments?[2] This money is not spent frivolously or for no good reason. The first duty of any government is to provide for the *security* of the nation. Each country therefore feels obliged to purchase weapons and maintain its armed forces at a prudent level, in case some threat of war or some dispute should arise with another country.

To get rid of these weapons, one must first be able to guarantee the security of each nation without them. In other words, it must be *guaranteed* that if a dispute should arise between two or more nations, for any reason whatever, then it can be settled by peaceful means, without the use of weapons. Only then will the nations feel safe enough to lay down their arms.

How can peaceful settlements be achieved in international disputes? Mechanisms are needed to provide conciliation and mediation services between the parties, in an attempt to bring them to an agreement amongst themselves. At the present time, such services are usually provided on an *ad hoc* basis, by a roving American Secretary of State for example. Henry Kissinger shuttled back and forth in an attempt to broker a peace deal between Israel and Egypt, and in 1997-1998 the U.S. negotiator Dennis Ross tried to keep the peace process alive between the Israelis and the Palestinians. In the last resort, however, if all mediation attempts fail and the protagonists still cannot reach an agreement, then a peaceful settlement can only be guaranteed by a process of *adjudication.* That is, some impartial court or tribunal must be set up which can judge between the nations in dispute, make a binding decision on the issue in question, and impose a peaceful settlement.

Hence one is led inevitably to postulate a complete framework of *international law.* A tribunal or *court* is needed, as outlined above, to arbitrate between nations in dispute; but the decisions of the court cannot be made in a vacuum, or at the whim of the tribunal members. They must be based upon an agreed set of principles or *laws.* These laws can only be established by some sort of international assembly or *parliament.* And in the last resort, if some nation should refuse to accept the judgement of the court, or simply invades the territory of somebody else, then there needs to be some sort of international police force or *security force* to enforce the law. We need to replace the "law of force" by the "force of law".

Adding these elements together, one finds the outline of nothing less than a world government. The most natural form of such a government would be a loose association of the presently existing nation-states making up a *world federation*, somewhat along the lines of the present European Union.

This line of argument was strongly urged by Albert Einstein:[3] *"In my opinion the only salvation for civilization and the human race lies in the creation of a world government, with security of nations founded upon law. As long as sovereign states continue to have separate armaments and armament secrets, new world wars will be inevitable."*

If a world federation can eventually be set up, and an effective system of international law established, then any need for nuclear weapons will have disappeared, and it will be possible to abolish them completely. In the long run, we can even look for the abolition of organized warfare itself. War is an archaic and primitive way of settling an argument, and should have no place in a civilized modern society. This happy state of affairs is not going to be reached overnight; but it is by no means an impossible dream. Already there are many instances of the increasing functional co-operation between nations which will help to bring it about.

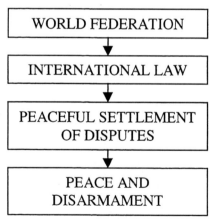

Figure 1.   *The argument for world federation. In order to get rid of nuclear weapons permanently, one must be able to guarantee that international disputes can be settled peacefully. This requires an effective system of international law, which implies a world federation.*

It hardly needs saying that the present United Nations cannot fulfill this role. The foundation of the UN was a major step towards a system of common security, and its peacekeeping functions are of inestimable value. The Secretary-General also plays an important part as a mediator in many international conflicts. But the UN is not a world government, and was never intended as such. Ultimately, a much more powerful organization is needed to provide an adequate guarantee of international security.

The Environment

In recent years, people have become more and more aware that the resources of the earth are limited, and that our global environment is being degraded to an alarming degree. One of the first harbingers of danger was Rachel Carson, who warned in her book *The Silent Spring* that the use of toxic chemicals such as DDT in the countryside was causing widespread destruction of birds and wildlife. There has been a depressing litany of subsequent disasters.

The atmosphere is perhaps the most fragile component of the environment, because its total mass is relatively small. The fumes from power stations and factories are releasing oxides of sulphur and nitrogen into the air, which are washed out again in the form of 'acid rain'. This acid rain is killing aquatic life in ponds and lakes, killing trees in forests, and even crumbling the stone of buildings in our cities.

It has been discovered that chlorofluorocarbons (CFCs), which we have also been releasing into the atmosphere, have begun eating away the ozone layer. CFCs are inert gases used in air-conditioning and refrigeration systems, but when they drift up into the upper atmosphere they are activated by light from the Sun, and begin to catalyze the chemical reduction of ozone. As a result, the total amount of ozone is estimated to be falling by half a percent per annum. Since it is ozone which protects us from the ultraviolet rays of the Sun, we can expect to see a rising incidence of skin cancers and ecological damage as a result.

By burning coal and oil, and cutting down forests, we are also releasing carbon dioxide and other greenhouse gases at an alarming rate. The total amount of carbon dioxide in the atmosphere is rising steadily, and is expected to double in the next century. These greenhouse gases act as a thermal blanket, and tend to increase the average temperature, via the 'greenhouse effect'. The earth's mean surface temperature has increased by 0.5° C in the last century, and is predicted by the Intergovernmental Panel on Climate Change to rise by a further 1 to 3.5° C in the next century.[4] This will cause glaciers and polar ice-caps to melt and contract, and the mean sea-level to rise by an estimated half a metre. There will also be a substantial shift in weather patterns. Until recently, nobody would have dreamed that human activities could have such drastic effects on the weather systems of the entire earth.

The rivers, lakes and oceans of the world are vast, but we have also reached the limits of their resilience. Marine life seems particularly vulnerable. Several species of whales have been hunted to the verge of extinction, and all around the world stocks of fish are disappearing rapidly, as fishermen destroy their own livelihood by overfishing. The global catch of fish peaked at 89 million tonnes in 1989, and has since declined to 85 million tonnes in 1995.[5]

Pollution of rivers and coastal waters is a major problem. Some waterways are little better than open sewers. One finds faeces, plastic syringes and other rubbish bobbing in the waves off Bondi beach in Sydney, or Fire Island in New York. The Adriatic Sea suffers from 'red tides', detergent foam and other serious signs of pollution. The Aral Sea has halved in size due to diversion of its feedwaters.

Lastly, there is the soil under our feet. The earth is groaning under the task of supporting its human population. The forests are disappearing worldwide at the rate of 11 million hectares per year, an area the size of Belgium or Iowa. In arid areas particularly, the soil is being eroded due to over-farming or over-grazing. Topsoil is being lost 20 to 40 times faster than it is being replaced, and large areas of farmland are being reduced to desert. As a result, starvation is endemic in regions such as the Sahel, south of the Sahara.

To divert somewhat from the main line of argument, there can be little doubt that the root cause of most of these problems is over-population, combined with industrialization. Human numbers have increased to a point where most of the fertile land of the planet has been taken up for agriculture, leaving hardly any room for other species of wildlife to survive. One of the great, slow tragedies of modern times is the crowding of many animal species into extinction, never to be seen again. The human population is already 6 billion, and is projected to double again to between 12 and 15 billion people by the year 2100. No doubt it will be technically possible to flog the earth into supporting this huge population; but in the long run we should probably be aiming to *reduce* the population to (say) half its present level, instead. The living space per person is already restricted: in Japan, there are hotel 'rooms' where you cannot stand upright, but have to crawl inside like a rabbit. One recent study at Cornell University has estimated the population which the earth can comfortably sustain at 2 billion people.[6]

Action must be taken to halt and reverse these continuing disasters. Even Margaret Thatcher eventually turned 'green' enough to demand salvation for the ozone layer. The main point to emphasize here is that these environmental problems affect everybody alike, and demand a *collective* response. We all breathe the same air, and to halt the greenhouse effect we are all going to have to stop producing so much carbon dioxide. It does no good for a single person to give up driving his car to work if the rest of us continue burning fossil fuel as usual. Lester Brown, the head of the Worldwatch Institute, remarks: "Ozone depletion, climate change, and oceanic pollution simply cannot be solved at the national level. Indeed, a world in which countries go their own way may not be worth living in."[7] Solutions to these worldwide problems can only be found by means of international agreements, with everybody acting in concert.

This is already happening to some extent. The International Whaling Commission, for instance, has set quotas on the numbers of whales that may be caught, and populations of some species such as right whales are already recovering. The Vienna Convention of 1985 and the Montreal Protocol of 1987 provide for the phasing-out of CFC production by industrialized countries, and their replacement by other gases. As a result, the tonnage of CFCs produced has already dropped to a third of what it used to be, and the problem of the ozone layer should eventually be resolved. But even if all CFC production were stopped tomorrow, it would still take the best part of a century for ozone levels to return to normal.[8]

Other problems such as the greenhouse effect are going to be much more difficult to solve, and will require some painful and difficult decisions. According to the Rio Convention of 1992, the signatory nations agreed to stabilize their greenhouse gas emissions at 1990 levels by the year 2000; but hardly any country will achieve that target. Less ambitious targets were set at the Kyoto Summit in 1997, when the developed countries pledged to reduce their emissions by 5% below 1990 levels by the year 2012; but already doubts are beginning to surface whether these new targets will be met. The limitation of greenhouse gas emissions implies restrictions on the use of fossil fuels for power generation and transport, which could have severe effects on the economic life of the country, and limit economic growth. This is likely to generate serious opposition from industry.

One proposal has been the imposition of a 'carbon tax' on the use of fuels containing carbon. This would provide an economic incentive for people to limit their use of energy, or else switch to renewable energy sources. Industrial lobbyists argue, however, that such a tax would make fuel and electric power more expensive, and reduce the competitiveness of the country in international trade, as compared with other countries which do not have the tax. Thus the proposals for a carbon tax have so far been defeated everywhere.

This example illustrates how hard it is to implement difficult decisions under an international system of voluntary consensus. If one country introduces a carbon tax and another does not, the second country gains an unfair cost advantage in international trade, and the whole system breaks down. Once again, there is an urgent need for a properly organized international parliament, where knotty decisions of this sort can be fully debated, and binding regulations can be formulated which will apply equally to all nations. The present system of reaching voluntary agreements under UN auspices is inadequate. To make the 'hard yards' on environmental issues, our global village needs a more effective village council.

Another obvious function of a world federation would be to administer the 'global commons' for the benefit of all. These are the areas of mankind's environment which belong to no single nation, such as the oceans, the skies, and outer space, where every nation should enjoy similar rights and accept similar obligations. Eventually, no doubt, Antarctica should belong in the same category. Many international conventions have already been ratified concerning these areas, such as the international Law of the Sea, which was arrived at after many years of negotiations in the United Nations.

Trade, Development and Finance

The volume of international trade and finance has increased to a staggering extent over recent years. A household in Australia, for instance, might own a car made in Japan, a washing-machine made in Germany, and a personal computer made in Taiwan. Major corporations are all transnational nowadays in their operations and outlook: a company with headquarters in New York may be looking to build a plant and expand its business in Thailand or China, or wherever labour is cheapest. Businessmen (and women) have become, willy-nilly, citizens of the world who may be required at a moment's notice to fly overseas to attend a business meeting or convention. It used to be said that when Wall Street sneezes, the rest of the world catches cold, but now you have to keep an eye on the Nikkei index as well.

All around the world, the current trend is towards lower tariffs and decreased barriers to trade, with the aim of achieving greater efficiency and productivity, and greater prosperity for all. A world federation could contribute even more to this process by removing obstacles and promoting trade, and providing better regulation of it. An example is provided by the success of the European Community in promoting trade within the European region.

There are also several problems in international commerce which call for solution by some world authority. One of them is the huge increase in speculation on the international currency market, which has a destabilizing effect on world affairs. International transactions have reached an almost frightening level, so that the central banks have become almost powerless to control the tide of money. The foreign exchange transactions recorded by the Bank of International Settlements now amount to around $1 trillion every single day. A single speculator on the New York market, dealing hundreds of millions of dollars at a time, can have a significant effect on the value of national currencies, and manipulate the market to his own advantage. Thus George Soros made his reputation and his fortune in 1992 when he defeated the Bank of England by betting against the British pound. Even the Federal Reserve Bank in America cannot control or withstand the market as a whole. One of the useful functions of a world federation might be to slow down and stabilize the speculative flow of money by imposing a small tax on international transactions. In the long run, the problem would be eliminated by the institution of a single global currency.

Another problem is that of tax evasion schemes such as 'transfer pricing', whereby corporations book their profits in some foreign tax haven rather than in the country where they were earned, in order to avoid paying their proper taxes at home. A world authority would be able to eliminate such abuses.

One serious political and moral dilemma is the so-called 'North-South' problem, or the ongoing transfer of resources from the underdeveloped Third World to the industrialized nations. The Third World nations of Latin America and Africa have borrowed many billions of dollars for development purposes, and now find themselves unable to repay the debt. Prices for commodities such as oil have fallen, and international interest rates have often risen, and so these countries are unable even to pay the interest on their loans. Like a family that has taken out too large a mortgage to buy a house, they are in a debt trap, and the consequence is poverty and hardship for their people. The nations of sub-Saharan Africa, excluding South Africa, currently owe some $220 billion in external debt, about four times their annual export income. Nearly 20% of their export income goes to servicing the loans, and still they have fallen into arrears to the tune of about $60 billion.[9] In 1993, African governments paid $402 million more to the International Monetary Fund than they received from it.[10] From time to time large chunks of Third World debt have been written off, as in the Mexican debt crisis, but after a while the same problem always seems to recur.

Problems such as these transcend national boundaries. Powerful global institutions have already been created, such as the World Bank and the International Monetary Fund (IMF). The germ of a world currency has appeared in the Special Drawing Rights issued by the IMF. Regular financial conventions are held, leading to agreements such as the General Agreement on Tariffs and Trade (GATT). It is only a natural extension of these developments to look for a world parliament to provide better oversight and regulation of international trade and finance. Then we could also undertake the difficult and thorny task of redirecting some small extra fraction of the world's resources towards development of the poorer countries, and relief for the millions living in wretchedness and poverty, or facing premature death from starvation or malnutrition.

Health, Education and Welfare

International organizations have a major role to play in welfare areas, as already witnessed by by the invaluable work of UN agencies such as the World Health Organization (WHO), the Food and Agriculture Organization (FAO), and the UN Educational Scientific and Cultural Organization (UNESCO).

The World Health Organization had its most famous triumph when it succeeeded in eradicating smallpox from the world. The only remaining examples of the bacterium are held in laboratories in England and Russia. The WHO also mounted a campaign to eradicate malaria by spraying the mosquitos which act as vectors for the disease.

This program had much initial success, but was not completed, and malaria is now as prevalent as ever. New outbreaks of diseases such as hepatitis and tuberculosis have occurred as by-products of the drug culture; and AIDS has presented an entirely new and frightening public health problem. New international programs with increased resources are needed to control these diseases.

The Food and Agriculture Organization, along with many non-government organizations such as Oxfam and World Vision, form the bulwark against famine and land degradation in the Third World. They are always there when drought or famine strike in Somalia or Mozambique, struggling heroically to meet the crisis on a shoestring budget. It is crystal clear that the world community is failing to meet its obligations, however, when it requires the efforts of the pop-star Bob Geldof to raise enough money to save hundreds of thousands of gaunt Eritreans from starvation. The US aid budget has fallen to 0.2% of GNP, against the UN target figure of 0.7%. Many other nations are dropping towards a similar level. Once again, a more effective world organization with greater resources is urgently required to do a proper job in this area.

Justice

Year after year, stories of killings, rapes, torture, arbitrary imprisonment and other gross violations of individual rights and liberties fill the world news. Bosnia and Rwanda are merely the latest in an endless catalogue of atrocities.

The United Nations does its best to prevent these crimes against humanity. The Universal Declaration of Human Rights was adopted by the General Assembly in 1948, and a large number of international conventions have been agreed since then, as we shall see later. UN resolutions have repeatedly condemned abuses of human rights such as the apartheid régime in South Africa; but a country can always disregard a UN resolution with impunity, if it does not mind the moral opprobrium of its neighbours. South Africa and Israel did so for years. To act as an effective guardian of people's rights, a world judicial system is required, with the jurisdiction and authority to uphold at least an agreed minimum set of basic human rights and dignities.

At a more mundane level, there is a need for an international police force to control the rising tide of international crime. Drug-smuggling, terrorism, and international fraud are common problems, and even the ancient trade of piracy still occurs here and there. Organized international crime syndicates such as the Mafia and the Triads seem to be on the increase. A joint police force more effective than Interpol is required to combat these threats.

Science and Technology

Scientific research has already become a global enterprise, and a very expensive one at that. In many fields it is becoming impossible for any single nation, except perhaps the USA, to afford the facilities needed to remain at the cutting edge of international research.

This prohibitive increase in cost first occurred in the field of particle physics. The world's premier accelerator laboratory at the moment is the European Centre for Nuclear Research, CERN, located near Geneva. Its main accelerator cost some $1.4 billion, and occupies a tunnel 27 kilometres in length hollowed out beneath the Jura mountains. The US at one stage set out to surpass CERN and build the next generation accelerator, dubbed the 'Superconducting Super Collider' (SSC) in a tunnel 50 kilometres in diameter near the town of Waxahachie in Texas. After spending $1.5 billion and almost completing the tunnel excavations, Congress discovered that the estimated total cost had risen to $12 billion, and decided to cancel the whole project. Many man-years of effort were thus wasted, and the whole field was dealt a blow from which it has still not recovered. Any future accelerators, costing such enormous sums of money, can only be built as co-operative ventures between many different nations.

A similar situation is becoming evident in other areas of science. Small national facilities become obsolete and are closed down, in favour of a few larger and more expensive facilities made available for international use. In astronomy, the Europeans are co-operating again to build the European Southern Observatory on a mountain-top in Chile. In space science, the US and Russia are collaborating to save money, and the planned International Space Station will be a joint venture of many nations. Even in biology, the human genome project will involve extensive international collaboration.

It is time that a single international research council and funding agency was set up to decide which major building projects should be funded, and where they should be built. Then the money available could be spent more wisely, and the facilities could be spread more equitably among the contributing nations. The European 'Framework' programme for scientific research, which currently disposes of about $4 billion per year, provides an example of what might be done.

Science involves universal truths, which transcend national boundaries. Good scientists are drawn from every race and creed, and they already form a very cohesive international community. At huge establishments like CERN, research workers from probably fifty different countries are present at any one time, all working together on their experiments. They already belong to a 'global village' of their own.

Conclusions

Most of our discussions have concentrated on the global difficulties and problems which need to be tackled by a 'village council'; but there are also many great opportunities for progress and advancement on offer. The potential benefits of world federation are huge. It may well take decades or even centuries for the full advantages to flow through, but in the long run we can look for the complete abolition of nuclear weapons, and even an end to the whole institution of large-scale organized warfare. The scarce resources and scientific expertise which are presently devoted to armaments can be redirected to more worthwhile ends. The global environment can be cleaned and repaired, and the human population stabilized at a sensible level, so that we can all live in pleasant and comfortable surroundings. The worst evils of absolute poverty and starvation in the Third World can be eliminated, and minimum levels of health, education and human rights can be established throughout the globe, giving room for millions of human beings to reach their full potential. These are not utopian pipe-dreams: the phenomenal advances of the nations of South-East Asia in recent decades have shown what can be done. International trade, travel, and business enterprises of all sorts would flourish as never before. Then we can look forward to a new era of peace and plenty, and to a new stage in the advance of human civilization.

The same bright picture of the future was painted by H.G. Wells more than seventy years ago in his great work *The Outline of History:* [11] *"There can be little question that the attainment of a federation of all humanity, together with a sufficient measure of social justice, to ensure health, education, and a rough measure of equality of opportunity to most of the children born into the world, would mean such a release and increase of human energy as to open a new phase in human history."*

Chapter 2

Some Snippets of History

How many years must the cannonballs fly,
Before they're for ever banned?
The answer, my friend, is blowin' in the wind,
The answer is blowin' in the wind.

Bob Dylan,
Blowin' in the wind.

The ideas outlined in the previous chapter are not by any means new. Philosophers, statesmen, religious leaders, lawyers, scientists, journalists and others have all discussed the idea of world federation over the centuries. There is an enormous literature related to the subject, and a comprehensive review would be a major task. Let us content ourselves with a few snapshots from history.

Early Beginnings

The concept of the 'global village' can be traced back to ancient times: "I am not an Athenian or a Greek," said Socrates, as quoted earlier, "but a citizen of the world."[1] It is easy to forget that all of civilized Europe was already united two thousand years ago, under the Roman Empire. By a decree of the Emperor Antonine, all people under the government of the Empire were made full citizens of Rome; and the philosopher Seneca urged citizens to regard the world as a common dwelling-place for all mankind.[2]

The need for a supranational authority to preserve the peace between nations has been recognized for hundreds of years. In mediaeval times, it was thought that the Holy Roman Empire, supported by the authority of the church, might provide such an authority. Dante discusses this idea in his book *De Monarchia*; and in the *Inferno*, Beatrice sings of an empire of Europe, divinely ordained to establish peace.

As one might expect, most schemes to preserve the peace have been inspired by the imminent threat of war. In mediaeval and Renaissance Europe, the driving force appears to have been fear of the the Turks, who were knocking on the gates of Vienna in 1529 and again in 1683. One very early scheme was proposed about 1306 by Pierre Dubois, a lawyer and adviser to Philip IV of France, who wrote a treatise entitled *De Recuperatione Terre Sancte* (The Recovery of the Holy Land). He advocated an alliance between the Christian states of Europe, led by France, to keep the peace between them and to reconquer the Holy Land from the Moslems. Each sovereign would swear a binding oath to keep the peace, and a *permanent court of arbitration* would be established to adjudicate disputes between them, along with a *General Council,* convened by the Pope, to discuss common problems. In the fifteenth century George Podiebrad, King of Bohemia, proposed a European Assembly of Princes, with a court and a treasury, to prosecute a holy war against the Turks. In the sixteenth century the Dutch scholar Erasmus, the Italian Pope Leo X and the English Cardinal Wolsey all suggested that European nations should ally themselves by a universal treaty, with arbitration of disputes and collective sanctions against transgressors, for defence against the Turks and to assure peace among themselves.

Then in 1617 the Duc de Sully, formerly Chief Minister to Henry IV of France, produced a somewhat peculiar scheme which he called *The Grand Design of Henry IV.* He proposed that the Hapsburg empire should be dismembered, and then a great federation should be formed of all the hereditary monarchies, elective monarchies, and republics of Europe, to preserve peace among themselves and (once again!) to mount a crusade against the hapless Turks. To settle religious problems, each state was to choose a single religion, either Catholic, Lutheran or Calvinist. He proposed that the federation should be governed by a Senate of 66 persons, commissioned every three years from the participating States. Here we see for the first time the idea of a *federation* of independent states, governed by a *representative assembly.* At about the same time, an obscure French scholar named Emeric Crucé published another scheme called *The New Cyneas*, which emphasized that war should be entirely superseded by a regulated system of arbitration; and for the first time he proposed the inclusion of non-Christian states, including even the dreaded Turks, who were to rank second only to the Pope in his proposed League.

In 1625, the great Dutch jurist Hugo Grotius wrote his famous treatise *De Jure Belli ac Pacis* (The Laws of War and Peace), which is commonly taken as the starting-point of modern *international law*. The book has been through 56 editions, and was a leading textbook for centuries. In it, Grotius discusses the idea of Natural Law, established by mutual consent between the members of a society, and aimed at the "utility of the community", i.e. the common good. Hence arises the "jus gentium", or Law of Nations: "There is some law common to all nations which applies both to the initiation of war and to the manner in which war should be carried on." [3] He discusses the concept of the "Just War", which may be undertaken by some nation to redress a wrong or injustice, and lays down permissible rules for the conduct of a war. He calls for clemency in victory, as the only way to a just and lasting peace. He does not propose any way in which the law might be *enforced*, but relies on mutual consent and "good faith" among the nations.

The ideas of Grotius became the cornerstone of the Peace Treaties of Westphalia, which finally ended the Thirty Years War in 1648. Lawyers mark this date as the beginning of the era of the modern nation-state. Not surprisingly, Holland has remained a centre of international law ever since: witness, for example, the World Court located at the Hague.

The next landmark scheme was due to William Penn. He was the son of Admiral Sir William Penn, a high official in the British Navy under Charles II, who figures prominently in the diaries of Samuel Pepys. The younger Penn flirted with Quakerism while he was at Christchurch, Oxford, and was sent down for 'heretical activities' after only a year in residence, which earned him a thrashing from his furious father. Young William officially joined the Society of Friends ('Quakers') in 1667. He became a leading spokesman for the sect, and a prolific author of pamphlets and treatises. This heretical faith brought him terms of imprisonment in both the Tower of London and Newgate at different times.

When the Admiral died, he was owed the sum of £16,000 by the chronically impecunious government of Charles II, and this debt was later discharged by granting a tract of land in America to his son. William founded there the model colony of Pennsylvania, with Philadelphia as its capital - the "city of brotherly love". He drafted a constitution for the colony providing for an assembly elected by all taxpayers, and guaranteeing religious toleration - highly advanced ideas for the time. He also insisted on fair treatment for the native Indians of the colony.

In 1692, during the wars of the Grand Alliance against Louis XIV,

Penn wrote a well-known essay entitled *Towards the Present and Future Peace of Europe*. This was not the most detailed or the most influential of the early peace plans, but it does contain a neat and concise statement of the guiding principle. The essay begins in ringing tones: "He must not be a Man, but a Statue of Brass or Stone, whose Bowels do not melt when he beholds the bloody Tragedies of this War ..". Penn goes on to discuss the 'Advantages of Peace', and the 'Means of Peace, which is Justice rather than War'; and then arrives at a conclusion[4] which is perhaps the first full and clear statement of the principle discussed in Chapter 1, and bears repeating once more:

"Peace is maintained by Justice, which is a Fruit of Government as Government is from Society, and Society from Consent."

There are clear echoes of Grotius here, and of the philosopher John Locke, in the references to government as established by the mutual consent of society. Penn next proposes that the "Sovereign Princes of Europe" or their delegates should agree to meet in a *"European Parliament"*, and there establish "Rules of Justice for the Princes to observe one to another, and thus prevent war". The meetings were to occur once a year; and if any Sovereign should refuse to submit to the Judgement of the Parliament, then the other Sovereigns should "Unite as One Strength" to compel his submission.

The Quakers, and other religious sects like them, have appeared in the forefront of movements for world peace, abolition of slavery, and other worthy social causes ever since this time.

A little later in France the good Abbé de Saint-Pierre put forward an elaborate and detailed proposal, in a *Plan for Perpetual Peace,* for the creation of a federation of European states designed to settle disputes peacefully, following on from the ideas of Sully. Unfortunately, he framed his propositions in an abstruse 'Cartesian' style, modelled upon proofs in geometry, and Parisian society laughed at him. In 1761, however, his ideas were taken up and reworked by Jean-Jacques Rousseau, the great philosopher of the French Revolution. Rousseau argued that the federation should be run by the *citizens* of the member states, not by the rulers, because the citizens bear the cost of war while the rulers reap the glory. In a later commentary, *Criticism on Perpetual Peace*, he voiced his fear that such a plan would never be adopted due to the selfishness of kings: "As for disputes between prince and prince, is it reasonable to hope that we can force before a higher tribunal men who boast that they hold their power only by the sword?" [5]

We may pause to remark that these schemes, which were regarded as visionary in their day, have essentially been realized three hundred years later in the European Union. The Union includes both the European Parliament as an elected Assembly, and the European Council acting as an 'Assembly of Princes'. It remains to be seen what will be the final balance of power between them.

Across the Atlantic, the American War of Independence eventually led to the federation of thirteen former British colonies into the United States of America in 1788. This great event was already seen as an example to Europe, although it occurred on a smaller scale, and took place among a more homogeneous population. George Washington wrote to the Marquis de Lafayette: "I am a citizen of the Great Republic of Humanity.. We have sown a seed of liberty and union which will gradually spring up throughout the earth. One day, on the model of the United States of America, there will be created the United States of Europe." [6]

In Germany, the gentle philosopher of Königsberg, Immanuel Kant, also looked forward to a Europe of free republics which would bind themselves to one another in friendly pacts, and thus ensure perpetual peace. "At the tribunal of reason", he wrote, "there is but one means of extricating states from the turbulent situation, in which they are constantly menaced by war; namely, to renounce, like individuals, the anarchic liberty of savages, in order to submit themselves to coercive laws, and thus form a society of nations which would insensibly embrace all the nations of the earth." [7] Then he declares: "The law of nations shall be founded on a federation of free states."

During the Napoleonic Wars, the English philosopher Jeremy Bentham declared that peace would ensue if England and France both disarmed, and gave up their overseas colonies. In France, the Comte de Saint-Simon proposed in 1814 that European federation should commence with a union of France and England, the most democratic powers, to be joined gradually by other nations. Saint-Simon proposed a *democratic* parliamentary system on the English model, consisting of a European government all complete with a King, a House of Lords, and a House of Commons, with similar governments for each of the subsidiary nations! In view of the circumstances at the time, both these proposals must be regarded as a little optimistic. The ideas of Saint-Simon did have a great deal of influence, however, and foreshadowed some important modern schemes.

In 1811, the German religious philosopher Karl Christian Friedrich Krause first distinguished the concepts of European federation and *world-wide government.* In *Das Urbild der Menschheit* (The Archetype of Humanity), he proposed regional federations of Europe, Asia, Africa, America and Australia. The European federation was to use the German language, and to have its capital in Berlin; and each regional federation was to be part of a sovereign world republic with its capital in Polynesia. No doubt the bureaucrats would be happy with a capital in Tahiti! But in any case, this work is looking remarkably prophetic, in view of the growing trend towards regionalism in the world today.

The Growth of International Organization after Waterloo

Practical mechanisms for international co-operation in Europe began to appear after the battle of Waterloo. At the Congress of Vienna, some modest sprouts of international law were produced by the nations of Europe in general assembly. The neutrality of Switzerland was guaranteed by the great powers, and a declaration concerning the freedom of navigation on rivers was adopted. Czar Alexander I of Russia, whose country had so nearly been overwhelmed by Napoleon's Grande Armée, took a natural interest in schemes to ensure peace. He organized the 'Holy Alliance', led by Russia, Austria and Prussia, whose intention was to promote Christian principles and obligate all nations to the arbitration of disputes. Unfortunately, the alliance later came to be seen as a bulwark of autocracy.

Meanwhile, the 'Concert of Europe', orchestrated by Metternich and Castlereagh, maintained peace on the continent for many years. This began as an alliance of the Great Powers who had been victorious over Napoleon: Austria, Prussia, Great Britain and Russia. Their leaders met at a series of Congresses and Conferences in the years after 1815, to discuss international problems and take measures to maintain the peace. The Concert was an obvious forerunner of both the League of Nations and the United Nations, and it established a pattern which has proved remarkably persistent right down to the present day.

Turning away from the European scene for a moment, we discover an interesting development in the Middle East at this period, namely the establishment of the Baha'i faith. It began as an offshoot of the Shi'ite Islamic religion in Iran, when a merchant named Sayyid Ali Mohammed (later known as the Bab, or 'Gate') announced in 1844 the imminent coming of the 'Hidden Imam', or messiah. He later proclaimed himself as the Imam, and attempted to promulgate a new system of holy law. Orthodox Muslims were outraged, and in 1850 the

Shah of Iran crushed the Babis, and executed the Bab.

One of the adherents of the Bab was Mirza Husayn Ali (later known as Baha'u'llah, the 'Glory of God'), who was the son of a rich and influential landowner and government official. He and his younger brother both joined the Babi movement in its early days, and the younger brother actually became its leader after the execution of the Bab. In 1852 the Baha was imprisoned for four months in the notorious 'Black Pit' of Tehran, and was then exiled to Ottoman Baghdad. He underwent mystical experiences and religious revelations during his time in the Black Pit, and afterwards spent two years of religious seclusion in the mountains of Kurdistan. In 1866 he split with his younger brother and founded his own Baha'i movement. He produced an immense volume of writings over the subsequent years until his death in 1892, while enduring further successive exiles to Istanbul, then Adrianople, and then Acre in Syria. His distinctive code of Baha'i religious law is detailed in *The Most Holy Book*.

A central precept of the Baha'i faith is its belief in a new world order in which the peoples of the world will be united to live together in peace and harmony. "The earth is but one country, and mankind its citizens" wrote Baha'u'llah; and again, "These fruitless strifes, these ruinous wars shall pass away, and the 'Most Great Peace' shall come".[8] There are by now some four million members of the Baha'i community around the world, helping wherever they can to bring about this new world order. In their high social ideals and their dedication to peace and justice, there seem to be strong parallels between the Baha'i offshoot of the Islamic religion, and the Quaker offshoot of the Christian religion. These are surely among the salt of the earth; and it is sad to relate that the Baha'is are still being persecuted and even killed in the birthplace of their faith, Iran.

In China at this period, the eminent scholar Kang Yu-Wei also looked forward to international establishment of the Confucian Era of Peace-and-Equality. "Now that we seek to save the human race from its miseries, to bring about the happiness and advantages of complete peace-and-equality, to seek the universal benefits of One World, we must begin with the destruction of state boundaries and the abolishment of nationalism .. This it is which Good Men, Superior Men, should day and night with anxious minds wear out their tongues in planning for." [9]

Back in nineteenth century Europe, as the Industrial Revolution began to take hold, the twin ideals of peace and progress burned brightly. The first organized Peace Societies began to be established in

1815 by the Quakers and other religious groups. The great themes
which are still current in the peace movement today were quickly laid
down. In the United States William Ladd advocated a Court of Nations
for the settlement of all international disputes by means of arbitration;
and a resolution to this effect was passed by the Senate of Massachusetts
in 1837. Proposals for *disarmament* were circulated.

In 1843 the first worldwide Peace Convention was held in London,
accompanied by ridicule and sarcasm in the Press. It culminated in a
public meeting of 2000 people. An international Peace Congress was
held every two years thereafter until 1853. The president of the 1849
Paris Congress was none other than Victor Hugo, who opened
proceedings with a magnificent address looking forward to the future
establishment of an United States of Europe. But soon the outbreak of
the Crimean War in Europe and the Civil War in America led to a
decline in the peace movement for some years.

The first international utilities began to be established in 1855 when
the International Telegraph Convention was signed, leading to the
formation of the Telegraphic Union in 1865. In 1874 the Universal
Postal Union was created, guaranteeing freedom of transit for mail
services, and setting uniform rates for postage. Other treaties and
conventions followed, covering all aspects of international
communications, travel and commerce.

At the same period, all sorts of special interest groups began to hold
regular international meetings, until Leonard Woolf wrote during the
First World War: "today there is hardly a profession or interest which
does not gather periodically .. from Chambers of Commerce to bird-
fanciers and film makers." [10] There was an International Federation of
Miners, and an International Union of Woodworkers; there was even an
'International Association for the Suppression of Useless Noises', and
an 'International Association for the Rational Destruction of Rats'. By
1914, there were already 450 non-government international
organizations in existence, helping to weave together the global village.

In 1863 the international Red Cross association was founded by the
great Swiss philanthropist Jean Henri Dunant, and the first Geneva
Convention was organized, which established rules for the treatment of
wounded soldiers in war, and the protection of hospitals and medical
personnel. Later Conventions were held in 1906, dealing with rules for
armed forces at sea; again in 1929, dealing with the treatment of
prisoners of war; and in 1949, dealing with the protection of civilians in
war. For his work in helping to soften the rigours of war, Dunant was

awarded the very first Nobel Peace Prize in 1901.

The search continued for ways to establish a Code of International Law. The House of Commons in Britain carried a motion in 1873 calling for a permanent system of International Arbitration, moved by Henry Richard. Some elaborate proposals appeared, such as the draft code produced by Professor J.C. Bluntschli of Heidelberg, which ran to 862 articles, and the two-volume work of Professor James Lorimer of Edinburgh. To implement these codes, Bluntschli once more proposed a federation of European states, while Lorimer outlined a plan for International Government.

The first embryonic world parliament, called the Inter-Parliamentary Union, was organized in 1886 by William Randal Cremer, a British labour leader, together with Frederic Passy, a French economist. It was composed of legislators from many countries, and played a role in the Hague Conferences which followed shortly thereafter. In 1904 the Union formally proposed "an international congress which should meet periodically to discuss international questions".

It was the Czar of Russia once again, Nicholas II, who convened the first Hague Conference in 1899. The aim was to limit the armaments that were being built at the time in great quantities (and at great expense), and to provide for peaceful settlement of international disputes. Representatives of 26 nations met at the first conference in 1899, while at a second conference in 1907 the representatives of 44 nations met, and argued with each other for four months. Since it required a consensus of opinion to achieve anything in practice, the results were rather limited. A Permanent Court of Arbitration (later to become the *World Court*) was set up at the Hague to provide optional arbitration of disputes; but as Leonard Woolf rather wickedly noted, the only matters which the conference could agree should *always* be referred to a judicial tribunal were "the interests of indigent sick persons, of the working classes, of dead sailors, and of writers and artists."[11] Some thirteen conventions were adopted to revise some of the customs and laws of war to eliminate unnecessary suffering; and three declarations were made, valid for five years, prohibiting the use of expanding ('dum-dum') bullets, asphyxiating gases, or bombardment from aerial balloons in warfare. The conference failed to reach any agreement on limiting existing armaments, or providing for compulsory arbitration of disputes. Nevertheless, it represented the first multilateral disarmament convention held at the official level in peace-time, and was an important forerunner of the League of Nations.

The latter years of the nineteenth century, and the early years of the twentieth century, marked the height of the age of imperialism. Bismarck tramped across the stage, Kipling wrote his stories of the White Man's Burden, and the great powers of Europe struggled for influence in the world at large. They competed with each other in raising conscript armies, in constructing 'dreadnought' battleships and other weapons of war, and in annexing colonies in Africa and Asia. The prevailing strategic doctrine was the Balance of Power, or what we should now call *deterrence*. It was neatly summed up by Captain A. T. Mahan, later to become an Admiral in the US Navy and a famous naval historian and strategist, who wrote in 1899:

"The immense armaments of Europe are onerous; but nevertheless, by the mutual respect and caution they enforce, they present a cheap alternative ...to the frequent and devastating wars which preceded the era of general military preparation."

Unfortunately the arms race continued to accelerate, and the deterrent eventually broke down with the outbreak of World War I, the 'Great War'. This developed into a mindless, brutal war of attrition in muddy trenches, with men being killed and mutilated on a scale that had hardly been dreamed of before. The total number of soldiers killed in the war has been estimated at 8.5 million, with another 20 million wounded, and about 10 million civilians also perished.

The League of Nations Between the Wars

People everywhere were stunned and horrified by the carnage of the First World War, and determined that it must never happen again: this must be "the war to end all wars". Schemes and societies to achieve a lasting peace after the war sprang up in many places. In the United States, a League to Enforce Peace grew up, led by the former President William Taft, and in Britain a League of Nations Society was established. Leonard Woolf wrote a two-volume report for the Fabian Society entitled *International Government*, which foreshadowed many features of the eventual League of Nations.

Ideas of this sort were taken up by President Woodrow Wilson of the United States, and set forth in his famous 'Fourteen Points' address[12] to a joint session of Congress on January 8, 1918. This address became the accepted statement of the war aims of the victorious allies. The major objectives , from our point of view, included the future *disarmament* of all nations:

IV. "Adequate guarantees given and taken that national armaments will be reduced to the lowest point consistent with absolute safety."

- and the formation of a *league of nations* to guarantee peace:

XIV. "A general association of nations must be formed under specific covenants for the purpose of affording mutual guaranties of political independence and territorial integrity to great and small states alike."

When the war ended, and the peace conference met in Paris, President Wilson insisted that formation of the League should be the first order of business. A Committee of nineteen members was set up to draft a Covenant for the League, with Wilson as chairman. Other notable contributors included the President's friend and advisor Colonel House, along with Lord Robert Cecil of Britain, Léon Bourgeois of France, and General Smuts of South Africa. Jan Smuts wrote *A Practical Suggestion*, which included a ringing declaration that the League should be thought of "not only as a possible means of preventing future wars, but much more as a great organ of the ordinary peaceful life of civilization, as the foundation of the new international system which will be erected on the ruins of this war."[13] The Committee did its work with great despatch, and produced a draft in only some thirty hours of meetings. The resulting Covenant became Part I of the Treaty of Versailles. But before examining the Covenant in more detail, we should comment on the remainder of the Treaty, which consists of the peace settlement imposed on the defeated Central Powers of Germany, Austria-Hungary and Turkey.

It is generally agreed that the Treaty of Versailles was a misguided agreement, and sowed the seeds of the Second World War. A swinging broadside against the Treaty was written by John Maynard Keynes, in his well-known book *The Economic Consequences of the Peace*. Forgetting the principle of clemency in victory which Grotius had laid down, statesmen such as Clemenceau of France and Lloyd George of Britain (and including, sad to say, one Billy Hughes of Australia) determined to exact vengeance for the sufferings of their people in the war. Under the peace settlement, the Austro-Hungarian empire was dismembered, and Germany and Turkey were shorn of their colonial possessions. The province of Alsace-Lorraine was transferred from Germany to France. Germany was disarmed, with her army cut to 100,000 men, fortifications on the Rhine dismantled, and conscription abolished. She was forbidden to possess submarines, tanks or aircraft for military purposes, and her merchant navy was confiscated, while the

British blockade continued for two years after the war. Finally, the allies demanded reparations for the damage done by the war, to the tune of some $32 billion, far more than the Central Powers could ever pay.

The Germans were thus humiliated and impoverished by the Versailles Treaty. Matters were made worse when in 1923 they defaulted on their reparations payments, and France and Belgium occupied the Ruhr basin. Galloping inflation in Germany followed, making the German currency worthless, so that at one stage it required a wheelbarrow full of currency to purchase a loaf of bread. The situation could not go on, and it was retrieved by the Dawes Plan of 1924 and the Locarno agreements of 1925, which set both Germany and France on the road to recovery; but the German people naturally hated the Versailles treaty and longed to see it reversed, and this was a major factor in Hitler's rise to power later on.

Let us turn now to the Covenant of the League of Nations. Since the League was in many ways simply an earlier and smaller version of the United Nations, we shall not spend too much time on it, but there are some instructive lessons to be drawn.

The Covenant of the League consisted of 26 articles. The first 7 of these dealt with the organization of the League, which is illustrated below.

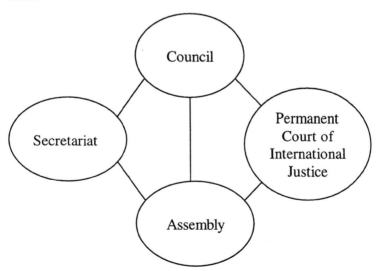

Figure 2. *The organization of the League of Nations.*

The major organs consisted of the Assembly, the Council, the Secretariat, and the Court.

- The Assembly consisted of representatives from all the Member states, and could deal with any matter within the sphere of action of the League: it was the precursor of the General Assembly of the UN. The Assembly met once a year in September, as an embryonic world parliament. In the heyday of the League, these were occasions of high drama, attended by Presidents and Prime Ministers.
- The Council was to consist of representatives of the victorious Great Powers, originally taken as the US, Britain, France, Italy and Japan, together with several representatives of lesser powers elected by the Assembly. The Council was the executive of the League, and had the primary responsibility for dealing with threats to the peace, and drawing up plans for disarmament. It met three or four times a year, or whenever required to deal with threats to peace. It was the precursor of the Security Council of the UN.
- The Secretariat provided bureaucratic support for the League, and consisted of the Secretary-General, Sir Eric Drummond, and about 600 staff headquartered in Geneva.
- A Permanent Court of International Justice, successor to the Hague Court, was set up to arbitrate disputes.

Each member of the Assembly and the Council had one vote, and decisions on matters of substance required the agreement of all members present (the 'unanimity rule'). Matters of procedure could be decided by a simple majority vote.

Articles 8 and 9 of the Covenant dealt with disarmament, in accordance with Woodrow Wilson's point IV. The disarmament of Germany was claimed to be only a beginning to more general disarmament among the great powers, and the Covenant required plans to be drawn up to bring this about.

It was recognized that disarmament could only occur if means were available to handle disputes, and Articles 10-21 were intended to deal with these aspects. Prominent among them were:

Article 10. "The Members of the League undertake to respect and preserve, as against external aggression, the territorial integrity and existing political independence of all Members of the League. In case of any such aggression, or in case of any threat or danger of such aggression, the Council shall advise upon the means by which this obligation shall be fulfilled."

Article 12. "The Members of the League agree that, if there should arise between them any disputes likely to lead to a rupture they will submit the matter either to arbitration or judicial settlement or to enquiry by the Council .."

Article 16. "Should any Member of the League resort to war in disregard of its Covenants .. it shall *ipso facto* be deemed to have committed an act of war against all other Members of the League, which hereby undertake immediately to subject it to the severance of all trade or financial relations .. [the article goes on to talk about "armed forces to be used to protect the Covenant of the League."]

Articles 22 -25 dealt with the improvement of social conditions, and provided for the League to take under its wing all previous international bureaux or commissions; while Article 26 dealt with amendments to the Covenant.

This was a very ambitious document. In theory, Article 10 provided a guarantee of the territorial integrity of every member of the League, as demanded by Woodrow Wilson. Article 12 provided for any dispute between Members to be submitted to arbitration, and Article 16 discussed the sanctions, including armed force, which might be applied against any nation that broke the Covenant. In theory, this should have provided a complete system of common security for all the Members of the League.

The trouble was, the theory was not supported by practical measures to carry it out or enforce it - the League had no 'teeth'. As mentioned above, the entire personnel of the League consisted of a few hundred men and women in the Secretariat. The budget of the League averaged a puny $5.5 million per year: Britain's contribution was a mere £150,000 per annum. At the Paris peace conference, Léon Bourgeois of France argued long and hard for an international armed force to be created in order to uphold the Covenant, but he was outvoted.

The League was therefore only a shell organization, totally reliant on the good faith of its Members to abide by and uphold the Covenant. If that failed, and a violation of the Covenant occurred, the offender could only be brought to book by the resolute and combined action of the other Member States. Would that be forthcoming?

In the event, the League was immediately dealt a crippling blow by the defection of the United States. President Wilson had failed to carry the Republican party with him in his proposals. The Americans felt that they had been dragged into a costly war in Europe which had produced no discernible benefits for themselves, and isolationist sentiment was growing. The Republicans, led by Henry Cabot Lodge, argued that Article 10 of the Covenant would only entangle the US in further foreign wars, and so the President was unable to muster the required two-thirds majority to ratify the Versailles Treaty in the Senate. Hence the US dropped out of the League which its own President had created.

Of the other great powers, Italy and Japan were before long taken over by militaristic governments absorbed in their own imperialist adventures. Germany was still disarmed and smarting under the Versailles treaty, and was not even a member of the League in the early days. That left only Britain and France to uphold the Covenant; and since both of them had suffered heavily in the Great War, they were not prepared to resort to arms on any but the most vital issues to themselves. France, indeed, was still obsessed by the latent threat from Germany. The defenders of the Covenant were looking a little thin on the ground.

For a while, nevertheless, the League was reasonably successful. At the first meeting in Geneva, there were 42 Member states represented; and at one time or another, a total of 63 states belonged to the League. The Council settled, or helped to settle, a number of disputes between smaller nations such as that between Finland and Sweden over the Aaland Islands, and others between Greece and Bulgaria (1925) and Colombia and Peru (1933). On one occasion in 1921, when Yugoslavia suddenly invaded Albania, the League was able to stop a war after fighting had actually begun. A meeting of the Council was held. A pending Yugoslav loan became non-negotiable on the London market, and Yugoslav exchange rates fell all over Europe - the Yugoslav troops quickly withdrew. This incident illustrates what can potentially be done by sanctions.

The League also did well on a number of economic and social issues. It directed the financial reconstruction of Austria, Hungary and Greece after the war, by means of loans. Under the leadership of the Norwegian explorer Dr. Fridtjof Nansen, it organized the relief and repatriation of many thousands of prisoners of war and refugees. It mounted programs to combat disease, white slavery, and the drug traffic. It set up a system of Mandates or trusteeships for the ex-colonies of Germany and Turkey, and promoted education in the poorer countries. These good works were among the most valuable functions of the League, and of course they have been continued and extended by the present United Nations.

On the issue of disarmament, however, the League had less success. When its members came to consider the question seriously, they ran into the old dilemma of disarmament versus security. How could each country ensure its own safety, if it gave up its weapons? A resolution of the 1922 Assembly stated: "in the present state of the world, many Governments would be unable to accept the responsibility for a serious reduction of armaments unless they received in exchange a satisfactory guarantee of the security of their country."[14] They obviously did not regard the guarantee provided by Article 10 of the Covenant as sufficient, without practical mechanisms to back it up. The Article was already becoming, in effect, a dead letter.

Some progress was achieved by the Washington Naval Treaty of 1922. Under this treaty, a fixed ratio of 15:15:9:5:5 was established between the capital ships and aircraft carriers of Britain, the United States, Japan, Italy and France respectively, and agreement was reached to scrap, or convert, some seventy vessels of war then afloat or partly built. After that, the disarmament issue was referred to a long series of committee meetings, with little result. A major Disarmament Conference was planned for 1932, but it was overtaken by events, and led to no substantive agreement.

It was in the mid-1920s that a remarkable figure appeared on the European scene in the person of Aristide Briand. He was a lawyer, a statesman, and a brilliant orator, who became Premier of France no less than 11 times. He believed that peace could only be assured by a reconciliation between France and Germany, first of all, and beyond that by a federation of all the states of Europe. Together with Count Richard Coudenhove-Kalergi and others, he was a leader of the pan-European movement at the time.

In 1925 Briand was Foreign Minister of France, and undertook a *rapprochement* with Germany. He found a ready partner in the German Foreign Minister, Gustav Stresemann, and together with the other European powers they forged the treaty known as the Locarno Pact. By this treaty, the signatories Britain, France, Germany, Italy, Belgium, Poland and Czechoslovakia bound themselves to achieve general disarmament. Germany and France renounced the use of war to alter the frontiers between them, and Britain and Italy bound themselves to guarantee the common boundaries of Belgium, France and Germany. The Rhineland was declared a neutral zone. All disputes were to be settled through the League.

The "spirit of Locarno" removed for the time the tension between France and Germany, and further progress was made in 1926 when Germany was finally admitted to the League of Nations. The first sitting of the Assembly that year, when Germany was admitted to its seat, was a great occasion. "C'est fini!" thundered Briand, to huge applause - the long series of bloody encounters between France and Germany was ended. Shortly afterwards Briand and Stresemann were jointly awarded the Nobel Peace Prize. But unfortunately, as we now know, there was one final encounter between the two countries yet to come.

Shortly afterwards, Briand concluded another agreement with F.B. Kellogg, the US Secretary of State, which was called the Kellogg-Briand Pact. Its purpose was to outlaw war entirely. Each party promised to renounce war as an instrument of national policy, and to settle all disputes or conflicts by peaceful means. The Pact was signed in Paris on August 27, 1928, by 15 states, and by 1936 it had been accepted by 65 states. As a practical instrument the Kellogg-Briand Pact was useless, and failed to prevent the various acts of aggression in the succeeding decade. It did mark an important long-term shift in public opinion, however, by establishing war as an outlaw act rather than a normal instrument of national policy, as it had been in the days of Macchiavelli or Clausewitz.

In 1930 Briand went even further, and circulated a *Memorandum on the Organization of a Federal Order of European Union*, in which the establishment of the long-awaited United States of Europe was made part of the official foreign policy of France. "Unite in order to live and prosper!" he urged. At that time, however, few of the other European nations were interested. The League Assembly dealt with the issue by the time-honoured procedure, and referred it to a Commission from whence it never emerged.

By then the international scene was growing darker. The Great Depression had begun, and economic hardship was leading to an upsurge in nationalism and xenophobia all over the world. Militarists were already in control in Italy, and were winning power in Japan, and in Germany Hitler's Nazi party was quickly gaining influence. All this spelt trouble for the League of Nations.

In spite of these overcast conditions, or possibly because of them, the 1930s saw the birth of the first organized movements for world government. One of the earliest was due to the great science fiction writer H.G. Wells. In 1913 he had performed one of his astounding leaps into the future with the publication of his novel *The World Set Free*. He portrayed a terrible war fought with "atomic bombs", after which the survivors formed a world government, which brought an end to war and ushered in an era of unprecedented social and economic progress. In 1933, he followed this with another book called *The Shape of Things to Come*, which again advertised the virtues of world government, and led to the formation of small and short-lived "Wellsian societies" around the world. In 1937, Rosika Schwimmer and Lola Maverick Lloyd founded the more permanent Campaign for World Government in the United States, and in Britain the Federal Union group was founded the following year. In 1939, the *New York Times* correspondent Clarence Streit published a book called *Union Now*, in which he advocated a union of the North Atlantic democracies, as a deterrent to Hitler and a prelude to a broader federation. The book created a great deal of interest and sold 300,000 copies, but was soon swept away by events.

In Japan a notable event occurred with the founding of the Buddhist society Soka Gakkai (the Society for Value Creation) by Tsunesaburo Makiguchi in 1930. Makiguchi was an educator and pacifist, who was later imprisoned for his beliefs and died during the Second World War. The society works for the abolition of war, and promotes global transnationalism and 'global governance'. It has since become a very powerful group, and has formed its own party in the Japanese parliament, called the Komeito or 'Clean Hands' party.

In the meantime, however, the League of Nations had met its downfall. The first major challenge arose when Japan overran Manchuria in 1931. China appealed to the League Council over this violation of its territory, and after long delay the Council condemned the Japanese action, causing Japan to withdraw from the League. But Manchuria was a long way from Europe, and neither Britain nor France felt able to challenge Japan on her home turf, while the US would do nothing to help. Thus Japan was left in control of the puppet state which she had set up in Manchuria, and the League was effectively defeated. It had come a cropper at the first hurdle, but since the events had taken place far from the European centre of interest, the blow was not yet seen as fatal.

A second major challenge arose when Mussolini invaded Ethiopia in 1935. Again the Council condemned the action after long hesitation, and invoked Article 16 of the Covenant to impose sanctions against Italy, which thereupon withdrew from the League. The sanctions proved to be completely ineffective. States outside the League would not agree to observe the trade embargo, while the French, fearing to drive Mussolini into the arms of Hitler, would not agree to extend the embargo to vital commodities such as oil. Once again the aggressor was left in possession of the field, and the League was defeated. After this it sank quickly into irrelevance.

By now Hitler had risen to power in Germany, becoming Chancellor in 1933, and openly beginning a program of German rearmament. From 1935 onwards, Britain and France were forced to begin rearming in response. For a time they tried desperately to appease the German dictator. They acquiesced as step by step he re-established the German armed forces, re-occupied the Rhineland, carried out the anschluss with Austria, carved off the Sudetenland from Czechoslovakia, and finally swallowed Czechoslovakia whole. "Peace with Honour!" proclaimed Neville Chamberlain, as he waved the shameful Munich agreement. But finally Britain and France were forced to make a stand when Hitler invaded Poland in 1939, and World War II began. By this stage the League had become politically moribund, and it played little or no role in these developments. It was officially wound up in 1946, when its baton was passed to the new United Nations.

The League of Nations was thus, in the end, a failure. Its structure was a rather primitive one, not unlike that proposed by Pierre Dubois back in 1306. The gap was too great between the high principles which were announced in the Covenant, and the feeble mechanisms which were assigned to uphold them in practice. German resentment at the unjust Versailles settlement, the onset of the Great Depression, and the rise of Fascism in the 1930s all produced tremendous stresses in the international system, which the League was totally unable to withstand. Nevertheless, the League did represent the first great experiment in establishing the collective security of all nations based on law, and its founders and supporters will go down in the honour-roll of history. Learning from the results of this experiment, the world resolved to do better next time, when the United Nation was set up.

What lessons can be drawn from the failure of the League? The history of these times illustrates two of the basic points which were already made in Chapter 1. First of all, disarmament alone is not enough to ensure peace. In fact, general disarmament is not even possible unless ironclad guarantees can be given which assure the security of each nation without recourse to arms. Because this security was lacking, the nations of the world found themselves unable to carry out the general disarmament which they had promised under the Covenant of the League.

Furthermore, security cannot be guaranteed merely by words on a piece of paper. Effective mechanisms and procedures to ensure peace and security must be put in place, backed up by adequate resources. In the final analysis, nothing less than a complete system of international law and government will do. Although Article 10 of the Covenant appeared on paper to guarantee the territorial integrity of each nation, we have seen that it meant very little in practice. There were no mechanisms or resources to back it up, except the voluntary efforts of the individual Member states. The resulting edifice crumbled at the first serious challenge. Not once did a member of the League take up arms to defend the territorial integrity of another member (at least until 1939, when the League had already collapsed). Not once did the Council of the League even recommend such an action.

The Rise and Fall of the World Federalist Movement after Hiroshima

The Second World War was eventually concluded in 1945, after the first atomic bombs were dropped on Hiroshima and Nagasaki. There were 25 million deaths among the military combatants on both sides, and another 30 million civilian deaths. The Soviet Union alone lost more than 20 million dead. The world's people resolved afresh to try and prevent such catastrophes in the future, and for this purpose created the United Nations in 1945, as a successor to the League, while in Europe the movements began that were to lead to the European Union. We shall examine both of these developments in some detail in the succeeding chapters.

This time around, a long-lasting peace was arrived at by the victorious Allies. Mindful of Grotius (and perhaps even more of Winston Churchill's famous motto: "In War: Resolution. In Defeat: Defiance. In Victory: Magnanimity. In Peace: Goodwill."[15]), they dealt generously with the defeated Axis powers. By schemes such as the far-sighted Marshall Plan, the US provided assistance to help Germany and Japan get back on their feet after the War. The result is that both nations have been model citizens of the world community, by and large, ever since.

The search for peace and disarmament was now given new urgency by the need to control the awesome new weapon that had been created in the atomic bomb. A fission weapon (or 'atomic bomb') is about a million times more powerful than a chemical weapon, in that a few kilograms of enriched uranium or plutonium have the explosive power of 10 kilotonnes of TNT. Thus it was that a single primitive bomb was able to demolish the entire city of Hiroshima, killing some 130,000 people in the process. In the minds of many people, this immediately conjured up a nightmare vision of future atomic wars in which the whole Earth might be devastated, and the human race destroyed. At the time, no doubt, such fears were highly exaggerated. In June 1946, for example, the entire remaining atomic arsenal of the US consisted of just nine bombs. But these apocalyptic visions were to become more realistic as time went on, and they provided the motivation for most of the schemes for peace and disarmament which now began to pour forth. Henceforwards, the pacifist movement, the movement for nuclear disarmament, and the movement for world government were to be bound up closely together.

Among scientists the leading figure in these movements was Albert Einstein, the greatest theoretical physicist of his time. He was a convinced pacifist, and worked for international peace and understanding all his life. Even in 1914 at the beginning of the First World War, when he was a young professor at the University of Berlin, he was one of a lonely band of four faculty members who wrote a *Manifesto to Europeans,* saying in part: "Never before has any war so completely disrupted cultural cooperation. It has done so at the very time when progress in technology and communications clearly suggest that we recognize the need for international relations which will necessarily move in the direction of a universal, world-wide civilization ... the time has come when Europe must unite to guard its soil, its people and its culture ... we shall endeavour to organize a League of Europeans." [16] Of course, amid all the war hysteria of the times, he and his friends were ignored.

After World War I, Einstein wrote and campaigned regularly for pacifist causes. In the 1930s, however, he was forced to flee Germany for America by the rising tide of Nazi anti-Semitism. He recognized that Hitler represented a threat to civilization, and had to be resisted, by force if necessary. He had a part in the making of the atomic bomb, through his famous letter with Leo Szilard to President Roosevelt, advising him that such a weapon was possible.

After the war against Japan was ended by the bombing of Hiroshima and Nagasaki, Einstein was one of a large group of scientists who were stunned and appalled by the lethal power of this new weapon which they had helped to create. Their feelings were summed up in the powerful words of Robert Oppenheimer:[17]

"In some sort of crude sense which no vulgarity, no humour, no over-statement can quite extinguish, the physicists have known sin; and this is a knowledge which they cannot lose."

They realized the unprecedented destruction which the bomb could wreak if used in future wars, and the need to prevent any such catastrophe if possible. A Federation of American Scientists (FAS) was organized by Leo Szilard to work towards this end, consisting initially of groups from the atomic laboratories at Oak Ridge, Chicago, Los Alamos and New York. The *Bulletin of the Atomic Scientists* was founded and edited by Eugene Rabinowitch, with its warning clock on the cover designed by none other than Edward Teller, and set at seven minutes to midnight. An Emergency Committee of Atomic Scientists was set up as a front and fund-raiser for the FAS, with Einstein as chairman, and including many eminent figures such as Harold Urey, Hans Bethe, Thorfin Hogness, Philip Morse, Linus Pauling, Leo Szilard and Victor Weisskopf. They issued a famous telegram:[18]

"Our world faces a crisis as yet unperceived by those possessing the power to make great decisions for good or evil. The unleashed power of the atom has changed everything save our modes of thinking, and thus we drift towards unparalleled catastrophe. We scientists who unleashed this immense power have an overwhelming responsibility in this world life-and-death struggle to harness the atom for the benefit of mankind and not for humanity's destruction."

It was Einstein's view, as quoted in Chapter 1, that the only solution to the problem lay in the formation of a world government; and he campaigned for this goal whenever he could. Some scientists thought likewise; others were less ambitious, and looked only for international control of atomic energy and atomic weapons under the UN. Many distinguished scientists around the world joined in this campaign against the Bomb. In Britain, an Atomic Scientists Association was formed, with Nevill Mott as its first president, and after him Rudolf Peierls. Men like Joseph Rotblat, P.M.S. Blackett, and the Australian Mark Oliphant became lifelong campaigners against nuclear weapons.In Denmark, Niels Bohr had tried to get the Allies to agree to international control even before the bomb was dropped. In Austria, Hans Thirring led the campaign.

It was in this immediate post-war period, in fact, that the movement for world government reached heights that have never been matched either before or since. Even while the war was in progress, a former Republican presidential candidate in Wendell Wilkie had published a book entitled *One World,* which sold 2 million copies. At the end of the war the journalist Emery Reves wrote *The Anatomy of Peace*, which became a bible of the world government movement. It contains a lively diatribe against nationalism and national sovereignty, and argues the need for universal democratic institutions to administer universal law: "War takes place whenever and wherever non-integrated social units of equal sovereignty come into contact"[19], declares Reves. "Peace was never possible .. until some sovereign source of law was set up over and above the clashing social units."[20] .. "Peace is law. It is order. It is government" [21] (in which we hear an echo of William Penn). He pours scorn on the fledgling United Nations as pathetically inadequate to the task.

The leaders of the world government movement in the United States included people such as Grenville Clark, a Wall Street lawyer; Norman Cousins, editor of the *Saturday Review of Literature*, and author of *One World or None;* Alan Cranston, who was to become a long-serving Senator from California; and Robert Hutchins, chancellor of the University of Chicago, where a *Preliminary Draft of a World Constitution* was developed. Organizations such as Americans United for World Government, World Federalists USA, and Student Federalists flourished, and merged in 1947 to form the United World Federalists, whose aim was primarily to strengthen the United Nations into a world government. Its first president was Cord Meyer, Jr., a young marine veteran, who wrote a book called *Peace or Anarchy.* The total membership of this umbrella organization swelled to 47,000 by 1949. Some 22 state legislatures passed resolutions endorsing world government. In the House of Representatives, 91 members introduced a resolution supporting world government as the "fundamental objective" of US foreign policy. One poll in 1946 found 63% in favour of world government, and 20% opposed to it.

A similar story was told in other countries. Leading campaigners in Britain included the philosopher Bertrand Russell, and an engineer and Member of Parliament named Henry Usborne, who founded a Parliamentary Group for World Government consisting of some 80 members in the House of Commons. He also organized a popular 'Crusade for World Government' which reached 15,000 members by 1950. Corresponding movements sprang up all over Western Europe, and indeed all over the world. In India, Mahatma Gandhi and Jawaharlal Nehru endorsed the idea. "Exactly what are we trying to do by atomic warfare?" asked Nehru sarcastically. "I cannot for the moment think of any objective which would not be swept away by 1,000 million people being destroyed or disabled".[22] Earlier, he had declared that "The world, in spite of its rivalries and hatreds and inner conflicts, moves inevitably towards closer cooperation and the building up of a world commonwealth. It is for this One World that free India will work."[23] In Italy, the Movement for European Federation and World Federation claimed 137,000 members in 1949.

In France, an extraordinary phenomenon occurred when an American comedian named Garry Davis, who had been a bomber pilot during the war and was the son of the popular bandleader Meyer Davis, renounced his American citizenship and proclaimed himself a citizen of the world. He camped in a pup-tent on a small strip of UN territory in Paris, and began an unauthorized speech from a balcony to the UN General Assembly calling for "One government for one world!", until he was dragged away by the guards. The "Little Man" became a sensation in Paris, and his ideas were endorsed by intellectuals such as Albert Camus, André Gide, and Jean-Paul Sartre. A registry of World Citizens was started, and reached a mark of half a million by 1950. Some 400 communities in France, Belgium, Denmark, West Germany and India were 'mundialized', or announced themselves as world territory, by mid-1951.

A coalition of world federalist organizations, with the clumsy title of the World Movement for World Federal Government (WMWFG) was established at a meeting in Montreux, Switzerland, in 1947. Its president was Lord John Boyd Orr, who was the first director-general of the UN Food and Agriculture Organization, and was awarded the Nobel Prize in 1949. By 1950, the movement claimed 56 member groups in 22 countries, with some 156,000 members.

The movement remained divided over tactics. The 'minimalists', mostly from the United States, sought a world government with powers limited to preventing war. The United World Federalists aimed to strengthen the UN for this purpose. The 'maximalists', mostly from Europe and elsewhere, favoured greater powers for the world body. Some favoured the establishment of regional bodies first, and the main advocates of a united Europe soon formed their own organizations and had little more to do with the WMWFG thereafter. Usborne's Crusade for World Government proposed direct popular elections to send delegates to a 'people's world convention'. Garry Davis insisted on keeping his World Citizens entirely independent.

Notwithstanding these internal arguments, popular support was strong. Opinion polls organized by UNESCO during 1948 and 1949 found world government was favoured by a majority of respondents in six countries (France, Italy, the Netherlands, Norway, West Germany and Britain - i.e. virtually all of Europe), and rejected in only three countries (Australia, Mexico and the United States). Parliamentary groups supporting world federalism numbered 100 members in Sweden, 110 members in Japan (including Prime Minister Yoshida), 200 members in France, and nearly 300 members in Italy. The constitutions of France, Italy, the Netherlands and West Germany were all *amended* to permit limitations on national sovereignty for the purpose of joining a regional or world federation.

This upsurge of enthusiasm was to lead to great results on the European front. But sadly, the federalist movement achieved no concrete result on the larger world scene before it was overtaken and submerged by the onset of the Cold War.

The US and the USSR had found themselves on the same side in World War II, and for a little while thereafter tension between them was low. The US government did indeed make some initial attempts to place atomic weapons under international control. Following the Acheson-Lilienthal Report, the so-called Baruch Plan was presented to the United Nations, according to which all aspects of atomic energy were to be placed under strict international control, enforced by "condign punishment"; while afterwards those nations possessing atomic weapons would destroy them. Unfortunately, the Russians regarded this as a trick to preserve the American monopoly of atomic weapons, and vetoed the proposal in the Security Council.

The two superpowers were now rivals for power and influence in the world, and were even more deeply divided by the difference between their respective capitalist and Communist ideologies. The USSR, according to Lenin's doctrine, looked forward to the collapse of capitalism; while the US developed a policy of 'containment' to prevent Communist expansion. The fear and suspicion between them grew rapidly. Already in 1946, Winston Churchill had warned of the "Iron Curtain" descending across Europe, as the Communists imposed their control in the East. In 1948 there was a face-off over the Berlin blockade, and in 1949 the Soviets surprised the Americans by exploding their first atomic bomb. In 1950 the Korean War broke out. All these events helped to drive the fear of Communism to fever pitch in the United States, culminating in the hysteria of the McCarthy era.

The United States was now strategically dependent on nuclear weapons. Unwilling to match the manpower of the Red Army on the ground, they were coming to rely on nuclear weapons to deter the

Soviets from any possible attack on Western Europe. After the Soviets exploded their atomic bomb, the US decided to go ahead and develop the H-bomb, or fusion bomb, one thousand times more powerful still. Robert Oppenheimer, Director of the Los Alamos project, strenuously opposed this decision, arguing that it would only lead to a new and terrible arms race in thermonuclear weapons, but his protests were brusquely dismissed by President Truman. The first H-bomb was exploded on the atoll of Eniwetok in 1952, obliterating an entire island one mile in diameter, and leaving a huge crater on the ocean floor.

The Communists, meanwhile, were promoting their own version of the peace movement. Ever fearful of an attempt by the West to crush them by armed force, as Lenin had predicted, they saw the peace movement as a useful brake to use against any such attempt. They denounced the West as "imperialists" and "warmongers", sponsored events such as the World Peace Congress in Paris in 1949, and set up the World Peace Council in 1950. Under state sponsorship, petitions for peace drew hundreds of millions of signatures in the East.

This had the unfortunate side-effect of bringing all the peace organizations in the West under suspicion of being "Communist fronts" or "fellow-travellers". The world federalists, indeed, were receiving fire from both sides. The Soviets were adamantly opposed to the idea of world government, calling it a plot of "imperialist forces which aspire to world domination." [24] The Daughters of the American Revolution, on the other hand, charged that world federalism was "the key to Russian domination of America"! [25] The *Chicago Tribune* claimed that the movement was led by "dangerous liberals and radicals", and behind them were "veteran followers of the Communist party line." [26]

The result was a rapid collapse of the peace movement as the Korean War continued. The membership of the peace societies dropped alarmingly. All but eight of the American states which had previously resolved to support world government had voted to *rescind* those resolutions by June 1951. The People's World Convention organized by Henry Usborne in 1951 was a fiasco. Cord Meyer became disillusioned, and afterwards began a distinguished career with the CIA! Garry Davis gave up his campaign for the time being and went home to America. Later on, however, he created the concept of a World Passport, and in 1960 published his book, *The World is my Country*. There are over a million world citizens currently listed with the International Registry of World Citizens, living in more than 105 different nations.

Among the atomic scientists, enthusiasm also dwindled, and many went back to their classrooms or laboratories. The Emergency Committee was disbanded in 1951. Edward Teller, with his Hungarian background, became a staunch Cold Warrior, and director of the H-bomb research program. Harold Urey also supported the development of the H-bomb. Robert Oppenheimer fell under suspicion for his opposition to the program, and was hauled up before a government inquiry, and stripped of all his government posts.

Other leading scientists, however, maintained their opposition to nuclear weapons. Looking forward somewhat, Linus Pauling was to gain the rare distinction of winning a Nobel Peace Prize to go with his Nobel Prize for Chemistry. The Russian Andrei Sakharov, father of the Soviet H-bomb, later became passionately opposed to such weapons and suffered internal exile for his beliefs. Albert Einstein continued his work for peace and world government, until in 1955, just a week before his death, he signed a famous Manifesto with Bertrand Russell and others: "Shall we put an end to the human race, or shall mankind renounce war?" [27] This led to the foundation of the Pugwash movement, which organizes high-level Conferences on Science and World Affairs, and aims to reduce the danger of nuclear war. Joseph Rotblat won the 1995 Peace Prize for his work with the Pugwash movement.

For the time being, at any rate, the peace movement which had sprung up in the postwar period had now withered away again. The world federalist movement was particularly affected by the Cold War, since federalist schemes were clearly impractical while the confrontation between the two superpowers continued; and so it became only a small strand of the broader nuclear disarmament movement from this time on.

The Cold War and the Nuclear Arms Race

Let us now move the story forwards somewhat more quickly towards the present day. The nuclear arms race continued through the 1950s, with the Soviets exploding their first H-bomb in 1953. The prevailing strategic doctrine was once again *deterrence*. It was perceived that the attempts at disarmament and appeasement after World War I had failed, and had only encouraged the Fascist dictators in their warlike adventures. The strategic pendulum thus swung back again, and each superpower was determined that it must possess enough weapons to ensure its own security, if not to overawe its rival.

The first period of mass protest against nuclear weapons did not occur until the late 1950s, when scares began over radioactive fallout.

One incident had occurred in 1954, when the Japanese fishing-boat *Lucky Dragon* was caught downwind of the Bravo H-bomb test in the Pacific. Twenty-three of its crew fell ill from radiation sickness, and one died. Later, reports began to appear of radioactive isotopes of cobalt and strontium being carried around the world in the atmosphere, and appearing in milk supplies. Demands were made to stop atmospheric tests of nuclear weapons. The Campaign for Nuclear Disarmament was founded in Britain in 1958, with Bertrand Russell, the novelist J.B. Priestley, and the left-wing MP Michael Foot among its leaders. The first Aldermaston march was organized at Easter that same year.

In view of the public concern, the US and Soviet governments began negotiations towards a ban on atmospheric testing. Then in 1962 the two superpowers confronted each other over the Cuban missile crisis, when they came closer to nuclear war than ever before or since. Chastened perhaps by this experience, they concluded the following year both the Hot-Line agreement and the Partial Test-Ban Treaty, which prohibited the testing of nuclear weapons in the atmosphere or under water, or anywhere that radioactive debris might spread outside the country undertaking the tests. This was the first major treaty for the control of nuclear arms.

The 1960s saw an arms race take off in a slightly different direction, involving the development of ballistic missiles. The US had received a shock in 1957 when the Soviets launched the first Sputnik satellite, and seemed to have jumped into the lead in missile technology. President Kennedy began a major effort to regain the lead in this area, with its centrepiece being the program to land a man on the Moon. This was duly achieved in July 1969, and represents one of the pinnacles of human achievement in this century, despite the mixed motives for the program's inception. Meanwhile, the war in Vietnam had soured relations between the superpowers even further, and little further progress in arms control could be achieved between them until the war ended.

A big step forward in arms control occurred on the international scene with the signing of the Non-Proliferation Treaty in 1968. This treaty is the centrepiece of attempts to control the 'horizontal proliferation' of nuclear weapons to nations other than the five which possessed them at the time: the USA, the USSR, Britain, France and China. Multilateral treaties of this sort will be discussed briefly in the next chapter; for the moment, we shall restrict our attention to bilateral treaties between the US and USSR.

It was during this time, as the nuclear stockpiles of the two superpowers grew to ever more frightening proportions, that the strategic doctrine of 'Mutual Assured Destruction' (MAD) was developed under Secretary of Defence Robert McNamara. This theory held that as long as each superpower knew that it would be devastated by the other one in the event of a nuclear war, then neither of them would dare to start such a war. A very stable posture of mutual deterrence would be achieved between the two nations, and so peace between them would be preserved. Gwynne Dyer has attempted to sum up the doctrine as "Don't do that, or I'll kill us both!" This implied the seemingly paradoxical corollary that anything which might hinder the "assured destruction" should be avoided. Neither side should attempt to develop a 'first-strike' capability which could disable its opponent's nuclear arsenal, and furthermore both sides should abandon any fallout shelter programs or missile defence programs they might be pursuing.

In 1972, after the end of the Vietnam War, some further important bilateral agreements were concluded. The Strategic Arms Limitation Talks resulted in the SALT I Interim Agreement, which for the first time placed a ceiling on the permissible number of ballistic missile launchers on each side. The Anti-Ballistic Missile (ABM) Treaty was signed about the same time. In line with the MAD doctrine, it placed restrictions on the *defensive* systems allowed to each side. The allowed number of interceptor missiles and ABM radars were restricted, and each side was allowed only one anti-missile launching site. The Soviets chose a site covering Moscow, while the US built a 'SPRINT' system covering the ICBM silos in North Dakota, but later abandoned it as useless.

A number of other agreements were reached during the 1970s: an Agreement on the Prevention of Nuclear War (1973), the Threshold Test-Ban Treaty (1974), the Peaceful Nuclear Explosions Treaty (1976) and the SALT II Treaty (1979). The aim at this time was never more than 'arms control' - that is, the placing of quantitative ceilings or upper limits on the numbers of various weapons systems permitted to both sides. The achievement of actual 'disarmament', or a reduction in weapons, seemed too much to hope for. Due to military ingenuity, such as the placing of multiple warheads on a single missile, and the development of new classes of missiles, the total number of weapons continued to rise inexorably throughout these years.

After 1979, and through the early 1980s, tension between the US and the USSR grew again. The Soviet intervention in Afghanistan, the deployment of new missile systems in the European theatre, and the accession of the hard-liner Ronald Reagan to the US Presidency all helped to sour relations, and no further bilateral arms control agreements were reached for nearly ten years. The US Senate would not even ratify the SALT II Treaty.

At their peak, the arsenals of the two superpowers contained a total of more than 50,000 nuclear warheads of all types, equivalent to an explosive power of between 3 and 4 tonnes of TNT for every man, woman and child on Earth. In theory, this might actually have sufficed to wipe out all human life on the planet in the event of a full-scale nuclear war, since it required approximately one tonne of TNT, on average, to kill someone in World War II. In practice this would not have happened, since the explosive impacts would be distributed very unevenly; but when combined with the effects of radioactive fallout and nuclear winter, the result would certainly have been the worst catastrophe ever to befall human civilization, with the deaths numbered in hundreds of millions.

The inhabitants of Europe were now confronted with a new and alarming situation, as intermediate-range missiles were deployed on both sides of the Iron Curtain. Soviet SS-20 missiles were installed in Eastern Europe, and NATO in response deployed batteries of Pershing II and Cruise missiles in Britain, Germany, Holland and Italy. Since the range of these missiles was only a few hundred kilometres, they reduced the early-warning time of a surprise attack to only some 7 minutes, which left no time for a considered response, and virtually mandated an 'automatic launch-on-warning' hair-trigger response system. The Europeans now found these new and dangerous weapons pointed at their heads from both sides, and located on their own territory, while they had little or no say in the matter.

The result was a huge new upsurge in the nuclear disarmament movement. Hundreds of thousands of people took part in mass protest marches through the cities of Europe. Groups such as the Women of Greenham Common in England became front-page news. Organized groups of professionals such as the Medical Association for the Prevention of War, Scientists Against Nuclear Arms, Teachers for Peace, and Lawyers for Peace sprang up and flourished all over the world. In 1982, the Pugwash Declaration was signed by 111 Nobel Laureates, calling on all peoples and all governments to strive to reduce the threat of nuclear war. Enormous pressure began to build up for the leaders of the superpowers to do something to halt and reverse the seemingly unstoppable nuclear arms race.

The End of the Cold War

For a while, nothing much seemed to happen. President Reagan began his ill-conceived 'Star Wars' program for research and development of defences against ballistic missiles. This was roundly condemned by expert groups such as the American Physical Society as impractical, expensive, and liable to lead to violations of the ABM Treaty and a new arms race. Then in 1982 it was discovered that a full-scale nuclear war would lead to the phenomenon of 'Nuclear Winter'.[28,29] Dust and smoke would be lofted into the stratosphere, and would obscure the Sun in the Northern Hemisphere for weeks and months, leading to freezing temperatures, crop failures, and mass starvation to add to the miseries of the survivors of the war. All this helped to heighten the public anxiety.

The breakthrough came in 1985, with the accession of Mikhail Gorbachev to the leadership of the USSR, when the Cold War finally thawed. Gorbachev believed in peace and nuclear disarmament, as well as 'Perestroika', or the restructuring of the Communist system. He achieved rapid results on both fronts! He also endorsed the concept of international law in an address to the General Assembly of the UN in December 1988, saying: "Our ideal is a world community of states which are based on the rule of law and which subordinate their foreign policy activities to law." [30]

This is not the place to recount the subsequent complete collapse of the whole Communist system and of the Soviet Union, leaving behind a social and economic chaos which has still not finally settled. The result was to leave the United States as the single dominant superpower for the time being. At the same time a watershed was reached in the search for nuclear disarmament.

The first fruit of the Gorbachev revolution was the Intermediate Nuclear Forces (INF) Treaty of 1988, under which all land-based intermediate-range nuclear missiles in the European theatre were removed or dismantled. This was the first actual *disarmament* measure since World War II, and although it affected only about 4% of the warheads existing at the time, it was a development full of promise and hope.

These hopeful developments have continued in subsequent years. The Strategic Arms Reduction Treaties (START I and II), signed in

1991 and 1993 respectively, have achieved dramatic reductions in the nuclear arsenals on both sides. Land-based ICBMs with more than one warhead are banned, which removes any first-strike capability from each side. The total number of missile warheads is due to be progressively reduced from about 10,000 to under 3,500 on each side by the year 2003, representing a total reduction by a factor two-thirds. A Comprehensive Test-Ban Treaty, which would forbid virtually all tests of new nuclear weapons, has been endorsed by the General Assembly of the UN. The strength of public opinion on the issue was re-emphasized in 1995 when the French began a series of tests on Mururoa: President Chirac was surprised and chastened by the world-wide storm of protest which resulted.

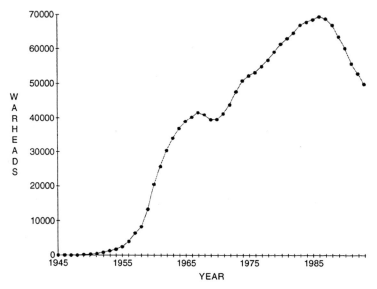

Figure 3. *World stockpiles of nuclear warheads since World War II, estimated by R.S. Norris and W.M. Arkin, "Bulletin of the Atomic Scientists", December 1993, p. 57. The total now includes many warheads retired or in reserve awaiting dismantlement. The 1993 Russian stockpile, for instance, comprised 15,000 active and 17,000 inactive and retired warheads. In 1995, there were estimated to be at least 20,000 warheads remaining in the operational inventories of the NPT nuclear weapon states.*[31]

The nuclear threat has thus been substantially reduced in recent years. Public anxiety has abated somewhat, and the clock on cover of the *Bulletin of the Atomic Scientists* has been moved back to seventeen minutes to midnight. Membership of peace societies and disarmament groups has dwindled away once more .

This does not mean that the problem of nuclear weapons has disappeared entirely, by any means. According to the START II Treaty, both Russia and the US will still be left with over 3,000 warheads in 2003. Other nuclear powers such as the UK, France and China show no disposition to give up their independent nuclear forces. In the intervening years since the NPT was signed in 1968, further countries such as India, Israel and South Africa have acquired the Bomb (although South Africa has since given it up). Still others have demonstrated ambitions to acquire it, such as Iraq, Libya, Iran, North Korea and Pakistan. In 1998, both India and Pakistan revealed themselves openly as nuclear-weapon states by a series of nuclear tests.

For the moment, nevertheless, tensions between the major powers are at extremely low levels, and we are experiencing a period of 'Pax Americana'. Led by the United States, the world community has intervened to halt a number of conflicts. Iraqi aggression was turned back by the Gulf War; some semblance of order has been restored in Cambodia and Bosnia; and some progress has even been made in the long-running conflict between Arabs and Israelis, and in recognizing the aspirations of the displaced Palestinians. No doubt many problems persist, such as ethnic conflicts, the problem of Islamic fundamentalism, and revolutionary struggles in Africa. But among the great powers, unusual harmony prevails.

World Federalism during the Cold War

Meanwhile, the world federalist movement had reorganized itself after the Korean War collapse. Henry Usborne and his group formed a World Association of Parliamentarians for World Government involving lawmakers from 10 countries, which campaigned for a review of the UN Charter; but when this failed to eventuate, the parliamentary group withered away for a time. In 1956 the WMWFG renamed itself more euphoniously as the World Association of World Federalists (WAWF), and later still it became the World Federalist Movement. The main body in America, the UWF, renamed itself the World Federalists Association (WFA) in 1965. WFA branches also exist in some 14 other countries around the globe, but their membership remains rather small.

Clarence Streit and his followers had already branched off from the main federalist movement. Streit continued to advocate a union of the North Atlantic democracies, as a prelude to world federation, and also to form a bulwark against Communism. In 1949 an Atlantic Union Committee was set up to promote these ideas, including prominent supporters such as Owen Roberts, a former justice of the Supreme Court, and William Clayton, a former Under-Secretary of State and architect of the Marshall Plan. The Atlantic Union movement gained a good deal of influence in governing circles during the period 1949 to 1959, but never gathered much popular support. Its present-day successor is the Association to Unite the Democracies, based in Washington.

New proposals for world government continued to appear from time to time. In 1958, Grenville Clark and Louis B. Sohn published *World Peace through World Law*, which remains the best known of the detailed schemes for world federation. It will be discussed further in the next section. Hugh Gaitskell, leader of the British Labour Party in the late 1950s, put forward an '*8-point programme for world government*'. In 1963, Pope John XXIII released an encyclical entitled *Pacem in Terris* (Peace on Earth), which discussed somewhat cautiously the need for a "supranational organization" to promote the "universal common good".

New associations to promote world government also continued to emerge. The Movement for Political World Union was founded by Dr. J.H.C. Creyghton in Holland in 1969, and gathered members in 50 countries. Dr. Creyghton published his ideas in a book called *International Anarchy*, and established an Emergency World Council as a preparatory step towards a world government. In America, the group Planetary Citizens was founded in 1970. Its president, Donald Keys, was the UN representative of the World Association of World Federalists. Planetary Citizens aims to increase people's awareness of their role as citizens of the planet, and it numbered about 200,000 members circa 1980. A complementary group is the Global Citizen's Association in Canada.

Academic programs on the subject also began to appear. Besides the group at the University of Chicago mentioned earlier, the Institute for International Order began an educational project in 1961 based on discussion of the Clark-Sohn model. The World Order Models Project (WOMP) was established in 1968 under the auspices of Harry B. Hollins of the World Law Fund, and directed by Saul Mendlovitz. Academic interest in the area has continued to spread ever since, and some discussion of the idea of world government is now found in standard textbooks on international relations and international law all over the world.

In 1977 a group called the World Constitution and Parliament Association, headed by Philip Isely, attempted to short-circuit the stalled process of evolution towards a world federation. They held a World Constituent Assembly meeting at Innsbruck in Austria, attended by participants from 25 countries, where a draft *Constitution for the Federation of Earth* was adopted, and submitted for ratification by individuals and governments around the globe. Some four million individuals are claimed to have indicated support in the succeeding period, but no governments have yet been persuaded. A world parliamentary group was re-established in the following year, by Nicholas Dunlop of New Zealand. Originally named Parliamentarians for World Order, it has since been renamed Parliamentarians Global Action. It now has some 1300 members worldwide.

The world federalist movement sank to a low ebb during the long siege of the Cold War. Membership of the World Federalist Association dropped as low as 5,000 at one point, although it had recovered to 12,000 by 1989. Joseph Baratta, a historian of the movement, commented bleakly in that year: "The ideal of a world federal state .. has been almost entirely forgotten. The very expression 'world government' has fallen out of use. Books on world politics no longer include a chapter on world government as the ultimate goal of some transitional strategy, and the topic has been dropped from the Encyclopaedia Brittanica." Nevertheless, he had been able to discover published works on world federalism from some 75 nations around the globe, including some 50 different prototype schemes, which demonstrate the worldwide appeal of the idea.

Detailed Schemes and Discussions

Let us now take a slightly closer survey of two or three of the more detailed schemes for world federation which have been put forward in the post-war period, and some of the discussions which have ensued.

The Chicago Committee to Frame a World Constitution, supported by Robert Hutchins and led by G.A. Borgese and Richard McKeon, produced an elaborate and far-reaching *Preliminary Draft of a World*

Constitution in 1947. It sets out the framework of a complete world government, with powers to collect taxes, regulate commerce, administer fiscal policy, regulate transport, etc., as well as control armaments and maintain the peace. It promised to eliminate poverty and ignorance: for example, all world citizens would be guaranteed free education to the age of twelve, and social security later in life. These were worthy aims, but they necessarily implied that the world government would take over many of the functions of the component national governments in fields like health, education, and welfare.

A plan like this, which involved major infringements of national sovereignty, was never very likely to achieve success. The *'realist'* school of political scientists, led by men such as Hans Morgenthau,[32] argued that politics is all about the pursuit of power, and that independent nation states will never willingly surrender their power and sovereignty to any other body, such as a world federation. We shall discuss whether this is really true in Chapter 6; but it certainly means that 'maximalist' schemes such as the Chicago draft were unlikely to succeed.

In order to counter the realist arguments, the United World Federalists concentrated their attention on 'minimalist' schemes: that is, on reforms of the United Nations organization at the minimum level necessary to enable it to keep the peace. The best-known scheme of this sort is the Clark-Sohn proposal, which did not actually appear until 1958.

Grenville Clark was a Harvard graduate, a partner in a prosperous Wall Street law firm, and a friend of Henry Stimson and Franklin Roosevelt. Together with the Harvard professor of law Louis B. Sohn, he constructed a detailed scheme for UN reform in *World Peace through World Law*. It takes the form of a revision of the UN Charter, Article by Article, together with some extra appendices, designed to prevent war, establish a system of world law, and allow complete disarmament. The plan includes the following major elements:

1) Membership of the organization should be *universal*, otherwise disarmament cannot occur. The plan therefore would not come into effect unless 5/6 of all nations consented;

2) The General Assembly would become an *elected* body, with 30 representatives for each of the four largest nations (by population) and so on down to 1 representative for each of the 21 smallest nations, making a total of about 750 representatives. The Assembly would have the power to make *binding laws* "strictly limited to matters directly

related to the maintenance of peace", but not on matters such as regulation of trade, immigration, etc., or the domestic affairs of any country. It could make "recommendations" on any subject relevant to the maintenance of peace and the welfare of the world's people;

3) The Security Council would be abolished, and replaced with an Executive Council or Cabinet of 17 members, elected from the Assembly;

4) *All* national armaments would be eliminated by stages over a six-year period, except for those needed for internal police purposes;

5) A World Police Force, or 'United Nations Peace Force', would be built up over the same period of time to *enforce* the world law and keep the peace. It should be a strong and effective fighting force in case of need, composed of some 300,000 - 400,000 men, with some nuclear weapons held in reserve;

6) Many organs and agencies of the present UN would continue, including the Economic and Social Council, and the Trusteeship Council. They would be strengthened where necessary;

7) Provisions were made for a Judicial and Conciliation System, and a UN Revenue System. The budget of the organization was estimated at about $95 billion. per annum (1980 prices);

8) Amendments to the Charter would require assent from 2/3 of the General Assembly and 4/5 of the member nations;

9) A later draft of the proposal included extra elements to protect the environment and manage the earth's natural resources, including an Ocean Authority, and a World Development Authority to assist underdeveloped areas.

The authors aimed to produce a detailed plan, adequate to the purpose, which could form a basis for future discussion. Any trespasses on national sovereignty were minimized, and they hoped that this would make the plan more immediately acceptable to national governments. In this they were disappointed, of course.

After the world federalist movement had collapsed during the Korean War, there were several academic attempts to analyse the reasons for its failure. The realists, as noted above, contended that world federation was only a pipe-dream anyway, because real world politics consisted of nothing but a naked struggle for power. Others, such as the theologian Reinhold Niebuhr, argued that the world was not ready for political unification, and further convergence between the world's cultures and philosophies was required first.[33] It certainly seemed that the world was not ready to embrace the idea of federation in a single great leap of faith. Thus people began to ask whether the same goals could not be achieved by a more gradual or evolutionary process. The main examples of this line of thought are the *'functionalist'* and *'regionalist'* schools. The latter will be discussed in Chapter 7.

The *functionalist* theory was first enunciated by David Mitrany in *A Working Peace System* (1943). He argued that the global village was already being bound together by the many international agencies and associations which already exist at a technical and functional level, such as the Postal Union, the Red Cross, the World Bank, the International Monetary Fund, and many more. As these organizations grow in numbers and power, the power of the international system also increases: "Sovereignty cannot in fact be transferred effectively through a formula", says Mitrany. "By entrusting an authority with a certain task, carrying with it command over the requisite powers and means, a slice of sovereignty is transferred from the old authority to the new." [34] Ultimately, he speculates, there will be universal binding rules of law covering all possible fields of endeavour. Political leaders would then be unable to declare war, because it would cause too much damage to the fabric of the international community. Similar ideas were discussed by Inis Claude in his classic study of international organizations, *Swords into Plowshares*. Keith Suter has painted a picture of power being transferred outwards from the nation state and into the non-government organizations, the transnational corporations, and the UN system. [35]

Mitrany is not in favour of grandiose schemes for world federation. In his picture the world would be run by a network of a thousand expert international committees, rather than by a single federal parliament. In practice, perhaps, both will be necessary.

Ernst B. Haas, in *The Uniting of Europe* (1958) and *Beyond the Nation State* (1964), formulated a theory which he called *'neofunctionalism'*. He argued that technical organizations can only be effective if they are intergovernmental, rather than nongovernmental, because they require a high degree of political support. This will only be forthcoming if they fulfill purely national objectives, as well as international ones. He performed careful case studies of the European Community and the International Labour Organization to support his thesis. His emphasis moved back again towards an ultimate goal of political unification, and it is this position, buttressed by the example of the European Union, which is probably the more orthodox position among integration theorists today.

The World Order Models Project (WOMP) began as a program of

study based on the Clark-Sohn proposal. It has involved a number of participants from all around the world, with its principal spokesmen including Saul Mendlovitz, Robert Johansen, Ali Mazrui, Rajni Kothari, Elise Boulding, Johan Galtung (founder of the Peace Research Institute in Oslo), and last but not least Richard Falk, professor of international law at Princeton.[36] They developed a number of criticisms of the Clark-Sohn proposal, from a somewhat left-wing or Third-World perspective. The proposal was characterized as a liberal, establishment, American viewpoint, which sidestepped political struggles in favour of constitutional or legal engineering. The most important criticism, however, was that the scheme concentrated solely on the prevention of war, and ignored other global problems that were of equal or even greater importance, especially for the developing world. The Clark-Sohn proposal had deliberately excluded all areas of concern except peace and disarmament, in order to minimize any trespasses on national sovereignty. Other global problems do need to be taken into account, however, if only because they may lead to disturbances of the peace. Many wars have started as disputes over trade and resources: for example, the wars of the British East India Company, or the Opium Wars in China. It was to try and meet criticisms like these, that the later version of the Clark-Sohn scheme did in fact include a development authority and environmental protection authority.

The WOMP team have concentrated their attention on the elements needed to achieve a *"just world order"*. They have identified a set of five major global problems that need to be faced:- war, poverty, social injustice, ecological instability, and alienation. Correspondingly, they see five major elements which are required for a just world order, namely: peace; economic well-being; social justice; ecological stability; positive identity and meaningful participation. These goals are broadly equivalent to those we have outlined in Chapter 1.

With their opening to Third World participants, the WOMP team have moved away from formal, legalistic schemes in favour of an emphasis on grass-roots initiatives and social movements among the oppressed , in accordance with a struggle theory of history. They have concentrated particularly on ideas including:

- demilitarization and alternative security;
- the emergence of a truly global civilization;
- global citizenship;
- the local-global relationship.

Sensitive perhaps to the criticisms of the realists, Professor

Falk has become quite scathing at times against 'naive and utopian' ideas of world federation. He declares, for instance: "The line of argument that leads from the present impasse straight to the future utopia, with no intervening opposition from present power-wielders, is sheer phantasy, the dream of a rationalist every bit as irrelevant to the politics of change as the most grandiose mystical vision of the kingdom of heaven. Linear thinking does not begin to comprehend the complexity of social and political reality and cannot serve as a source of either precept or insight into the future of the planet." [37]

This criticism is directed not so much at the federalist goals themselves, but at those who neglect the problem of how to reach those goals, which is known as the problem of "transition". In *The Study of Future Worlds*, published in 1975, Falk himself pictures a "preferred world" for the 1990s, which includes a "central guidance framework" headed by a World Assembly consisting of three houses, an Assembly of Governments, an Assembly of Peoples, and an Assembly of Organizations and Associations. He sees the transition process as consisting of three stages. Stage 1 involves raising political consciousness, and achieving consensus on the world order problems and goals listed above. Stage 2 involves translating this consensus into a politically effective movement; and stage 3 involves the actual transformation of political structures to achieve institutional change, and some degree of "central guidance". Falk hoped that each stage might occupy about a decade.

The last scheme which we shall mention is the *Constitution for the Federation of Earth* constructed by Philip Isely's group.[38] It provides for a World Parliament, an Executive, Administration, Judiciary, Enforcement System, and 'Ombudsmus' (or 'Complaints Desk'), together with an 'Integrative Complex' of essential research, planning, and facilitative agencies. The World Parliament consists of three Houses:

- A House of Peoples, representing the people of the earth directly, with up to 1,000 representatives distributed in proportion to population;
- A House of Nations representing the nations of the earth, with each nation having one, two, or three representatives depending on its population level;
- A House of Counsellors, numbering 200, nominated by teachers and students at universities and colleges within each region.

The powers of the world parliament are specified, and cover a broad range of functions, including the maintenance of peace, protection of human rights, promotion of equitable development, regulation of world trade and communications and so on, together with protection of the environment, and "solution of all problems which may be of global concern or consequence." Member nations are guaranteed the freedom to determine their internal political, economic and social systems as they choose. Powers not specified by the constitution are reserved to the member nations. A Bill of Rights for individual citizens is included. The scheme thus provides a blueprint of a complete functional government for our global village. It appears to be a reasonably sound proposal, on the face of it, and would address most of the world order values. It secured no great support among the governing élites, however, and thus had no chance of being adopted.

Conclusions

The movement for world federation reached an astonishing peak of enthusiasm in the years between the ending of World War II and the onset of the Korean War. Many political leaders and parliamentarians endorsed the idea of world government, and opinion polls in a number of countries found a majority of voters in favour of it. Although this burst of enthusiasm lasted only a short time, it demonstrated that wide community support can potentially be generated for these ideas, given the right leadership and direction. If people can be convinced that there is a feasible and practical way to achieve world federation, which will preserve their national and cultural identities, then they will be prepared to support it.

Such a federation was clearly *not* possible while East and West were locked in the mutual fear and antagonism of the Cold War, and the movement dwindled to a low ebb during that time. Stockpiles of nuclear weapons built up steadily on both sides, until they reached frightening and absurd proportions. At last the growing public alarm and worldwide protest produced a break in the cycle, and the emergence of Mikhail Gorbachev and the signing of the INF and START Treaties signalled the end of the Cold War. The number of nuclear warheads has finally begun to decrease, and public anxiety has also lessened.

Yet even when START II is fully implemented in 2003, around 10,000 strategic nuclear warheads will still remain, carrying the equivalent of about one tonne of TNT for every soul on earth. This is still enough to devastate the planet. The nuclear threat has been reduced, but not eliminated by any means.

Where are we headed for now? It seems unlikely that complete nuclear disarmament can possibly be achieved in the present circumstances. Each superpower will insist on retaining a *minimal deterrent*, sufficient to wreak unacceptable devastation on any attacker, and to maintain the balance of Mutual Assured Destruction. At present there is no other way of guaranteeing their own security against other nuclear-armed states. There is some argument as to whether a minimal deterrent consists of a few hundred or a few thousand warheads; but the US and Russian arsenals will remain well above that level in 2003 in any case.

If the superpowers try to reduce nuclear armaments below this critical level of minimal deterrence, they will confront again the age-old dilemma: How can a nation guarantee its security if it throws away its weapons? This dilemma appears in a particularly acute form for nuclear weapons, because they are still the most powerful and effective weapons of war, and the possession of them still carries enormous prestige and political "clout". This makes them very much harder to get rid of than chemical or biological weapons, for instance. As we saw in Chapter 1, the only real answer lies in the creation of a universal system of common security based upon international law, which amounts to some sort of world federation.

The other great problems of poverty and starvation, environmental degradation, resource depletion and social injustice are still with us, and some are becoming more acute every year. Piecemeal attempts are being made to deal with them, but the task could be performed much more effectively by a supranational authority. Thus the need for a world federation remains as strong as ever. The fact is that the collapse of Communism and the ending of the Cold War has removed the principal obstacle. We should now be taking advantage of the present mild climate in international affairs in order to push on towards a proper federal system. Surely it need not require another great war, or some other catastrophe, to galvanize us into action?

History warns that the present lull will not last for ever. New tensions and new disputes are bound to break out eventually between the different sovereign states. We should take advantage of the international fine weather to continue building up, wherever possible, better mechanisms of collective security and international law. We should promote the ideals of global co-operation and citizenship, and of international justice and harmony, and we should try to avoid the old narrow and nationalistic habits of thought which have brought us to so many catastrophes in the past. These "changes in our way of thinking" have indeed been proceeding at a rapid rate in recent years. The ways of the old imperial or colonial eras are now dead and almost forgotten, so that the flag-waving attitudes encountered in a novel by Rudyard Kipling or a history by Arthur Bryant will seem merely quaint to a modern reader. Young people, especially, are becoming more and more international in their outlook; and this factor may well provide the key to a whole new era of peace and prosperity in the world's history.

In the long run, I believe, the formation of a world federation is inevitable. The whole course of history has consisted of the creation of larger and larger political units. Families have been welded into tribes, and tribes have been welded into nations, with many different stages in between. One day the nations will undoubtedly be welded into a world community, and we see many of the forerunners of that event around us today.

The process of amalgamation has been a gradual one, of course, and has suffered many a setback as the Goths or the Vandals have rolled back the tide of civilization for a time. If we look at the evolution of feudal England or France, for example, the power of the central government was only slowly established. The kingdom was made up of subsidiary duchies, and each duke or baron had his own personal armed forces and system of local government. Many bitter wars were fought between them as they contended for power, such as the Wars of the Roses in England, which ended in the deaths of most of the Plantagenet line; but eventually the primacy of the king was established, and the dukes gave up their private armies and their claims to independent authority. In Scotland, the Highland clans were not finally made subject to the central government until after Bonnie Prince Charlie was defeated in 1745. Yet now, order can generally be maintained within the nation by nothing more than a police force, armed with batons.

We may probably expect a similar process to occur as the new world federation emerges. Individual nations will be jealous of their power, and doubtful of the ability of the central government to protect them, and they will not be willing to disband their armed forces all at once. We may expect conflicts and wars to continue for a period, until eventually the authority of the central government will become fully established, the armed forces of the individual nations will wither away, and the forces required to maintain peace and security will dwindle into a mere police force.

How long will this process take to occur? Arnold Toynbee (1948), Andrei Sakharov (1968) and Saul Mendlovitz all bravely predicted that world government would be established by the year 2000, the end of the millenium. That prediction is now looking a little shaky! Freeman Dyson, in the book *Weapons and Hope*, predicted it might take from 50 to 400 years: that seems a more realistic estimate, and may even prove to be conservative. Gene Roddenberry of the science fiction TV series *Star Trek* assures us that a federation will certainly be in place by the twenty-third century AD.

Chapter 3

The United Nations

"I am convinced that the Great Framer of the World will so develop it that it becomes one nation, so that armies and navies are no longer necessary ... I believe that at some future day, the nations of the earth will agree upon some sort of congress which will take cognizance of international questions of difficulty and whose decisions will be as binding as the decisions of our Supreme Court are upon us."

Ulysses S. Grant

Let us now take a look at the global security organization which currently exists, namely the United Nations. After briefly recalling its foundation, structure, functions and history, some of the shortcomings of the organization will be listed, and the attempts which have been made to reform it will be sketched.

Foundation, Structure and Functions

Even while World War II was still going on, plans were being made to set up a new security organization to succeed the League of Nations. Franklin Roosevelt was determined that the US would not be left out this time, and made sure that the State Department played a leading role. After preliminary discussions, mainly between Britain and the US, a detailed plan was prepared in Washington under Secretary of State Cordell Hull. The principal Allied powers, comprising the US, Britain, Russia and China, then met at conferences at Dumbarton Oaks in August 1944, and at Yalta in February 1945, to hammer out an agreed draft of a Charter for the new United Nations on the basis of the US plan.

The new organization was designed to be stronger than the old League of Nations, but was very similar in structure. It had a Council, an Assembly, a Court and a Secretariat, just like the old League. It was also supposed to be equipped with an armed force to keep the peace. The great powers were to be given special responsibility for maintaining peace and security, and were given permanent seats on the Security Council for this purpose. The arrangements between them reflected very clearly the conditions of the wartime Alliance. It was recognized that no effective action could be taken unless all the great powers were in agreement on the matter concerned. The old voting rule of unanimity which had applied in the League was dropped, but it was replaced by the infamous 'veto' provision, whereby no decision could be taken by the Security Council if any one of the great powers disagreed with it.

At the same time, new international organizations were being set up for other purposes. The Bretton Woods Conference in July 1944 created new financial institutions in the International Monetary Fund (IMF) and the International Bank for Reconstruction and Development (the World Bank), aiming to lay the foundations of a new world monetary system, and to provide finance for the reconstruction of post-war Europe and the development of emerging economies. Each body had an independent board, with a weighted voting system that gave the US a dominant voice in both institutions. Their headquarters were sited in Washington. In the same year the Food and Agriculture Organization was established, and a new International Civil Aviation Organization (ICAO) was set up.

The draft UN Charter was presented to a Conference of all the allied powers, great and small, at the San Francisco Conference in April 1945. President Roosevelt had just died, the war against Japan was still going on, and the first atomic bomb had not yet been dropped on Hiroshima. Some 282 delegates from 50 countries attended, including representatives of both American political parties.

Talks went on for two months, before the Charter was finally signed on June 26, 1945. The smaller powers were somewhat concerned at the dominant role which the great powers had given themselves, and tried to enhance the powers of the general forum, the Assembly. They did succeed in having some changes made. The General Assembly was given a wider scope of matters for discussion, and an Economic and Social Council (ECOSOC) was added as another principal organ of the UN, supervised by the Assembly. Some allowance was made for regional security arrangements; and a Trusteeship Council was also added, to supervise dependent territories such as the old mandated territories or new territories captured from the Axis powers.

The most controversial question concerned the veto. The smaller powers wanted the power of veto reduced, and it was decided that the veto could not be used to prevent a subject from even being *discussed* in the Security Council. A group led by H.V.('Doc') Evatt of Australia and Peter Fraser from New Zealand argued that a permanent member should not be able to block resolutions proposing *peaceful* settlement of disputes, and also should not be able to veto amendments to the Charter. But on both these points the Big Five stood firm, and would not budge.

The Charter was quickly ratified by most signatories, and came into force on 24 October, 1945. It begins with the famous, solemn preamble:

" We the peoples of the United Nations, determined

to save succeeding generations from the scourge of war, which twice in our lifetime has brought untold sorrow to mankind, and

to reaffirm faith in fundamental human rights, in the dignity and worth of the human person, in the equal rights of men and women and of nations large and small, and

to establish conditions under which justice and respect for the obligations arising from treaties and other sources of international law can be maintained, and

to promote social progress and better standards of life in larger freedom,

and for these ends

to practice tolerance and live together in peace with one another as good neighbours, and

to unite our strength to maintain international peace and security, and

to ensure, by the acceptance of principles and the institution of methods, that armed force shall not be used, save in the common interest, and

to employ international machinery for the promotion of the economic and social advancement of all peoples,

have resolved to combine our efforts to accomplish these aims.

Accordingly, our respective Governments, through representatives assembled in the city of San Francisco, who have exhibited their full powers found to be in good and due form, have agreed to the present Charter of the United Nations and do hereby establish an international organization to be known as the United Nations. " [1]

There follow 111 Articles of the Charter itself, and another 70 Articles of the Statute of the International Court of Justice.

The principal organs of the United Nations are as follows.

The Security Council

The Security Council is the most powerful body in the UN, and carries primary responsibility for the maintenance of peace and security. Its decisions on these matters are binding on the other members of the UN. It consists of five Permanent Members (the United States, Britain, Russia, France and China), and ten non-permanent members elected for two-year terms by the General Assembly. Each member has one vote, and decisions can only be made with the affirmative votes of nine members. For non-procedural matters, the affirmative votes must include *all* the permanent members. This means that any Permanent Member can block or *veto* a decision on non-procedural (i.e. substantive) questions.

The General Assembly

The Assembly is the main deliberative forum of the UN. It consists of representatives from all the Member states, each having one vote. It may consider and discuss any matter within the scope of the Charter. The Assembly oversees the regular work of the UN, carried on through its various committees and agencies and in the Secretariat. It also controls the budget. Decisions on important questions, such as recommendations on peace and security, admission of new Members and budgetary matters, require a two-thirds majority vote. Other decisions require only a simple majority. Unfortunately the resolutions of the Assembly have no legally binding force on members, although they do carry a certain amount of moral authority.

The original members of the UN numbered 51 states, but by 1993 the total number had risen to 185.[2]

The Economic and Social Council

ECOSOC co-ordinates the economic and social work of the UN, together with the specialized agencies and institutions. The Council has 54 members, elected for three-year terms. Each member has one vote, and decisions are reached by a simple majority. The Council also consults with more than 600 non-governmental organizations which are concerned with economic and social matters.

The Trusteeship Council

This Council was set up to supervise the administration of non-self-governing trust territories, with the aim of advancing them towards independence. All of the original 11 Trusteeships have now been terminated, and the task of the Council has thus been completed.

The International Court of Justice

The Court is open to any member of the UN, and can give advisory opinions when asked by other organs of the UN. It consists of 15 Judges, who serve terms of nine years, and are elected by the General Assembly and the Security Council. Like its predecessors, the Court sits at the Hague. In reaching its decisions, the Court takes into account treaties and conventions recognized by the contesting parties, and the general principles of international law and custom. The decisions of the Court have no binding force, unless the Members have voluntarily bound themselves in advance to accept the jurisdiction of the Court. Where a party fails to comply with a binding judgement of the Court, "the Security Council may .. take such action as it may deem necessary to give effect to the judgement."

By 1994, a total of some 72 cases had been submitted to the Court, and 22 advisory opinions had been requested.[3]

The Secretariat

The Secretariat is the civil service of the UN, and administers its programs and policies. Its head is the Secretary-General, who is appointed by the General Assembly on the recommendation of the Security Council. The Secretariat now consists of a staff of about 14,000 men and women from some 170 countries, with its headquarters in New York.[4] The first Secretary-General was Trygve Lie of Norway.

The Secretary-General was seen as more than just an administrator: he was given the right to bring to the attention of the Security Council any matter 'which in his opinion may threaten the maintenance of international peace and security.' This was to be used later in attempts to expand his role.

Some other features of the UN merit a brief discussion:
a) Military Staff Committee
Article 47 of the Charter provides for a Military Staff Committee to be established, consisting of the Chiefs of Staff of the five Permanent Members, which should assist the Security Council concerning military requirements for the maintenance of international peace and security. It was envisaged that a military force would be placed at the disposal of the Security Council.

Figure 4. *The organizational structure of the United Nations (after "Toward World Order", by Vandenbosch and Hogan).*

b) Specialized Agencies

In addition to the many agencies operating directly under the UN, there are a number of separate and autonomous agencies related to the UN by special agreements. We have already mentioned the Telecommunications Union (ITU), founded in 1865; the Postal Union (1874); the ILO (1919); the IMF and World Bank, founded in 1944. Some other important agencies were established immediately after the war. The UN Educational, Scientific and Cultural Organization (UNESCO) was established in 1946 to advance human culture, especially in the Third World. The UN Children's Fund (UNICEF) was created by the General Assembly in the same year, with semi-autonomous status, and supported by voluntary financial contributions. The World Health Organization (WHO) was formally established in 1948, with its headquarters in Geneva.

c) Budget

The regular programme budget of the UN totalled $2.6 billion in the 1994-95 biennium.[5] Member states are assessed on a scale based on their capacity to pay. The maximum assessment per member is 25% of the budget, charged to the USA, while the minimum assessment per member is 0.01%. Extra assessments are made to cover peacekeeping commitments around the globe. Many other UN activities are financed by voluntary contributions outside the regular budget. These cover various specialist agencies for relief and development such as UNICEF, UNHCR, etc. Many member states are in arrears on their assessments. In December 1994, only 75 out of 184 Members had paid their assessments in full. Unpaid contributions totalled $1.8 billion for the regular budget, and $1.3 billion for peacekeeping operations.[6]

d) Amendments

The Charter can be amended by a vote of two-thirds of the Members of the General Assembly. The amendment must then be ratified by two-thirds of the Member States, including all five Permanent Members of the Security Council. The permanent members can thus veto any amendments. Only very minor amendments have ever been made to the Charter, in order to reflect the increasing membership of the UN. In 1965, membership of the Security Council was raised from 11 to 15, and the number of affirmative votes needed to reach a decision was raised from 7 to 9. The membership of ECOSOC was also raised from 18 to 27 in 1965, and in 1973 it was increased again to 54.

In essence, the new United Nations is very similar to the old League of Nations. It depends on an alliance of the five Big Powers to keep the peace, and requires that they must all be in agreement before any effective action can be taken on matters of peace and security. It is not a world government, and was never intended to be one. It has no elected parliament, and no power to make binding international law, except with the concurrence of its member states. Article 2 of the Charter states explicitly: "The Organization is based on the principle of the sovereign equality of all its Members."[7] In other words, it is a league or "confederation" of sovereign states.

History and Development

Rather than attempt a chronological history of the United Nations, which would be little to the purpose anyway, we shall limit ourselves to some notes concerning particular aspects of the subsequent development and activities of the organization.

Peacekeeping

The first object of the UN, listed in Article 1 of the Charter, is "To maintain international peace and security, and to that end: to take effective collective measures for the prevention and removal of threats to the peace, and for the suppression of acts of aggression or other breaches of the peace, and to bring about by peaceful means, and in conformity with the principles of justice and international law, adjustment or settlement of international disputes or situations which might lead to breach of the peace."[8]

The principal responsibility in this area lies with the Security Council. Chapter VI of the Charter provides that international disputes which are "likely to endanger the maintenance of international peace and security" can be brought to the attention of the Security Council or General Assembly. They may then *recommend* peaceful means of settling the dispute, and encourage the parties to seek a solution by "negotiation, enquiry, mediation, conciliation, arbitration, judicial settlement, resort to regional agencies or arrangements, or other peaceful means of their own choice."

If the dispute enters a more serious stage, and the Security Council determines that "a threat to the peace, breach of the peace or act of aggression" exists, then Chapter VII of the Charter empowers the Council to take any measures up to and including "such action by air, sea and land forces as may be necessary to maintain or restore international peace and security." All Members of the UN undertake to make such forces available to the Security Council on its call.

Unfortunately, the veto provision was to hamstring the activities of the Security Council almost from the start. As soon as World War II ended, suspicion and distrust began to develop between West and East, giving rise eventually to the Cold War. The USA and the USSR found themselves at loggerheads on many issues, and whenever this occurred, the Security Council would be paralyzed and unable to take action.

The first instance of this occurred as soon as the question of a standing security force for the UN was considered. This was supposed to provide the 'teeth' for the UN, which were so conspicuously lacking in the League of Nations. At its second meeting in January 1946, the Security Council directed the Military Staff Committee to draw up plans for such a force. A Committee was appointed, consisting of representatives of the five Chiefs of Staff, but it proved impossible to reach any agreement. The United States wanted a substantial and effective military force of twenty divisions, 4000 aircraft, three battleships, six aircraft carriers, and supporting forces;[9] but the Soviet Union, realizing that control of the force would remain in Western hands for the foreseeable future, favoured a much smaller force. The West wanted the ability to station these forces at UN bases around the globe, but the USSR wanted the component troops to be stationed exclusively in their home territories. The Soviets also wanted contributions of equal size from each permanent member, while the West argued that the forces need only be 'comparable' in size. Finally, the West wanted the forces to be kept in being permanently, while the USSR wanted them withdrawn to their own territories shortly after the ending of any emergency.

These differences would not seem to be insurmountable, but the Security Council was unable to resolve them, and so the security force never came into existence at all. The Military Staff Committee was left without any useful function. Its members have continued to hold a ceremonial meeting once each month for one minute, right up to the present day, but no business is ever transacted.

The veto provision has meant that the Security Council has been unable to take effective action in any military conflict involving one of the five great powers, or their proxies. Thus the UN played virtually no

part in the Vietnam War, where the US was involved, or in the
Afghanistan conflict, where the Soviet Union was involved. It also had
little part in the early struggles for independence in the colonies of
Britain and France, such as the Mau-Mau rebellion in Kenya, or the
fight for independence in Algeria. In the case of Indonesia, on the other
hand, where only the Dutch were involved, the Security Council did
play an important role in smoothing the path to independence in 1949.

The one great exception to the general rule given above was the
Korean War. At the time when the war broke out in June 1950, the
Soviet Union was boycotting the meetings of the Security Council,
which had refused to admit Communist China to the Chinese seat on the
Council in place of the Nationalists. As a result, the USSR was not
present to apply its veto when the Security Council authorized the use of
force against the North Koreans. A military force was quickly
established under the UN flag, led by the United States under General
Douglas Macarthur, with contingents from a total of 16 members of the
Western alliance. They soon pushed the North Koreans back above the
38th parallel, which formed the boundary between the two Koreas, and
then further back almost to the Chinese border. At this point, the
Communist Chinese entered the fray, and drove the UN forces pell-mell
back again into the South. At one point the US seriously considered the
use of nuclear weapons against them, as declared in a press conference
by President Truman.[10] But eventually the UN forces managed to rally
and repel the Chinese and the North Koreans, until a ceasefire was
finally declared at the original line of demarcation, the 38th parallel.

After this episode, the Soviet Union made sure that it was present to
veto any proposal of which it disapproved in the Security Council. The
Security Council then remained virtually paralysed for the entire period
of the Cold War, extending for some forty years. It did not authorize
another major intervention by an armed force until the Gulf War in
1992, after the Soviet Union had collapsed.

Lacking any security force of its own, and with the Security Council
often deadlocked by disagreement between the great powers, the United
Nations has not been very successful in preventing or halting armed
conflict in the post-war period. There have been more than 150 local
wars around the globe since 1945, resulting in something like twenty
million deaths.[11] In Cambodia alone, the gruesome Pol Pot régime was
responsible for the massacre of about 1.5 million people, according to
recent press reports. The UN has been forced to rely mostly on
diplomatic means to halt conflicts, using the moral authority of the

Security Council, or the 'good offices' of the Secretary-General as a mediator or conciliator. But it has also evolved an extremely valuable role as a *peacekeeper*, in a way which was not at all anticipated in the Charter.

The first major peacekeeping operation occurred in connection with the Arab-Israeli war. In 1947 the General Assembly proposed the partition of Palestine, which at that time was a British Mandated territory, into an Arab State and a Jewish State. On the 14th May 1948 the UK relinquished its Mandate, the Jewish Agency proclaimed the State of Israel, and Arab forces immediately opened hostilities against it. After a period of fighting, and intense diplomatic activity, the two sides agreed to a truce proposed by the Security Council. It was to be supervised by a Mediator, Count Folke Bernadotte of Sweden, with the assistance of military observers.

A special unit called the United Nations Truce Supervision Organization (UNTSO) was set up for this purpose, initially consisting of 21 observers from each member state of the Truce Commission (Belgium, France and the United States), together with five senior staff officers from Sweden. The observers were unarmed, and their purpose was not to enforce the truce by means of arms, but merely to report any violations, and to act where possible as impartial 'umpires' to investigate and settle any complaints.

The initial four-week truce was followed by further fighting, and a period of unrest ensued during which Count Bernadotte was assassinated by Jewish terrorists, to be replaced by Ralph Bunche. Eventually an Armistice Agreement was reached between Israel and the four neighbouring Arab states, Egypt, Jordan, Lebanon and Syria. To supervise the armistice, UNSTO was increased in size to a body of some 600 observers. It has continued in existence to this day, and in 1992 consisted of about 300 personnel drawn from 19 different countries.

Peacekeeping operations have been mounted by the UN in many different quarters of the globe since then. The purpose of these operations is not to apply military force, but rather to prevent the occurrence of further conflict after some sort of truce or ceasefire has been reached between the warring parties. The UN mission may supervise a ceasefire, provide a buffer between the opposing forces, or assist in troop withdrawals. Alternatively, it may help to implement the final settlement of a conflict by supervising elections or helping to implement a disarmament agreement, perhaps.

The mission generally involves military personnel, but may include civilians as well. The operations are classified either as 'observer' missions, in which case the personnel go unarmed, or else 'peacekeeping' missions, where the forces are equipped with light defensive weapons, which they are only empowered to use in self-defence. This means that the operations can only be set up with the consent of all parties to the conflict. It is vital that the peacekeepers be seen as completely impartial, and they are usually drawn from the smaller members of the UN, such as the Scandinavian countries. During the Cold War, in fact, the great powers were mostly excluded from these operations, but that restriction has now been dropped. The military personnel are provided on a voluntary basis by the Member states, and over 60 countries have taken part in peacekeeping operations up to date. The UN interim force in Lebanon (UNIFIL), to take an example at random, included contingents from Canada, Fiji, Finland, France, Ghana, Iran, Ireland, Italy, Nepal, the Netherlands, Nigeria, Norway, Senegal and Sweden.

The missions are financed by obligatory contributions levied on the member states. Ideally, each mission should be only a temporary operation, while a permanent solution to the conflict is worked out. In several cases, however, no permanent solution has yet been found, and the peacekeepers have remained in place for many years. In the Middle East, there have been six wars connected with the Arab-Israeli conflict since 1948, and five UN peace-keeping operations have been established, three of which (UNTSO, the Golan Heights, and Lebanon) are still active. Other missions have been in place in Kashmir since 1949, and in Cyprus since 1964. The total expenditure on peace-keeping missions is comparable with the regular UN budget in size, and amounted to $3.2 billion in 1994.[12]

There were thirteen peace-keeping operations set up by the United Nations in the forty years 1948-1988, and this work was recognized by the award of a Nobel Peace Prize to the peace-keeping forces in 1988. With the end of the Cold War, the pace has picked up, and another 21 such operations were authorized by the Security Council in the period 1988-1994. Some notable recent successes of the UN missions have included supervision of political reforms in El Salvador, monitoring of national elections in Nicaragua and Haiti, and the assistance of Namibia towards independence. In Cambodia, the UN succeeded in brokering a peace agreement, and set up the United Nations Transitional Authority (UNTAC) which organized elections, repatriated 350,000 refugees, and began the rehabilitation of the country, which is still slowly proceeding.

The value of these missions is enormous, in controlling and preventing conflict, and reconstructing war-torn countries. The benefits can hardly be measured in monetary terms, but they are surely many times more than the costs. Observer missions have generally cost no more than a few million dollars each, although the cost of UNTSO has mounted to more than $300 million over forty years. The most expensive mission to date has been that to Cambodia (UNTAC), which at $2 billion[13] is only a small price to pay for the rescue of an entire country from war.

There are severe limitations, however, on those situations in which a UN mission can be useful. If any of the parties to the initial conflict is still determined on fighting, the UN peacekeepers are powerless to stop them. This was graphically illustrated in 1982, when Israeli tanks rolled contemptuously straight through UN checkpoints on their way to the invasion of Lebanon. It has been demonstrated again recently in Bosnia, where numerous truces and ceasefires were violated by Serb or Muslim forces whenever they saw an advantage to be gained. Members of the UN peacekeeping force (UNPROFOR) were at various time shot at, wounded, killed, or taken hostage. Being unable to use force except in self-defence, they were powerless to stop the fighting, until the United States intervened in strength on its own account, and pressured the warring parties into a peace agreement at Dayton.

Some other recent UN operations which have been unsuccessful were the ill-conceived intervention in Somalia in 1992, and the civil war in Rwanda in 1993. The objective was good in both cases. In Somalia, the UN was having difficulty in getting assistance to 1.5 million starving drought victims, because of lawlessness and fighting between the rival factions of General Mohammed Farah Aideed and Ali Mahdi Mohammed. The United States, with Security Council authorization, mounted 'Operation Restore Hope', with the idea of using force if necessary to control the warring factions and protect food convoys on their way to the relief camps. This was not strictly a 'peacekeeping' mission, because the UN troops were authorized to use force under Chapter VII of the Charter, and the precondition of consent by the warring parties was not met. The UN troops became embroiled in fighting in Mogadishu and elsewhere. A number of servicemen from Pakistan, Italy and the US were killed, and hundreds of Somalis were also killed by fire from the UN troops. The operation failed to prevent further conflict between the rival warlords, and was generally a political and public relations disaster.

In Rwanda, the UN had set up refugee camps for victims of the tribal warfare between the Hutus and the Tutsis; but at one stage UN troops had to stand by helplessly while thousands of people were massacred in the refugee camps under their guard. A total of perhaps one million people were slaughtered in the country as a whole. Such incidents provide stark evidence of the weaknesses of the UN system.

Decolonization

A second major objective of the UN, stated in Section 2, Article 1 of the Charter, is: "To develop friendly relations among nations based on respect for the principle of equal rights and self-determination of peoples, and to take other appropriate measures to strengthen universal peace." [14]

In accordance with this principle of *self-determination*, the UN has consistently demanded that colonialism must be eliminated, and that colonial peoples must be helped and encouraged along the path to independence. Chapters XI, XII and XIII of the Charter deal with these questions. Chapters XII and XIII describe the Trusteeship System which was set up to administer the former colonial territories of the defeated powers in World Wars I and II. A total of 11 Territories were placed under the guardianship of the Trusteeship Council after the Second World War: all of them have since attained independence, or freely associated themselves with another country.

Chapter XI of the Charter consists of a Declaration regarding Non-Self-Governing Territories, i.e. the colonial possessions of all the other UN members, such as Britain and France. According to this declaration, the colonial powers "accept as a sacred trust the obligation to promote the well-being of the inhabitants of these territories, and to develop self-government". The UN had no power to impose a particular timetable for independence, but it continued to press the issue by means such as the Declaration on the Granting of Independence to Colonial Countries and Peoples in 1960, and the establishment of a Special Committee on Decolonization in 1961. It campaigned strongly against the white minority régime in Rhodesia, for example, and in favour of the independence movements in many other colonies.

By now this battle has been largely won. The great European colonial empires of the past have disappeared, and a total of 80 nations formerly under colonial rule have joined the UN as independent States since 1945. They make up nearly half the current membership. Of 72 non-self-governing territories listed in 1946, only 17 remain, and these consist of small island territories, with a total population of only 2 million people. Some of them certainly represent contentious issues for the future: the list includes American Samoa, East Timor, New Caledonia, Bermuda, Gibraltar, and several more.

Human Rights

A third great objective of the UN is included in Section 3, Article 1 of the Charter: "To achieve international co-operation in promoting and encouraging respect for human rights and for fundamental freedoms for all without distinction as to race, sex, language, or religion."[15] No further provisions were made to pursue this objective in the Charter; but the UN has consistently acted to "promote and encourage" human rights ever since.

This issue had already arisen at the foundation of the League of Nations back in 1919. During the Versailles negotiations the Japanese delegate, Baron Makino, asked for a sentence to be inserted in the Preamble to the Covenant to state that the members of the League endorsed the principle of the equality of nations and the just treatment of their nationals. This seemingly inoffensive and reasonable proposal caused deep embarrassment to the United States, Australia and New Zealand, because it indirectly asserted the principle of racial equality, whereas those three countries had all enacted racially discriminatory laws which limited immigration from East Asia. The British and Americans therefore refused the Japanese proposal, much to the dismay of Baron Makino, and there was even a question for a while whether Japan might refuse to join the League. Let us note in passing that the Japanese position finally won the day a quarter of a century later, when the principle of equal rights was incorporated in the UN Charter.

After the Second World War, in which terrible acts of genocide, torture and other atrocities had been committed, there were demands from many quarters for a more effective system of protection for individual human rights. A prominent figure among these campaigners was Eleanor Roosevelt, wife of the former US President Franklin Roosevelt. In 1946 the Economic and Social Council set up a Commission on Human Rights, consisting of eighteen members. Its purpose was to draft an international bill of human rights, to become a benchmark, or "a common standard of achievement for all peoples and all nations." This work resulted in the Universal Declaration of Human

Rights, which was adopted by the General Assembly without dissent on the 10th of December, 1948. That date has been observed as Human Rights Day ever since.

An important issue was raised by the Soviet Union in the debate over the Declaration: namely, whether the UN would be interfering in the domestic affairs of its Member states by attempting to guarantee the human rights of individual citizens. Article 7 of the Charter lays down expressly that: "Nothing contained in the present Charter shall authorize the United Nations to intervene in matters which are essentially within the domestic jurisdiction of any state." This argument did not deter the majority of UN members, who held that there were certain basic human rights that no state has the right to violate; but in the end the Soviet Union and other Communist countries abstained from voting on the Declaration.

The Declaration contains a comprehensive list of human rights drawn largely from Western democratic models. It begins with a simple proposition in Articles 1 and 2, echoing Rousseau, which says: "all human beings are born free and equal in dignity and rights", and are entitled to rights and freedoms "without distinction of any kind such as race, colour, sex, language, religion, political or other opinion, national or social origin, property, birth or other status." It is thus asserted that there are certain natural human rights which are 'inalienable': no state has the right to violate them.

Articles 3 to 21 of the Declaration set out the civil and political rights to which all human beings are entitled. They include basic personal rights such as the right to life, liberty and security of person, the right to marry and found a family, and the right to own property. There are basic civil rights such as freedom from slavery and torture, freedom of thought, conscience and religion, and freedom of movement. Legal rights include freedom from arbitrary arrest or exile, the right to a fair trial, and the right to be presumed innocent until proven guilty. Political rights include freedom of opinion and expression, the right to peaceful assembly and association, the right to take part in government, and equal access to the public service.

Articles 22 to 27 of the Declaration deal with social and cultural rights. They include the right to work, and to form and join trade unions, the right to education, the right to an adequate standard of living, and to social security, and the right to rest and leisure.

The Declaration thus provides a broad and comprehensive package of human rights to which the people of the world may aspire. It is only a statement of principle, however, and its adoption was merely the start of a long process which then began, of drafting international covenants which should put these rights into binding legal form. Each covenant has the same status as an international treaty. It may be ratified or not by each UN member as it sees fit; but once ratified, the covenant forms a binding legal obligation.

There was a time lapse of almost twenty years before agreement could be reached on the precise terms, but at last two covenants were adopted unanimously by the General Assembly on 16 December, 1966. They were the International Covenant on Economic, Social and Cultural Rights, and the International Covenant on Civil and Political Rights. Together with two extra Optional Protocols and the Declaration itself, they make up what is called the International Bill of Human Rights. It took another ten years, until 1976, until these Covenants entered into force. By 1994, some 130 States had ratified them, comprising somewhat over two-thirds of the UN members. Each party to a Covenant submits periodic reports on its compliance, which are considered by an 18-member Human Rights Committee. The First Optional Protocol to the Covenant on Civil Rights allows for complaints to be received by the Committee from individuals who consider that their rights have been violated. To date 80 Members, or only about one-half of UN members, have ratified the Protocol. Findings of the Committee are made public, and have led to several changes in national laws, as well as the release of a number of prisoners, and compensation paid for various human rights violations.

A Second Protocol, adopted by the General Assembly on 15 December 1989, aims at Abolition of the Death Penalty. To date, only 26 Members have agreed to be bound by it.

In addition to these general provisions on human rights, the UN has campaigned very strongly against racial discrimination. A Declaration on the Elimination of All Forms of Racial Discrimination was adopted in 1963, and an International Convention on the same topic came into force in 1969. By 1994 there were 142 States party to it. An 18-member Committee on the Elimination of Racial Discrimination was set up, which receives reports and may consider complaints by groups and individuals (by now the *modus operandi* of the UN should be clearly evident!).

The UN was particularly active in opposing the apartheid system of racial segregation practiced by South Africa from 1948 onwards. A Special Committee against Apartheid was established in 1962, and an arms embargo against South Africa was instituted in 1963. There were repeated condemnations of police killings of demonstrators such as occurred in the Sharpeville massacre of 1960, and South Africa was excluded from the UN in 1974. An International Convention declaring apartheid a crime against humanity came into force in 1976. World Conferences were held in 1978 and 1983, and a Programme of Action was drawn up. The South Africans still remained obdurate, and the UN could not force them to change their policy.

The UN tried to increase the pressure. Calls for sanctions, including an oil embargo, were discussed in 1979. In 1988 an International Convention against Apartheid in Sports came into force, reinforcing an earlier Declaration of 1977. The South African rugby team, their beloved Springboks, were excluded from international competition together with the cricket team. This had more effect than perhaps anything else, as the pariah status of their country was brought home to ordinary white South Africans. Combined with a drying-up of international investment capital, this brought about an eventual change of heart in the government of President de Klerk. The major apartheid and security laws were finally lifted in 1991, and the first nationwide election under universal suffrage in 1994 saw Nelson Mandela take power as President, bringing an end to the apartheid era.

Other Conventions involving human rights include those on Elimination of Discrimination against Women (1979); against Torture (1987); on Rights of the Child (1989); and Rights of Migrant Workers (1990). A Centre for Human Rights has been established in Geneva.

It is clear that the UN has been engaged in a slow process of building up a body of conventions, which will provide a comprehensive structure of international law in the field of human rights. It is also clear that it will be a long time before the law's writ is recognized all over the world. Approximately a third of the members of the UN have not ratified any of the human rights conventions; and the UN can do nothing to enforce them in any case, except apply moral pressure. Horrible violations of human rights are still commonplace, such as the recent tortures, rapes, and mass executions of prisoners reported in Bosnia; and other examples can be seen on the news virtually every day.

International law

Article 13 of the Charter charges the General Assembly to "initiate studies and make recommendations" for "encouraging the progressive development of international law and its codification."[16] To help carry out this task, the General Assembly set up the International Law Commission in 1947, which now has 34 members, and meets for one session of two or three months each year. Its purpose is to prepare draft conventions on topics of international law.

The General Assembly is not a legislative body, and has no power itself to make binding international law. The way in which it works is as follows. First, it may adopt a Declaration of principles on the topic at hand. Then, a concrete legal document, in the form of a Convention, will be hammered out during a long and tedious succession of committees and conferences, which are necessary in order to reach some sort of consensus on the detailed terms and provisions. The draft convention is then adopted by a vote of the General Assembly, and opened for ratification by the individual Member states. When the number of ratifications reaches a certain predefined level, the convention enters into force, and thereafter becomes a legally binding treaty between those states which have ratified it. The whole process may extend over many years. A Committee or Commission will often be set up to implement or administer the convention. We have already mentioned examples of some conventions which have been formulated on the topic of human rights.

The centrepiece of UN lawmaking up to date has been its work on the Law of the Sea, a topic which dates all the way back to Hugo Grotius. In 1958, the First UN Conference on the Law of the Sea was held, and approved four Conventions on the topic. Unfortunately the conference was unable to reach agreement on one basic question, namely the width of the territorial sea off the coast of each maritime nation. The old standard width was 3 miles, which was about as far as an old-fashioned cannon could carry; but many states wanted it extended to 6 or 12 miles. Thus the 1958 Conventions were never brought into force.

A Sea-Bed Committee was set up in 1967 to draft principles on the use of the seabed and its resources. The resulting Declaration of Principles was adopted in 1970, declaring that the seabed and its resources beyond the limits of national jurisdiction are "the common heritage of mankind", to be reserved for peaceful purposes. It was decided that a single, new Convention was needed to encompass all the related aspects of the Law of the Sea. Conferences and negotiations continued for twelve years until the final text of the new Convention was approved at a conference on 30 April 1982, by a vote of 130 in favour to 4 against, with 17 abstentions.

The Convention covers all aspects of the ocean and its uses: navigation and overflight, resource exploration and exploitation, conservation and pollution, fishing and shipping. It defines territorial seas over which coastal states may exercise sovereignty as extending 12 nautical miles from the coastline. It also defines an "exclusive economic zone" (EEZ) extending 200 nautical miles from the coast, in which coastal states have rights over natural resources such as oil deposits, and may control marine research and environmental protection. All states enjoy traditional freedoms of navigation, overflight, scientific research and fishing on the high seas. Exploitation of the seabed is to be under the control of an International Seabed Authority, located in Jamaica. Disputes are to be referred to an International Tribunal for the Law of the Sea, located in Hamburg, Germany.

The Convention was to come into force when it had been ratified by 60 member states. It was another twelve years before the necessary ratifications were received, so that it was not until November 1994 that the Convention finally entered into force. By May 1995 it had received 75 ratifications. In the meanwhile, however, it has acted as a *de facto* guide to conduct for the member states: for instance, 128 states have proclaimed territorial seas out to 12 miles, and 112 states have proclaimed a 200-mile EEZ. A few states have been greedy, and claimed rights beyond those allowed by the Convention.

Another major part of the 'global commons', which has become steadily more important, is outer space. The UN has been very concerned that the arms race might extend into outer space, leading to a 'Star Wars' scenario with orbiting missiles, bombs and battle stations. The General Assembly set up a Committee on the Peaceful Uses of Outer Space in 1959. Five Treaties, Conventions and Agreements have entered into force, concerning the Exploration and Use of Outer Space (1966); Rescue of Astronauts, Return of Astronauts and Return of Objects Launched into Outer Space (1967); Liability for Damage Caused by Space Objects (1971); Registration of Objects Launched into Outer Space (1974); and Activities of States on the Moon and Other Celestial Bodies (1979). The titles sound like something from a science fiction novel, but their objects are perfectly serious. The placing of nuclear weapons, or other weapons of mass destruction, in orbit or on the Moon is forbidden by the 1966 Treaty. Principles governing the use of artificial earth satellites have also been adopted.

A third region which *ought* to be part of the global commons, but is not, consists of the continent of Antarctica. This area is for most practical purposes uninhabitable, but it is subject to territorial claims by a number of countries, and as such it is not subject to UN control. In 1959, however, an Antarctic Treaty was signed between all the interested parties, under which it was agreed that the continent will be reserved for peaceful purposes only, so that no military bases or nuclear weapons may be established there. This was actually the very first of the postwar arms control agreements. One may hope that the various parties will eventually agree to jointly resign their rather tenuous territorial claims, and transform Antarctica into another part of the global commons, free of nationalistic ambitions. It could then be turned over to UN administration for the benefit of all mankind, and for the protection of its fragile environment.

One final important area of international law concerns trade. The UN set up a Commission on International Trade Law (UNCITRAL) in 1966. It has concentrated on matters to do with the international sale of goods, international payments including electronic fund transfers, and shipping. A number of conventions on these topics have been adopted over the years from 1974 to 1989. Other conventions adopted or under discussion have concerned subjects such as diplomatic relations, the law of treaties, the prevention and settling of disputes, mercenaries, and terrorism.

The *International Court of Justice* was set up to provide judicial settlement of international legal disputes, as mentioned previously. Only states can bring cases before it, not individuals. According to Article 38 of the Statute, it may make decisions on the basis of international conventions recognized by the contesting states, and also based on international custom, the international principles of law, and precedents in the form of previous judgements and teachings.

The Court has no power of compulsory jurisdiction, although several delegates at the San Francisco Conference in 1945 argued strongly that it should have. The Statute does contain an 'optional clause' in Article 36, however, which provides that states at any time may *voluntarily* declare that they recognize the compulsory jurisdiction of the Court on any question of international law. Fewer than half of the UN members have done so, and most of those have attached conditions or reservations, or set time limits to their agreement. The US accepted the Court's jurisdiction in 1946, subject to termination after 5 years, or on 6 months notice. Britain and France also accepted the compulsory jurisdiction of the Court, with reservations, but the Soviet Union did not. Under Article 36, the Court has the power to determine whether it has jurisdiction in a particular case, or not.

As it turns out, the Court has been little used. Some 72 cases have been submitted to it from 1945 to 1994, or a little over one per year, and 22 advisory opinions have been requested by other organizations. Eleven cases are still pending, which indicates that the pace is picking up a little. Most of the cases have concerned relatively minor matters. Some have been territorial: in 1953, for example, the Court found in favour of Britain in a dispute with France over the sovereignty of some small Channel islets. Others have concerned the law of the sea, as when in 1974 the Court found that Iceland was not entitled to exclude fishing vessels from Britain and Germany from certain waters off its coast. In 1989, Nauru filed a claim against Australia for the rehabilitation of areas on the island which had been devastated by phosphate mining. This claim was eventually settled out of court.

The most contentious case was probably that concerning Nicaragua. In 1979, the Somoza dictatorship in that country was overthrown, and replaced by a left-wing Sandinista government. The United States under President Reagan, via the CIA, supported a group of 'contra' rebels against the new régime, and at one time actually laid mines off Nicaraguan ports, despite the fact that the Sandinistas had won a democratic general election in 1984. Nicaragua complained to the Security Council, which reaffirmed her right to decide her own future without external interference. Nicaragua also filed suit against the US in the World Court in 1984. The US denied that the Court had jurisdiction, but the Court found that Nicaragua's application was admissible, and in June 1986 it ruled that the US was in violation of international law, and should pay reparations to Nicaragua. The United States refused to recognize this ruling, and has subsequently refused to recognize the jurisdiction of the Court under the 'optional clause'.

This whole episode forms a sorry blot on the international reputation of the USA. But it also illustrates again the weakness of the UN system. The Court could do nothing to enforce its judgement. Under Article 94 of the Charter, each member undertakes to comply with the decisions of the Court; but if any party to a case fails to comply with such a judgement, the other party "may have recourse to the Security Council", which may "make recommendations or decide upon measures to be taken to give effect to the judgement." Since the US is able to veto any decision of the Security Council, it is in a position to put itself above the law. By doing so in this case, it severely weakened the very structure of international law which it had itself promoted in 1945.

The important issues leading to war have generally not appeared before the Court. When their 'vital interests' are concerned, states have usually been unwilling to trust the outcome to the judgement of the Court. In principle, for example, the Court could have decided whether Iraq had any title in law to sovereignty over Kuwaiti territory in 1990; but Saddam Hussein preferred to try the law of force rather than the force of law, and sent his armies marching in. On this occasion he miscalculated, and the UN system, led by the United States, eventually threw him out again. Other conflicts have had no legal character at all. In Vietnam, for instance, the struggle was between two political systems, with participants on both sides willing to give their lives in the cause. There was no possibility that the issue could be settled in a court of law.

Disarmament

Disarmament was not seen at first as a major objective for the United Nations. At the end of the Second World War, it was believed that disarmament and appeasement in Europe between the wars had opened the way for Hitler's schemes of conquest, and so the prevailing doctrine was to maintain a strong military deterrent against any threat. Thus the Charter commits the Security Council and General Assembly only to making plans for the "regulation of armaments".

We have seen how the advent of the atomic bomb changed all that, and how calls for nuclear disarmament were starting to become urgent by the late 1950s. In 1959 the UN proclaimed the goal of "general and complete disarmament under effective international control"[17] as its ultimate aim. This was hardly a practical objective at the time: it was a catchphrase which was commonly used in documents of the period, particularly by the Russians, and was designed mainly for propaganda purposes. Nevertheless, it provided a signpost, and the UN has been working in that direction ever since.

The major forum for the negotiation of multilateral treaties on arms control and disarmament is the Conference on Disarmament, which was established in Geneva in 1962. It currently has 40 member states, including all five nuclear-weapon states. It is not formally part of the UN system, but it meets on UN premises, is supported by the UN Secretariat, reports annually to the General Assembly, and includes many of the UN delegates among its representatives, so that for all intents and purposes it might as well be considered as part of the UN. The multilateral treaties concluded at the Conference, and elsewhere, now form a substantial framework of restrictions against weapons of mass destruction. They can be grouped into four categories.

The first category consists of treaties banning weapons of mass destruction from the global commons. They include the Antarctic Treaty of 1959, the Outer Space Treaty of 1967, and the Seabed Treaty of 1971. They ban the placement or testing of nuclear bombs and other weapons of mass destruction in Antarctica, on the ocean floor, in orbit around the Earth, or on celestial bodies such as the Moon. These treaties were agreed quite early, because nobody really had any such nefarious intentions at that time.

A second, very important category consists of treaties banning whole classes of weapons of mass destruction. The Biological Weapons Convention of 1972 bans the development, production or stockpiling of all forms of microbiological agents or toxins such as anthrax. The ENMOD Convention of 1977 prohibits the use of "hostile environmental modification techniques" that might cause phenomena such as earthquakes, tidal waves, or changes in climate. The Inhumane Weapons Convention of 1981 places restrictions on the use of mines, booby traps and incendiary weapons. And finally, the Chemical Weapons Convention of 1993 bans the development, production, stockpiling and use of chemical weapons such as mustard gas, or nerve gases such as sarin. It provides for the progressive destruction over a 10-year period of the huge stockpiles built up previously by the great powers. It represents another great step forward on the road to disarmament, and the reduction of international tensions.

A third category is made up of regional arms control or disarmament treaties. The first of these was the Treaty of Tlatelolco of 1967, which created a nuclear-weapons-free zone in Latin America and the Caribbean. Another is the Treaty of Rarotonga (1985), setting up a nuclear-free zone in the South Pacific. We may also mention here the very important Treaty on Conventional Armed Forces in Europe which was signed between members of NATO and the Warsaw Pact in 1990 at the Conference on Security and Cooperation in Europe (CSCE). By this treaty the Warsaw Pact was terminated, and upper limits were placed on conventional forces in Europe, which resulted in the demolition of thousands of tanks and other weapons of war on both sides of the old Iron Curtain. Regional treaties are currently under discussion in several other areas of the world.

Finally, there are the treaties which place restrictions on the nuclear weapons already in existence. The first of these was the Partial Test-Ban Treaty of 1963, already discussed in the previous chapter, which bans all nuclear explosions in the atmosphere, in outer space, or under water. It marked the first major breakthrough in nuclear arms control. Next came the Non-Proliferation Treaty of 1968, which we shall discuss below. And last but not least is the Comprehensive Test-Ban Treaty (CTBT), which was endorsed by the General Assembly in 1996, but has not yet been ratified. This will be the coping-stone of the nuclear arms-control régime, and will ban all physical tests of nuclear weapons whatever. Assuming that it is observed, this Treaty will make it almost impossible for any state to develop and test new systems of nuclear weapons.

The United Nations itself has worked very hard to assist these efforts at disarmament. It has held Special Sessions on Disarmament in 1978, 1982 and 1988. It reconstituted the Disarmament Commission in 1978, consisting of all the member states, which meets for a month each year to discuss principles of disarmament. It has also set up Regional Centres for Peace and Disarmament, which have been given somewhat remote locations, such as Lomé in Togo, Lima in Peru, and Kathmandu in Nepal. Finally, a Register of Conventional Arms was opened in 1992, to record data on international arms transfers.

Of all the arms control treaties, the most crucial is probably the Non-Proliferation Treaty (NPT). Its purpose is to prevent 'horizontal proliferation', or the spread of nuclear weapons technology beyond the original five 'nuclear-weapon states' which possessed the Bomb in 1968, namely the USA, USSR, Britain, France and China. The treaty amounts to a bargain between the nuclear and non-nuclear states. Under Article II of the Treaty, the non-nuclear-weapon states undertake not to "manufacture or otherwise acquire" nuclear weapons. In return, the nuclear-weapon states undertake to assist them in the peaceful uses of atomic energy (Article IV), and also guarantee to "pursue negotiations in good faith" to achieve nuclear disarmament (Article VI).

The NPT was ratified by three of the nuclear-weapon states, the USA, USSR and Britain, but not by France or China. The latter two powers regarded the treaty as discriminatory, and designed to preserve the 'nuclear hegemony' of the superpowers, as the Chinese like to put it. Nevertheless, France declared that she would act as if she were a party to the treaty, while China declared that she would not help other states to acquire nuclear weapons. Of the non-nuclear-weapon states, most ratified the treaty, so that total ratifications had reached 178 by 1995,[18] making it the largest multilateral pact in existence. A group of seven so-called 'threshold' states, which harboured nuclear ambitions, did not initially sign the treaty. These were Argentina, Brazil, India, Pakistan, South Africa, Spain and Israel.

A common criticism of the NPT in the early days was that the superpowers had done nothing to implement their part of the bargain, under Article VI, to bring about nuclear disarmament. This criticism has lost much of its force since the end of the Cold War, and the signing of the START Treaties. France and China finally joined the NPT in 1992, and when the treaty came up for renewal after 25 years in 1995, the parties agreed to extend the treaty indefinitely.

Overall, the treaty has been reasonably successful, in that horizontal proliferation has not occurred quite so rapidly as people once feared it might. In the years since the NPT was signed, only three or four more states are known to have acquired the Bomb. India exploded what it called a "peaceful nuclear device" in 1974. It was revealed by Mordechai Vanunu that Israel now possesses up to 100 nuclear warheads: Vanunu was imprisoned for life for his pains. President de Klerk disclosed that South Africa had built six nuclear bombs by the end of 1989, but they were later dismantled. All these states adopted a 'bomb-in-the-basement' policy. The weapons are built as a deterrent, or for use in times of need, but no public announcement of the fact is ever made. The idea is presumably to minimize the damage to world public opinion, and to avoid touching off a corresponding nuclear arms race in neighbouring countries.

A political 'chain reaction' has nevertheless been slowly occurring in the nuclear weapons game. China was the first Asian nation to acquire the Bomb, in 1964, in order to stake her claim to superpower status. But India feared and distrusted China, especially since the 1962 surprise attack when the Chinese seized a huge expanse of Indian territory in the Himalayan mountains. Thus India began its own nuclear weapons program, despite the earlier pacifist declarations of Jawaharlal Nehru. When India carried out its "peaceful nuclear explosion" in 1974, it was Pakistan's turn to feel threatened. India and Pakistan, divided over religion, have fought several wars in Kashmir and Bangladesh since their partition in 1949. The Prime Minister, Zulfikar Ali Bhutto, declared that Pakistanis would "eat grass" if necessary, but they would get the Bomb too. Despite heavy American pressure to prevent them, they eventually succeeded in their object. In 1998, both India and

Pakistan became declared nuclear weapon states, as they openly carried out a series of nuclear tests.

Other states have from time to time demonstrated ambitions to own nuclear weapons. They include Argentina, Brazil, Iraq, Libya, Iran, Taiwan, and the two Koreas. According to newspaper reports, the military establishments in both Argentina and Brazil began the construction of nuclear weapons facilities, but these programs have since been halted by the present civilian governments. Colonel Gaddafi of Libya has publicly promised millions of dollars to anyone who can help him acquire a nuclear bomb. In Iraq, the Israelis bombed the Osirak nuclear reactor in 1982 because they believed it was being used to produce weapons-grade nuclear fuel; and in the aftermath of the Gulf War further evidence was found of a clandestine nuclear weapons program. UN sanctions are still in place against Saddam Hussein because of his refusal to enter into safeguards against weapons of mass destruction. Another crisis arose in 1991 when North Korea threatened to withdraw from the NPT, amid reports that it was trying to build a Bomb. The North Koreans were eventually dissuaded after a strong campaign and the promise of valuable incentives by the US. The US has also had to lean heavily on other client states such as Taiwan and South Korea to prevent them embarking on a bomb program.

A worrying feature of these attempts is that a number of the 'would-be' nuclear-weapon states are actually parties to the NPT, namely Libya, Iraq, Iran and North Korea. This demonstrates once again that an arms-control treaty is only a 'piece of paper', which depends on the mutual confidence and voluntary compliance of the parties to the treaty for its effectiveness. It can be destroyed by the violations of parties to the treaty, or by threats posed by states which do not accede to it. It is possible that the entire arms-control régime could break down in a period of crisis, in the same way that it did in the 1930s in Europe. Many people fear that if creeping proliferation continues from one country to the next, a time will come when nuclear weapons will be used again in combat, and a general holocaust might possibly ensue.

Another worrying trend is the continuing arms race in ballistic missiles. These are seen as a potent symbol of power in the modern world, and a thriving trade seems to have developed in them. Many countries around the world are actively seeking to build or acquire short-range, intermediate-range, or even intercontinental missile systems. Iraq and Iran are also known to possess chemical weapons, the 'poor man's atomic bomb', while Libya has also been engaged in a large program to produce them. The struggle for disarmament is not yet over, by any means.

Functional Agencies

Most of the day-to-day work of the UN is carried out through its various functional agencies and programmes, which generally report to the Economic and Social Council (ECOSOC). Some of these bodies have been set up by the UN itself, while others (the 'specialized agencies') are separate and autonomous organizations, related to the UN by special agreements. Together they make up what is called the 'UN family' or the 'UN system'. The larger agencies typically dispose of budgets around $1-1.5 billion per annum, made up of separate levies or voluntary contributions from the member states. Thus the total funds expended by the UN system (including peacekeeping funds, but excluding loans) probably amount to around $10 billion each year, even though the regular programme budget is only $2 billion.

There are a bewildering variety of UN activities, and we cannot do more than mention a few highlights. For a start there are the technical agencies, such as the Postal Union and the Telecommunications Union, which regulate and co-ordinate everyday international activities such as postal deliveries, telephone and radio traffic, shipping, aviation, and many more. Their work is basically invisible to the ordinary citizen like you or me, but it is clearly essential to our daily life in the modern world.

The main focus of the UN's work, however, is on economic and social progress in the developing countries (i.e. the Third World), where two-thirds of the world's people live. Many of them have to endure poverty, hunger, disease and ignorance. The goal of the UN is to eradicate or at least alleviate these problems: and it has some remarkable progress to report. Let us glance at some particular aspects:
a) Health
The World Health Organization (WHO) was established in 1948 to raise standards of health world-wide. It has achieved some spectacular successes. In 1967 it started a ten-year campaign to eliminate smallpox by a programme of inoculations around the world. By the end of the 1980s the disease had indeed been eradicated, and the only surviving examples of the virus were held in research laboratories in Atlanta, Georgia, and Novosibirsk, Russia. Even these are now due to be destroyed in 1999.

About 15 million children under the age of five die around the world each year. In conjunction with UNICEF, WHO has been mounting a major campaign against six of the common childhood diseases: diphtheria, measles, poliomyelitis, tetanus, tuberculosis and whooping cough. In 1991 it was announced that 90% of children in the developing world are now immunized against these diseases. The incidence of measles and tetanus has been roughly halved since 1980, and polio has been almost eradicated in several regions. Further programmes are under way to combat a list of tropical diseases such as malaria, leprosy and schistosomiasis. A new global health problem has arisen recently with the AIDS epidemic, which is especially severe in Africa. WHO has begun a programme to control and prevent the disease, but it is perhaps too early to tell what success it will have.

b) Education

The UN Educational, Scientific and Cultural Organization (UNESCO) was set up in 1946 to promote education, science, culture and communications around the world. Its major activity is educational, in training teachers and helping to build and equip schools.

The UN Children's Fund (UNICEF) promotes community-based programmes in education, as well as health care and midwifery. It has a budget of about $900 million per annum, made up entirely of voluntary contributions, three-quarters from governments and one-quarter from private citizens. In 1990 it set itself a goal to cut infant and maternal mortality and malnutrition in half by the year 2000, and to achieve completion of primary school by at least 80% of the world's children. UNICEF was awarded the Nobel Peace Prize in 1965.

c) Disaster Relief

The UN does its best to provide emergency relief for those in need around the globe. The UN High Commission for Refugees (UNHCR) continues the work begun by Fridtjof Nansen under the League, and spent $1.2 billion in 1993 helping refugees. The World Food Programme spends most of its budget ($1.6 billion in 1993) on relief food aid to the starving in sub-Saharan Africa and elsewhere. In 1991 it shipped 4.8 million tons of food.

The work of the UN complements that of many dedicated non-government organizations in these areas. The International Red Cross, Médécins Sans Frontières, World Vision, Oxfam and many more like them make heroic efforts in the struggle against poverty and disease. Bilateral aid programs are also very important. The World Food Programme only provided one fourth of the total food aid shipped globally in 1991.[19]

Crop failures and famine in the early 1970s led to establishment of the World Food Council in 1974, which addresses these problems. It co-ordinates the work of the World Food Programme and also the Food and Agriculture Organization (FAO) and the International Fund for Agricultural Development (IFAD), which promote and invest in rural development, with the aim of eliminating hunger. Great strides have been made in Asia, but it is estimated that sub-Saharan Africa still faces a 40% shortfall in food production.[19]

d) Trade

The General Agreement on Tariffs and Trade (GATT) is the multilateral treaty which lays down rules for international trade, and aims at the reduction of trade barriers. Negotiating 'rounds' in Tokyo (1973) and Uruguay (1986) each produced large (30%) cuts in tariffs. International trade with developing countries is also promoted by the UN Conference on Trade and Development (UNCTAD).

e) Development

Economic development in the Third World is a major priority for the UN. Besides the FAO and IFAD, which promote agricultural development, it has established the UN Development Programme (UNDP), with a budget of $1.4 billion in 1993, and the UN Industrial Development Programme (UNIDO). The sums available to these organizations are very modest, however, by comparison with those available to the multinational corporations, whose direct foreign investments totalled $225 billion in 1990.

Asian industrial production has taken off in recent decades, following the example set by Japan. This has been due largely to the hard work of the locals, and partly to their attracting foreign investment from the multinationals - the UN can claim little of the credit. The smaller 'Tiger' economies of South-East Asia have rapidly approached Western standards of living, while the larger nations like China and Indonesia have also boomed. Even India has begun to feel the stir of life along her economic keel as she opens herself to outside investment and competition. These are astonishing success stories, and will soon qualify much of Asia to be removed from the 'Third World' category. The recent financial crisis has halted progress for the time being, but is likely to prove only a temporary setback. Africa is a harder nut to crack, however, and the efforts of the UN are increasingly being concentrated there.

f) Finance.

The World Bank was set up in 1945 to raise standards of living in developing countries by providing them with loans for development. One of its arms, the International Development Association (IDA), even provides interest-free loans to some of the very poorest countries. The International Monetary Fund (IMF) was established to co-ordinate exchange rate policies, and to help member states correct balance of payments problems by providing them with temporary loans. It acts as a sort of financial 'policeman', and makes its loans subject to stringent conditions which the member state must adopt to put its financial house in order. Some huge problems have arisen over recent years as a number of Third World countries have run up debts which they cannot repay. Examples were quoted in Chapter 1.

The United Nations has also undertaken programmes in many other areas, such as family planning, the environment, drug trafficking, and others too numerous to go into here.

Shortcomings of the UN

Some of the great achievements of the UN system have been recounted above. Let us now run over some of its shortcomings.

The first group of problems concerns the unsatisfactory operation of the organization as it stands at present. To begin with, there have been perennial complaints about the stultifying and inefficient bureaucracy of the UN. Shirley Hazzard, who spent ten years working in the UN Secretariat, wrote a devastating critique of it in *Defeat of an Ideal*. She describes how staff are recruited on the principle of 'proportional representation' for each member state, with little regard for qualifications. There is no reward for merit and no avenue for promotion for General Service staff, whereas the top members of the Professional Service enjoy large salaries and a lavish round of cocktail parties and other entertainments. In the early days, a McCarthyite purge was carried out among the American employees, to eliminate anyone even remotely suspected of Communist sympathies. At one stage, an office of the FBI was even established within the UN Headquarters building itself. The result of all these factors has been low morale, obstruction, and stagnation among the staff. A startling amount of paper is produced, but very few concrete results emerge.

Another common criticism is that the organization lacks leadership and direction. In a study of the UN development system carried out in

1969, Sir Robert Jackson remarked: "For many years, I have looked for the 'brain' which guides the policies and operations of the UN development system. The search has been in vain .. There is no group (or 'Brains Trust') which is constantly monitoring the present operation, learning from experience .. and provoking thought inside and outside the system."[20] Shirley Hazzard pictured Jackson "raking the administrative cavity in a vain search for the missing encephalon." Brian Urquhart and Erskine Childers[21] wrote a more recent report calling for more effective leadership from the top. They advocate a more rigorous selection process for the Secretary-General, with more effective delegation of authority, and a streamlining of the senior echelons of the Secretariat.

Secretary-General Boutros-Ghali began to respond to some of these problems in recent years. Soon after his apppointment in 1992 he made substantial cuts in the higher-level posts within the Secretariat, and reorganized their lines of responsibility. One of his declared aims was to fight corruption and over-staffing within the bureaucracy.[22]

The General Assembly suffers from the fact that it has little power and little responsibility, and has become in large part a forum for propaganda. Its proceedings are enveloped in clouds of diplomatic and legal phraseology, so that most people know very little and care even less what goes on there. As the years have gone by, the balance of the Assembly has been changed by the entry of many new ex-colonial states from the Third World. The United States has often found itself outvoted and under criticism, much to the irritation of the US Congress. The Congress, in turn, has delayed or refused to pass appropriations for the UN. In 1985, the US and Britain withdrew altogether from UNESCO, charging it with gross mismanagement, waste, and politicization.

Many of the member states are perennially late in paying their dues to the UN, with the result that the organization is in a chronic state of financial crisis. In May 1996, it was owed $3.6 billion, of which the US share amounted to $1.9 billion. It has had to dip into peacekeeping funds to keep going, and is periodically threatened with bankruptcy unless the arrears are paid up.[23]

The second group of shortcomings, which are more of interest to us here, concerns the very severe deficiencies of the UN as compared with what we might like it to be, an effective world federation with power to regulate international affairs and maintain international peace. These include:

The power of veto

Any of the five permanent members of the Security Council can block a decision, rendering the Council impotent and powerless to act. In its neutral peacekeeping role, the UN has been restricted largely to mopping-up operations after the hostilities are over. On the few occasions when the UN has sanctioned intervention in force, such as in Korea, the Gulf War, Somalia or Bosnia, it has acted basically as an appanage to the United States, providing the seal of approval to an American-led operation. Now the USA is a benevolent and high-principled nation by historical standards, but even she is capable of lapses into self-interested actions of doubtful morality, such as the CIA machinations in Chile and Nicaragua. No true internationalist can be satisfied with a system where the world's peace and security depend on a single country, or even a group of countries.

Lack of legal jurisdiction

The World Court has no power of compulsory jurisdiction. As we have seen, it has been little used, and has had virtually no impact on the major issues of war and peace.

Lack of military force

The UN has no security forces of its own, and depends on voluntary contributions from the member states for its peacekeeping activities. The Military Staff Committee is a cipher, and has been given no resources and no useful function. Thus the UN has no means of guaranteeing security for its members, or preventing conflict before it occurs.

Lack of resources

The members of the UN, and particularly the US Congress, love to criticize the UN for waste and inefficiency. No doubt a good deal of waste, and even corruption, does go on within the UN system - as it does within almost any organization. But the overriding fact is that the total resources we give to the UN are minuscule, and laughably inadequate for the job we would like it to do. It has often been pointed out that the regular core budget of the UN, at a little over $1 billion per year, is less than that of the New York City Police Department. If the NYPD has trouble maintaining peace on the streets of New York, how can we expect the UN to maintain peace over the entire world?

The fact that the UN's resources are inadequate has been tacitly recognized by the extra levies and voluntary contributions provided to the individual agencies of the UN, which raise the total budget of the UN system to something in the vicinity of $10 billion per annum. But voluntary contributions are never enough to properly satisfy a social need. If we truly expected the UN to function effectively as a world security system, it would need a budget comparable with the defence budget of a superpower such as the United States, i.e. something more like $250 billion per annum. The budget of the European Union, for instance, is already around $100 billion per year.

A similar conclusion applies to the human resources of the UN. The Secretariat numbers some 14,000 people: but a big international company like IBM has been known to retrench more people than that in a single year. It is worth noting that the same parsimoniousness applied to the old League of Nations. The League Secretariat was a lean and efficient operation of only a few hundred people, run on a shoestring budget of only $5 million per annum. Nevertheless, it was constantly accused of reckless extravagance. The British Foreign Secretary, Austen Chamberlain, once made a solemn complaint to the Council over an expenditure by the Health Organization costing the British Treasury less than £1,500.[24]

Constitutional Rigidity

Amendments to the Charter require the agreement of all permanent members of the Security Council, and two-thirds of the members of the Assembly. In practice, this makes it almost impossible to pass any amendments. This has hitherto prevented the UN from evolving and growing as it possibly might have done, and as the European Union has done over the same period. The organization is like a plant bound in an iron pot, with no room to grow. It has found one or two chinks, through which it has thrust new shoots such as the peacekeeping operations, but in the main its growth has been stunted.

The General Assembly

The General Assembly has multiple problems, stemming perhaps from the fact that the great powers did not envisage a very important role for it when they drafted the original plan for the Charter. The first problem is the fact that the Assembly has no power to make binding international law, but can only pass recommendations or resolutions. Although they carry a certain amount of moral weight, these resolution can be ignored with impunity by the member states. South Africa and Israel did so for many years.

The result is a certain debasement of the political currency at the UN. Representatives can spout propaganda and pious platitudes without being responsible for putting their ideas into practice. Resolutions are passed by hundreds every year, but they often have little effect.

Another problem is the misrepresentative character of the Assembly. The principle of sovereign equality for all members announced in the Charter means that each nation gets one vote in the Assembly. Thus little San Marino, with 24,000 people and paying 0.01% of the budget, has an equal voice with the USA, which has 260 million people and pays 25% of the budget. The US found itself voting with the majority in the General Assembly only 15% of the time through the 1980s. The small nations have undue influence in the Assembly, and this is why the USA gets impatient with the UN, and ignores many of its resolutions and conventions.

The last and greatest problem is that the representatives in the General Assembly are not popularly elected. They are diplomatic representatives, and must act as mouthpieces for their governments at home. Their first loyalty is to their native countries, not to the UN, although individually many of them are also dedicated to internationalist ideals. They do not have the independence, or the loyalty to the organization, or the room for initiative that an elected representative would have. Thus the UN lacks the heart, and the brain, and the will, that it ought to have. This is not meant to denigrate the efforts of the many devoted representatives and staff there. It is a structural weakness in the organization itself.

Attempts at Reform

Many proposals and attempts have been made over the years to reform and strengthen the UN. We are particularly interested here in proposals for major reform, involving modifications to the UN Charter which might lead to a federal structure.

The United World Federalists in America have concentrated their efforts on amending the UN Charter to produce a 'minimal' world federation. The Clark and Sohn proposal gave a detailed blueprint, article by article, of what the amended Charter might look like. Large numbers of other proposals were also made.[25]

Hopes in the early days were pinned on Article 109 of the Charter, which stipulated that the question of a conference to review the Charter should be placed on the agenda of the tenth General Assembly in 1955. At that date, unfortunately, the Cold War was in full swing, and when the question came to be discussed the majority opinion in the Assembly was that any attempt to amend the Charter might destroy the UN entirely. As a result, no review conference was convened.

It was then hoped that the twentieth anniversary would provide another opportunity, and new plans were drawn up. A group called the Committee to Study the Organization of Peace prepared a number of reports and recommendations. Another group in the United States called the Conference Upon Research and Education in world government (CURE) held discussions over 16 years, whose ideas have been nicely summarized by Everett Millard in *Freedom in a Federal World*. But these hopes were again disappointed.

The General Assembly itself set up a Special Committee on the Charter in 1975 to consider proposals for amendments. Unfortunately, this committee had no more success in effecting change than the non-government organizations, largely because four out of five permanent members of the Security Council were opposed to its establishment in the first place. The Committee continued to meet annually through the 1980s, but was generally unable to agree on substantive and specific recommendations for action.

An interesting proposal was made by Richard Hudson of the Center for War/Peace Studies in New York in 1976. He suggested that a resolution of the General Assembly should become *binding* on the member states if it satisfied three criteria: that two-thirds of the member states voted for it, and also that the positive votes represented both a majority of the world's population, and a majority of the financial contributions to the UN. This "Binding Triad" proposal would require only a small modification of the UN Charter, and would represent a significant step towards a true world parliament.

The Campaign for UN Reform, founded by Walter Hoffmann as the political arm of the World Federalists Association in the US, has worked very hard towards change. By lobbying in the US Congress, it induced President Carter to produce a *Report on the Reform and Restructuring of the UN System* in 1978, which endorsed some minor changes. The

Campaign for UN Reform itself produced a well thought-out and constructive 14-point program for making the UN more effective.[26] It addressed the shortcomings listed above, and also advocated improvements in the UN programmes on human rights, disarmament, the environment, development, resources and finance. Many of these programmes have indeed been strengthened in recent years.

The fiftieth anniversary of the founding of the United Nations was celebrated in 1995. Once again, some modest proposals for change were made in a report called *Our Global Governance* by the Commission for Global Governance (the Carlsson-Ramphal Report). Once again, nothing in the way of Charter reform eventuated.

We have noted above that the UN Charter is very rigid, and difficult to amend. The calling of a review conference in itself requires the vote of two-thirds of the General Assembly and nine members of the Security Council. No formal review conference has in fact ever been held. The only amendments to the Charter which have ever been passed are trivial changes to enlarge the Security Council (1965) and ECOSOC (1965 and 1973).

In recent years, efforts have been concentrated on a less ambitious proposal to address the lack of democratic representation. The idea is to make the UN more democratic by adding on a second Assembly which would represent the peoples of the world.[27] The Second Assembly might be made up of representatives of non-government organizations, or it might consist of representatives from the legislatures of the member states, or it might be directly elected by the people. It could be classified as a 'subsidiary organ', providing input to the General Assembly, without requiring any formal amendment of the Charter. This is very much a second-best solution, since the Second Assembly would be a subsidiary, and have even less power than the General Assembly does. Phillip Isely has made the unkind comment that "it would be like grafting a leg to a dead horse."[28] Nevertheless, a Second Assembly would at least provide some sort of democratic voice within the organization.

These ideas were discussed at the first Conference on a More Democratic UN (CAMDUN) in New York in 1990,[29] convened by groups including the International Network for a UN Second Assembly, the World Citizens Assembly, Concerned Citizens Speak and WorldCOPE. A second conference was held in Vienna in 1991,[30] and a third in Accra in 1992. It was proposed that a UN Expert Group should be set up to study these proposals in detail, but so far no action has resulted.

Meanwhile, the World Citizens Assembly has been organizing unofficial meetings to discuss world issues in parallel with the UN General Assembly sessions, in the hope that such a gathering might eventually receive recognition as a Second Assembly.

Summary and Conclusions

The United Nations can pride itself on some remarkable achievements over the years. It has developed an effective role as a peacekeeper in limiting conflicts, or preventing their re-occurrence. The process of decolonization has been virtually completed. Many devastating diseases have been reduced or even eliminated, and heroic efforts have been made to combat starvation, poverty and lack of development in the Third World. A comprehensive network of treaties and conventions has been slowly built up to establish basic human rights, and to control or eliminate weapons of mass destruction. These are steadily establishing new legal norms, or standards of international behaviour. As Secretary-General Boutros-Ghali has said, the UN is "an instrument of peace, justice and cooperative development among nations; it is the repository of hope for humanity and the future. That hope deserves our deepest continuing commitment." [31]

Yet the organization remains much too weak. It has no power to make binding international law, and no compulsory jurisdiction. It has no security forces of its own, and its financial resources are too small by a factor of ten or even a hundred. As a security organization, it can be paralysed by a veto in the Security Council; and even when the Security Council has taken action, it has generally been following in the wake of the United States.

The greatest deficiency in the United Nations, however, is its lack of elected representatives. It has nobody to provide the independent voice, and the drive for progress and reform, which the system needs. Many people have called for more leadership from the Secretary-General, but the responsibility for the effectiveness and progress of the world organization should never rest on the shoulders of any single individual. An elected Assembly is urgently needed to provide more courage and drive within the system.

The network of nuclear arms-control treaties, centred on the Non-Proliferation Treaty, is by now quite comprehensive. Yet these treaties rely very heavily on the backing of public opinion and on mutual confidence for their effectiveness. They can never provide an absolute guarantee of nuclear security. A state can always opt to stand outside the treaty system; or a party to a treaty such as the NPT may undertake clandestine violations of the treaty, with no effective barrier or penalty to prevent it. In a time of crisis, the whole arms-control system could break down. This does not seem very likely just at present, when the prospects for peace are the best they have been this century; but the consequences could be absolutely horrifying if it did occur. We must therefore double and redouble our efforts to build a better security system, taking advantage of the present sunny weather in international relations.

Unfortunately, the UN has so far proved virtually impervious to constitutional reform. Countless proposals for change have been made over the fifty years of its existence, some large, some small. Some improvements have been made at the administrative level, and continued gradual progress has been made in the peacekeeping system, and the coverage of international treaties and conventions. But inertia and constitutional rigidity have completely blocked, up till now, all attempts to strengthen the UN Charter.

Chapter 4

Europe

"I belong to the party of civilization, the party of the twentieth century: from it will spring the United States of Europe, then the United States of the World."

Victor Hugo

In considering how to design and build any new system, it is always useful to refer to some model or prototype. Supposing that our purpose was to build a democratic world federation, what previous models could we find?

There are many federal systems to choose from in the world today. William Penn in 1692 quoted the example of the United Provinces of Holland. For the past two centuries, however, the most obvious model has been the federation of the United States of America. This was discussed in the inspirational little book *Planethood* by Benjamin Ferencz and Ken Keyes, for instance. It took some five years after the War of Independence had been won, from 1783 to 1788, before the founding fathers could hammer out a new Constitution for the United States and get it ratified: the fascinating story of those times has been re-told recently by Carl van Doren in *The Great Rehearsal.* Yet the federation of the United States was an easy task compared to world federation, since it only involved the union of thirteen small and relatively homogeneous ex-British colonies.

Since the end of the Second World War, a new example has slowly been unfolding before our eyes, as the great and ancient nations of Europe gradually move towards some sort of European federation. This process is still going on, and nobody can be sure exactly what its end-point will be. But it is a process full of promise and hope for the world, and surely provides the best example for our purposes. Let us examine it more closely.

The Schuman Plan

The first organized movement for European union was begun by Richard Coudenhove-Kalergi, who was half Japanese and half Hungarian, and a Count of the old Holy Roman Empire. He published his book *Pan-Europa* in 1923. We have also seen how Aristide Briand made an abortive proposal for European Union to the League of Nations in 1930. By the time the Second World War began, the movement was well established in most of the countries of Europe. Branches of the Pan-European Union were founded in Germany, France, and the United Kingdom. In 1929 Ortega y Gasset published another famous book, *The Revolt of the Masses*, calling for a great nation to be constructed from the peoples of Europe. In Britain the Federal Union group was established in 1939.

Then the Second World War intervened, bringing death and disaster to many millions of people. This had been the fifth major war between France and Germany in 200 years, and the people of Europe collectively resolved that this nuisance should henceforth cease. It was widely recognized that the way to prevent war in the future was by some form of European integration, and a great deal of discussion and correspondence along these lines was carried on within the Resistance movement and among the governments in exile, even while the war was still in progress. In July 1944, delegates from various national resistance movements issued a *Declaration of the European Resistance Movement*, which stated in part that "Federal Union alone could ensure the preservation of liberty and civilization on the Continent of Europe, bring about economic recovery and enable the German people to play a peaceful role in European affairs."[1]

After the war public support for both European federation and world federation swelled rapidly. The European Union of Federalists, led by Professor Brugmans of the Netherlands and Henri Frenay of France, soon claimed a membership of 150,000 in France, Italy, the Netherlands and Belgium. European federalists also figured prominently at the great conference in Montreux in 1947. Count Coudenhove carried out a survey of European parliamentarians in 1946, and found more than half of those in France, Italy, Belgium and Holland favoured some form of federation, while only 3% opposed federation on principle.[2] This groundswell of public opinion was now given political expression by a gallery of remarkable European statesmen.

The first was Winston Churchill, a soldier, statesman, historian, amateur painter and bricklayer, and descendant of the great Duke of Marlborough, who had led Great Britain through World War II. He hardly needs any further introduction. A second was Robert Schuman, who hailed from the border region between France and Germany. Small and spare, he was born in Luxembourg, and became a lawyer in the town of Metz, in the debatable land of Alsace-Lorraine. In World War I he worked in the German civil administration; whereas after the war, when Alsace-Lorraine became part of France, he was elected a member of the French Chamber of Deputies. In World War II he was arrested by the Gestapo, but escaped and went into hiding. After the war ended he re-entered parliament and became Foreign Minister in the government of Georges Bidault.

In Italy the leader was Alcide De Gasperi, another man of the frontiers. Born in the Tyrol, he became a member of the Austrian Parliament in 1911, and then a Catholic member of the Italian parliament after World War I. He was arrested by Mussolini in 1927, and afterwards took refuge for many years as a librarian in the Vatican. He re-emerged into Italian politics after World War II as leader of the Christian Democrats, and became Prime Minister in 1945. A foundation plank of the Christian Democrat platform was a call for a 'federation of freedom-loving Europeans', and Article II of the 1947 Italian Constitution declared that:

" *Italy consents, on condition of parity with other states, to limitations of sovereignty necessary to an order for assuring peace and justice among nations; it promotes and favours international organizations directed towards that end.* " [3]

In Belgium there emerged the commanding figure of Paul-Henri Spaak. A powerful and emotional speaker, he bore a striking resemblance to Winston Churchill. He determined to enter politics while still at school, following a family tradition. In 1916, at the age of 17, he tried to escape from occupied Belgium, and was imprisoned by the Germans. After the war, he became a lawyer and joined the Belgian Socialist party. In 1932 he entered Parliament, and in 1938 became Belgium's first Socialist Prime Minister. In World War II, he took refuge in London, and acted as Foreign Minister of the Belgian Government in exile. "I am often told", he said later, "that I look like Winston Churchill and speak English like Charles Boyer. But I wish it were the other way round." [4]

Spaak and his colleagues in exile believed in European unity, and as a first step they envisaged a customs union linking Holland, Belgium and Luxembourg (the Benelux countries). In 1946, Spaak went to see the Dutch Prime Minister, and together they told their officials to settle the technical problems within six months. The Benelux customs union was duly established, and marked the first concrete step towards European union. The Benelux countries have remained in the vanguard of European integration ever since - which is natural enough, since they have been crushed underfoot every time the greater powers went to war.

In Germany the driving figure was none other than Konrad Adenauer, the 'old fox', who became the first post-war Chancellor of Germany. He was born in Cologne in 1876, studied law, and entered politics, becoming Mayor of Cologne in 1917, and President of the Prussian State Council in 1921. He was always an internationalist by conviction, and put forward a proposal as early as 1923 for a 'Franco-German Economic Community' leading to a 'European Common Market' and even a 'Coal and Steel Union'![5] Between the wars he was a prominent member of the Catholic Centre Party, detested by the Nazis. He was deposed as Mayor in 1933 and arrested, and after his release was forced to live quietly near Bonn. After the Stauffenberg plot in July 1944 he was again imprisoned for several months. Then the war ended, and he became leader of the Christian Democratic Union. In 1949 he became Chancellor of West Germany, after a cliff-hanger election which he won by a single vote, having characteristically voted for himself. There he remained for fourteen years, until he retired in 1963 at the age of eighty-seven.

The guiding spirit behind most of the major developments, however, was Jean Monnet. It was fitting, perhaps, that a Frenchman should lead the way towards a united Europe, following in the grand tradition of Pierre Dubois, Sully, the Abbé de St. Pierre, Rousseau, Saint-Simon, Hugo and Aristide Briand. Jean Monnet was the son of a brandy merchant in the town of Cognac. He was short and sturdy, and was said to resemble Hercule Poirot in appearance. He was not a strong speaker, and preferred to work behind the scenes. He had been everywhere, and knew everyone, and was an organizer and 'fixer' (in the best sense) of absolute genius. The story is told that at one stage he bought a converted farmhouse outside Paris with a thatched roof. A field owned by a neighbouring peasant farmer intruded into the property, but the previous owner could not convince the farmer to sell it, and neither could Monnet at first. He solved the problem by buying a better field elsewhere in the village, and offering it to the farmer in exchange. The offer was instantly accepted.[6]

Monnet's career was one of almost incredible variety. After leaving school, he went to the Canadian backwoods as salesman for the family brandy company. Returning to France in World War I, he found out that Britain and France were bidding against each other for scarce raw materials. Aged only 26, he arranged a meeting with the French Prime Minister, René Viviani, and proposed a joint procurement system for the Allies. The idea was accepted and Monnet helped to organize it as an official of the Board of Trade. Thus his reputation was made.

In 1919, while still only 30, Monnet was asked to become a Deputy Secretary-General of the new League of Nations by Britain and France, and was given an honorary knighthood by the British. In the space of three years, he helped to settle a dispute over Upper Silesia, and to implement a recovery programme for starving Austria. He then resigned from the League of Nations, to rescue the family firm from bankruptcy. He became an investment banker, and helped to stabilize the Rumanian currency. He made a fortune on Wall Street, then lost it again in the 1929 crash. He helped to reorganize the Chinese railways. He was sent by the French government to the US in 1938 to buy American warplanes.

When war broke out in 1939, he was appointed to co-ordinate French and British arms purchases. He was one of the prime movers behind Winston Churchill's eleventh-hour offer of union between France and England, just before the fall of France. Afterwards he went to America again to buy war supplies for Britain. He became a close friend of John J. McCloy, Harry Hopkins, and many others, and was credited with a major part in promoting the 'Victory program' of aircraft production in the United States, and also the Lend-Lease scheme. After the war, he persuaded General de Gaulle to agree to his 'Monnet Plan' for the postwar modernization of France, and was appointed 'Commissaire au Plan' to help carry it out. His record in establishing international co-operation was already an astonishing one.

A first step towards European unity was made by Winston Churchill in a speech at the University of Zurich in September 1946. "We must build a kind of United States of Europe", he said. "The first step must be a partnership between France and Germany."[7] He paid a handsome tribute to the earlier work of Count Coudenhove and Aristide Briand. Four months later, he became chairman of the United Europe Movement in the UK.

In 1947, an 'International Committee of the Movements for European Unity' was set up, and it organized a grand 'Congress of

Europe' at the Hague in May 1948, which was attended by 750 delegates and statesmen from all over Europe. Winston Churchill presided at the Congress, and resolutions were passed calling for political and economic union in Europe, with a European Assembly, and a European Court of Human Rights. It was agreed to found a group called the European Movement to press these ideas, with Duncan Sandys as its first President. After many negotiations, these initiatives led to the Treaty of Westminster in 1949, which established the Council of Europe.

Despite Sir Winston's initiative, the attitude of Britain towards the idea of federation remained ambivalent. England had not experienced the full horrors of war, such as invasion and occupation by a foreign power, since the days of William the Conqueror. Whereas Germany had lost 3.75 million killed in the war, representing 5 percent of her entire population, Britain had lost only one-quarter as many in proportion, and had emerged the final victor.[8] She was still firmly wedded to what remained of the British Empire, including her many colonial possessions and the countries of the British Commonwealth, and she was still attached to her 'special relationship' with the United States. She was not ready to contemplate a full political union with the other nations of Europe. The most she would accept was a 'confederation', or a glorified alliance with the other European powers, and not a true federation. If the others wanted to go further, they would have to do it on their own.

This was reflected in the eventual Statute of the Council of Europe. Two bodies were established, a Committee of Ministers consisting of the foreign ministers of the member states, and a Consultative Assembly consisting of representatives appointed by the various national parliaments, providing a "means through which the aspirations of the European peoples may be formulated and expressed." They met once a year at Strasbourg. Ten nations were included at first: France, Britain, the Benelux countries, Denmark, Norway, Ireland, Italy and Sweden. Ten more were to join later on, namely Iceland, Germany, Greece, Austria, Turkey, Cyprus, Switzerland, Malta, Spain and Portugal, making twenty in all. The first meeting in August 1949 was a grand affair, with Churchill and many other powerful dignitaries among the delegates. Paul-Henri Spaak was elected as first President of the Assembly.

Unfortunately, the new Council of Europe had no legislative power: it was a sort of mini-United Nations within Europe. The Assembly could only make recommendations to the Committee of Ministers, and so became just another 'talk-shop'; while the Committee of Ministers was empowered only to make recommendations to the member governments. Like the UN, the Council performed some useful technical tasks, and established a European Convention for the Protection of Human Rights, and a European Court. But as a political body, it was all but useless. Within two years, Spaak had resigned in disgust. Regarding the Committee of Ministers, he wrote: "Of all the international bodies I have known, I have never found any more timorous or more impotent."[9] It was clear that something more was needed.

The Americans, led by people such as George Kennan, Senator Fulbright, General George C. Marshall, Secretary of State John Foster Dulles, and President Truman himself, were all in favour of European federation. They were anxious to re-establish a strong Europe, and if possible a united Europe, as an ally and a buffer against the Soviet Union. Since they were not themselves involved, they could see the merits of a federation, on the American model, to prevent future wars. From a distance, it all looked easy. To help the process, they set up the Marshall Plan in 1947, which channelled an enormous total of over $20 billion in grants and aid towards European reconstruction over a period of several years. To administer the plan, the Organization for European Economic Co-operation (OEEC) was set up in 1948, which later became the OECD. A private American Committee on United Europe was incorporated in 1949. In the same year, the North Atlantic Treaty Organization (NATO) was created, establishing a military alliance between North America and Western Europe.

It was at this time, while federalists were mulling over their disappointment in the Council of Europe, that Jean Monnet stepped in. The problem of Germany was now becoming urgent. The Federal Republic had recently been created, with Konrad Adenauer as its first Chancellor, and industrial production was beginning to recover.

The question was how to integrate the new Germany into the polity of European states. Adenauer himself proposed, in interviews and speeches at this time, that a political union should be formed between France and Germany, to be open also to Britain, Italy and the Benelux countries.[10] Monnet now came up with a more practical and carefully limited proposal, which came to be known as the *Schuman Plan*.

The scheme Monnet put forward was to amalgamate the coal and steel industries of France and Germany, together with any other interested parties, under a single authority. These industries provided the basic sinews of war, and once they were amalgamated it would become virtually impossible for the two countries to go to war against each other ever again. The functions of the common authority might later be expanded in a gradual and stepwise fashion, to form the basis of the hoped-for European federation.

Monnet sent a copy of his scheme to the French Prime Minister, Georges Bidault, but it was mislaid in a drawer. Meanwhile, he showed it to the Foreign Minister, Robert Schuman, who accepted it almost at once. On 9 May 1950, Schuman presented it formally to the French Cabinet, who approved it, and that afternoon he announced it to the press. Meanwhile, copies had been sent to Germany and the US, and Adenauer's agreement had been obtained. The Benelux countries and Italy soon joined in. Britain, however, was not initially informed, and the Foreign Secretary, Ernest Bevin, was hostile to the whole idea. Britain could not be persuaded to join.

The Schuman Declaration included the following passage, which announces the underlying intention of the plan:

"Europe will not be made all at once, or according to a single general plan. It will be built through concrete achievements which first create a de facto solidarity .. The pooling of coal and steel production will immediately provide for the setting up of common bases for economic development as a first step in the federation of Europe." [11]

This is very much a 'functional' approach, in accordance with ideas which were first becoming fashionable about that time. The anniversary of the declaration, on the 9th May, is now celebrated as 'Europe Day' each year.

The following month, delegations from 'the Six' gathered in Paris to draft a detailed treaty. The work took nine months, under the leadership of Jean Monnet, and resulted in the Treaty of Paris establishing the European Coal and Steel Community (ECSC) signed in 1951. The Treaty was then the subject of long and heated debates in all six national parliaments, but was eventually ratified and came into force in 1952. It provided for a common market in coal, coke, steel, iron ore and scrap, and established five main organisms:

- a 9-man High Authority, to run the organization from day to day;
- a Council of Ministers from the member states, to approve overall policy;
- a 78-member Common Assembly chosen by and from the national parliaments, which could make recommendations to the Council;
- a Consultative Assembly consisting of producers and users of coal

and steel products, to provide technical advice;

- a supreme Court of Justice with seven judges and two advocates-general.

The ECSC was clearly over-engineered for a mere industrial association: the Common Assembly and the Court were included in anticipation of its evolution into a full European federation. Monnet himself was elected as the first President of the High Authority, and threw himself energetically into the task. The common markets in coal and steel were opened in 1953.

Monnet did not rest on his laurels. Having set in motion plans for a European economic community, he next began to formulate separate plans for a European Defence Community (EDC) and a European Political Community (EPC).

The Korean War had by now begun, and the US was proposing that Germany should be rearmed, in order to contribute to European defence. The French were alarmed at this prospect, and suggestions were made by several people that German forces should only be raised within the context of a common European army. Monnet sent a plan to the French Defence Minister, René Pleven, for an EDC very much along the lines of the Schuman Plan, with a European army administered by a Commissariat, a Council of Ministers, and an Assembly and a Court which were to be shared with the ECSC. This draft proposal was presented to the French National Assembly by René Pleven in October 1950, and became known as the Pleven Plan. Again, a treaty-making conference was convened in Paris, and the resulting EDC Treaty was signed in May 1952.

The ECSC itself decided to draft another treaty providing for a European Political Community, and by March 1953 the draft was ready. It envisaged a European Executive Council, a Council of national Ministers, a Court, and a Parliament consisting of a Senate chosen from the national parliaments, together with a People's Chamber elected by the citizens as a whole. It seemed that a federal Europe was almost built already.

It was now that the wheels began to fall off the process, and opposition began to be felt. The EDC Treaty was at length approved by the legislatures in Germany, Holland, Belgium and Luxembourg, but not in Italy or France. The British would have nothing to do with it. Opposition came from both the Left and the Right. The Communists objected to the creation of a European army which could only be aimed at the Soviet Union; while the ultra-nationalists, such as the Gaullists in

France, objected to the loss of sovereignty which would be involved in committing part of the national forces to a European army. The war in Korea had now ended, and the need for an integrated defence force seemed less urgent. De Gasperi's government in Italy had fallen, and in France a more conservative government was in office, which included several Gaullists. The EDC Treaty was presented to the National Assembly by the new Prime Minister, Pierre Mendès-France, but he was himself lukewarm about it. In the event the Assembly voted to reject the Treaty by 319 votes to 264, with 43 abstentions including Mendès-France himself. The idea of a common European defence force had been dealt a mortal blow, from which it has still not recovered forty years later. The EPC Treaty made even less progress. The draft treaty was not approved by the Foreign Ministers of the Six, and after the defeat of the EDC it was tacitly dropped.

A less ambitious plan for defence co-operation was prepared by the British, and signed in October 1954. It created the Western European Union (WEU), which amounted to a military alliance of the European nations. It has acted essentially as a forum for discussion, and has been completely overshadowed by NATO, to which all the actual forces were attached until recently.

The Common Market

European federalists were generally dismayed by the defeat of the EDC Treaty, but Monnet and Spaak were not discouraged. They determined in early 1955 that Europe must be relaunched. The Benelux countries prepared a memorandum suggesting that the coal and steel community should be extended to form a common market covering the whole economic field. Spaak arranged a meeting of the Foreign Ministers of the Six, who supported the idea, and they set up a Committee to work out detailed proposals, headed by Spaak himself. Meanwhile, Jean Monnet stepped down from his Presidency of the High Authority of the ECSC, and formed a private 'Action Committee for the United States of Europe' to push things along. This committee was to continue its campaign for another twenty years, until 1975.

Spaak's committee began its meetings in Brussels in July 1955, and produced a report by March 1956 which was approved by the ECSC Assembly and the Foreign Ministers of the Six. The Committee was then commissioned to draft some actual Treaties. Spaak drove them hard. On one occasion, when the experts could not agree on the tariff to be applied to imported bananas, he lost his temper. "I give you two hours", he said. "If it's not settled by then, I shall call the press in and announce that Europe won't be built after all, because we can't agree about bananas!" [12]

By March 1957 the two Treaties were ready, and were signed in Rome. By January 1958 they had been ratified by all the Six, and entered into force. One of the Treaties established the European atomic agency Euratom, and the other established the European Economic Community (EEC), usually called the Common Market. The EEC was based in Brussels, and its first president was Walter Hallstein, a protegé of Konrad Adenauer who had been Rector of Frankfurt University before being appointed head of the German Foreign Office. He was another ardent pro-European.

The structure of the EEC followed what was by now the standard European pattern. It consisted of:

- a 9-man Commission, headed by Walter Hallstein, to run the day-to-day operations;
- a Council of national Ministers, to approve overall policy;
- a Court of Justice;
- the European Parliament of 142 members.

The Court and the Parliament were shared as common institutions between the ECSC, Euratom and the EEC.

As a means of promoting economic growth, the Common Market was an immediate success. By mid-1961, the tariff barriers between the Six had been almost halved, trade between them had increased by 70 percent, and overall production was up 20 percent.[13] An 'economic miracle' was occurring, and the practical benefits of European integration were becoming obvious for all to see.

Britain had still been reluctant to take part, and had refused to join the Treaty of Rome. In 1960 she formed a rival organization, the European Free Trade Association (EFTA), made up of Austria, Denmark, Norway, Portugal, Sweden and Switzerland. This was a much smaller and more widely scattered group than the Common Market, however, and it did not have the same striking success.

Britain now began to reconsider her position. Selwyn Lloyd, the Foreign Secretary, actually admitted in 1960: "I believe we made a mistake in not taking part in the negotiations which led to the formation of the coal and steel community."[13] John Kennedy had become President in America, and he gave strong encouragement for Britain to join the Common Market. At last in July 1961, Harold Macmillan announced to the House of Commons that Britain would begin negotiations to join the EEC, and Ireland and Denmark quickly did the same. The British negotiators were led by Edward Heath.

There were some difficult obstacles to overcome. Britain was concerned about her Commonwealth partners, and wanted to preserve access for their products such as New Zealand butter, at least to the British market. She was also concerned about the farm support program, one of the major priorities of the EEC, which was likely to be a drain on the British taxpayers, and of little benefit to the efficient British farmers. Negotiations dragged on for over a year, until they were brought to a sudden halt by the even more formidable obstacle of Charles de Gaulle.

General de Gaulle was a towering figure in French politics. He had been leader of the Free French during the war, and served briefly as the first French President after the war; and in 1958 he was dramatically returned to power during the Algerian crisis. He was a nationalist first and foremost, and stood always for the power and glory of France, and he had no sympathy for supranationalist ideas. He and his party had opposed the Schuman Plan, the Common Market, and Euratom. He was impatient with the British hesitations, and suspicious of their ties to America. He was also offended when Britain purchased American Polaris missiles instead of collaborating on a missile development program with the French. On 14 January 1963 he announced that Britain was not ready to join the Common Market because of her links with overseas countries, and instructed his Foreign Minister, Maurice Couve de Murville, to break off negotiations. One German delegate is said to have sat weeping at the table as the negotiators left the conference in Brussels.[14]

De Gaulle was to stifle further progress towards European integration for the best part of a decade. In 1965, the European Commission proposed some improvements in the EEC, consisting of a farm finance package, independent financing for the EEC, and greater powers for the European Parliament. The French wanted the farm finance package, but not the rest, which would have extended the supranational powers of the EEC. Once again, Couve de Murville broke off the negotiations, and the French actually boycotted the meetings of the Council for several months. Again in 1967, the British under Harold Wilson applied to join the Common Market. Once more the proposal was vetoed by Charles de Gaulle. The only forward progress occurred when the European structure was rationalized, and the ECSC and Euratom were merged into the EEC in 1967 to form a single entity, which was henceforwards simply called the European Community (EC).

In 1969 General de Gaulle finally resigned, to be succeeded as President by the much more progressive Georges Pompidou. Pompidou called a summit meeting of European leaders at the Hague, where it was agreed to widen the community by inviting Britain and others to reapply for membership. Here and at a subsequent meeting in Paris in 1972 some important new goals were laid down. It was agreed to deepen the community by aiming for full economic and monetary union, and eventually political unification as well. The Community was given its own independent sources of revenue, made up from agricultural levies, customs duties, and value added tax, and the budgetary powers of the European Parliament were strengthened.

In 1970 the British under Edward Heath applied for the third time to join the EC, along with Ireland, Denmark and Norway. Their applications were approved, and Britain, Ireland and Denmark were finally admitted in 1972. The Norwegian people, however, voted by a narrow majority at a referendum not to join, whereupon their government promptly resigned. In later years, Greece (1981) and Spain and Portugal (1986) were also to join the EC.

Further progress was impeded by the economic crisis caused by the OPEC oil shock. Attempts had been made to limit fluctuations between the European currencies, in preparation for monetary union, but these had to be abandoned in 1974. Britain was also unhappy about the scale of her contributions to the Common Agricultural Policy (CAP), and did not feel she was getting enough in return. Her conditions of entry to the EC were re-negotiated by Harold Wilson in 1974, and her continued membership was put to a national referendum in 1975, which approved it.

Another important summit meeting was held in Paris in 1974, at the invitation of Valéry Giscard d'Estaing, who had become President of France after Pompidou's death, and had previously been a member of Monnet's Action Committee for the United States of Europe. Three notable decisions were taken. Firstly, it was agreed to institute direct elections for the European Parliament: this was finally implemented in 1979. Secondly, it was agreed to explore ideas for European Union: this led nowhere for a time. Finally, it was agreed to hold regular summit meetings to discuss community policy, forming a European Council of Heads of Government (not to be confused with the earlier Council of Europe!). This in itself was a recognition of the increasingly important role of the EC. From this point on, all important decisions about the future of the community were to be taken at meetings of the European Council.

In 1979, moves towards monetary union were restarted by Roy Jenkins, then President of the Commission. The monetary 'snake' was reinstated, restraining currency fluctuations within a narrow band. The European Monetary System (EMS) was set up, and a European Currency Unit (ecu) was established, based on a basket of currencies of the member states.

The European Union

One of the members of the first elected Parliament in 1979 was Altiero Spinelli from Italy. Spinelli had early in life been a member of the Italian Communist Party, and was interned by Mussolini's régime for a total of sixteen years. He was one of the founders of the 'Movimento Federalista Europeo' in Milan in 1943, and was later Secretary General of the European Federalist Movement from 1948 to 1962. He served on the European Commission from 1970 to 1976, before being elected to the Parliament. He was keen to promote reform of the EC, aiming towards a complete union.

In 1980 Spinelli founded the 'Crocodile Club', a group of parliamentarians named after a restaurant where they went to dine in Strasbourg. They succeeded in having a *Draft Treaty for European Union* drawn up, which was adopted by the Parliament on 14 February 1984 by 231 votes to 31, with 43 abstaining. The structure it proposed was much more far-reaching than the one recently adopted under the Maastricht Treaty. It gave the Union responsibility for foreign affairs and defence, and also education, research, and cultural matters. It was thus a rather 'maximalist' proposal, although it did adopt the so-called principle of *'subsidiarity'*, according to which the union "shall only act to carry out those tasks which may be undertaken more effectively in common than by the Member States acting separately."[15] It called for free movement of people, goods, services and capital within the union. The Council of Ministers and the Parliament were to be given equal weight in making decisions. The Parliament had no power to put this Draft Treaty into operation itself, but the European Council agreed to set up an Ad Hoc Committee to study the proposals.

Attitudes towards European integration followed a consistent pattern within the European Council throughout the 1980s. The original Six were consistently in favour of further integration. A strong bond was

formed between the giant figures of Helmut Kohl of Germany and
François Mitterand of France, which provided the engine for progress,
steadily supported by the Benelux countries and Italy. The latecomers to
the community were much less enthusiastic, particularly Britain,
Denmark and Greece. The leader of the opposition was Margaret
Thatcher, the 'Iron Lady' from Britain. She was a true-blue
Conservative, who saw herself as cast in the Churchillian mould,
charged with restoring Britain's self-respect and economic prosperity
after decades of decline. Like de Gaulle, she wanted nothing to do with
further supranational adventures, and attended European Council
meetings with her famous handbag at the ready. In the early 1980s she
campaigned strongly for a reduction in Britain's financial contributions
to the Community, and succeeded in obtaining agreement for a
substantial rebate in 1984.

Another force for progress was Jacques Delors, who became
President of the Commission in 1985, and moved immediately to
revitalize its somewhat decayed bureaucracy. He proposed a seven-year
timetable for removing the remaining trade barriers within the
Community, in order to achieve a single market. He also oversaw the
drafting of the Single European Act, which provided the first major
changes to the EC structure since the Treaty of Rome. Both measures
were approved by the Council, and the Act came into force in 1987.

The Single European Act gave formal status to the European
Council, and gave greater voice and influence to the Parliament. The
member states agreed to harmonize their economic and monetary
policies, and to standardize policies concerning taxes, employment,
health and the environment. A Court of First Instance was established to
hear appeals against EC rulings. Most importantly, a system of weighted
voting on some issues was introduced into the Council of Ministers
instead of the previous unanimous voting rule which had given an
effective power of veto to each member state.

In the late 80s, the Common Agricultural Policy was rationalized. It
had previously accounted for fully two-thirds of the entire EC budget,
resulting in the accumulation of huge surpluses of agricultural products:
the 'butter mountain', the 'wine lake', and so forth. Under a new
scheme introduced in 1988, payments under the CAP were limited, and
agricultural subsidies began slowly to decrease.

As preparations continued for the coming single market, calls for
greater European unity in other areas were made. The Commission
prepared a three-stage plan for achieving economic and monetary union

(EMU), and proposed a social charter on human rights. West Germany and France proposed an intergovernmental conference (IGC) to discuss these ideas, and to begin work on a treaty to incorporate them. Margaret Thatcher voiced strong opposition to any further European integration, but in so doing she split her own Conservative party, and this was partly responsible for her being voted out of office and replaced by John Major in 1990.

The Treaty on European Union was signed in Maastricht on 7 February 1992. It was then put up for ratification by the member states. A referendum was held in most countries, and in some cases the result was very close. In France the treaty was approved by a thin margin of only 3.4%, while in Denmark the first referendum was actually lost, and a second vote had to be engineered later to get the treaty through. In Britain the government did not dare to put the issue to a referendum, and John Major had to battle the treaty through the parliament clause by clause. Nevertheless, by October 1993 the treaty had been ratified by all twelve member states, and came into effect.

The Maastricht Treaty transformed the EC into the European Union (EU), and established the single market. All trade barriers were eliminated, so that for example the customs post at Dover was removed and 500 Customs inspectors were put out of work. European citizenship was granted to the citizens of each member state, with freedom to live, work or study anywhere within the Union. Provision was made for full economic and monetary union by 1999. Enhanced powers were given to the European Parliament, and commitments were made towards a common foreign policy and defence policy for the Union. The treaty also included a Social Chapter, which Britain decided not to ratify at first.

The Treaty was also designed to reassure the Member states that their sovereignty was not threatened. Article F of the Treaty states: "The Union shall respect the national identities of its member states." The principle of subsidiarity is enshrined within the Treaty, and is interpreted in a rather stronger sense than in the Draft Treaty, so that whatever can be done locally, regionally or nationally should not be done at community level.[16]

New states have since applied to join the Union. Austria, Sweden and Finland were admitted to membership at the beginning of 1995: thus the Union now has a total of 15 member states. Switzerland and Norway were invited to join, but their citizens voted to reject membership at a national referendum in each case. There is also a long queue of further states in the Mediterranean and Eastern Europe who have applied for membership. Turkey, Cyprus, Malta, and Morocco have been granted associate status, but their applications for full membership have been deferred. In the case of Morocco, the application was rejected outright, on the grounds that she is not a European state. The applications of the former Soviet satellites Bulgaria, Hungary, Poland, Romania, the Czech Republic and Slovakia have been regarded favourably, but some appropriate economic criteria must be met before they can be accepted.

The Current Situation

The years since 1993 have largely been occupied in attempting to digest the provisions of the Maastricht Treaty. A certain amount of public disenchantment with Europe has set in. The strict financial criteria required by the timetable for monetary union have been blamed for causing budget cuts and unemployment. The parliamentarians in Strasbourg are seen as overpaid and underworked (quite unfairly), and the bureaucracy in Brussels is blamed for officious interference in the affairs of everyday life. Regulations from Brussels have dictated the shape of electrical plugs, the type of apples which can be grown in Denmark, and even the approved shape of cucumbers. Such pettifogging restrictions cause a good deal of public resentment, whereas the huge but rather intangible benefits of European integration are harder for the man in the street to see. Could it be that Europe won't be built after all, because they can't agree about cucumbers?

The deadline for monetary union, with the establishment of a European Central Bank and a common currency (the 'euro'), is 1 January, 1999 at latest. A recent public opinion poll has shown public support for a single European currency is presently 67% in France, but only 40% in Germany, with 52% opposed. In Britain, 58% are opposed.[17] Britain has in fact reserved the right not to join in the third phase of EMU (i.e. the single currency), and Denmark has already decided not to join it. On the issue of an eventual United States of Europe with a federal government, there is substantial support but not a majority, with 41% in favour in Germany and 45% opposed, 38% in favour in France and 52% opposed, and only 27% in favour in Britain, with 57% opposed.[17]

The present lack of any common European policies on foreign affairs and defence was starkly exposed by the recent crisis in Yugoslavia. The United States for a long time left Europe to sort out this problem in its own backyard. The Europeans, however, could not agree what ought to be done, and apart from sending envoys to try and mediate a settlement, they completely failed to find any effective measures to halt the conflict. It was only when the US and NATO stepped in that the war in Bosnia was ended by means of the Dayton accords.

Britain remains politically divided over Europe. Opposition to Europe has hardened within the Conservative Party, but the new Labour Government of Tony Blair appears more sympathetic to the European ideal.

A new Inter-Governmental Conference on EU Reform began in Turin in March 1996. All aspects of the Maastricht Treaty were open for discussion, except the provisions for economic and monetary union, which are supposedly already settled. A central topic was to be moves towards a Common Foreign and Security Policy (CFSP), as called for under the Maastricht Treaty. Should Europe continue to rely on NATO for its defence, or should it create an independent European force? There have been proposals to merge the old Western European Union with the EU, and make it the military arm of the union, but there is also strong opposition to such a move. Britain and Holland fear it would undermine NATO; and Austria, Finland, Ireland and Sweden argue it would threaten their neutrality.[18] France has also proposed the appointment of a high diplomatic representative to act as spokesman for the Union on matters of defence and foreign policy. In the end, very little progress was made on these issues in the new Treaty of Amsterdam, although Britain did end her opt-out on the Social Chapter of the Maastricht Treaty.

The European Commission, under its new President Jacques Santer, prepared a report for the IGC entitled *Reinforcing Political Union and Preparing for Enlargement*. Its proposals included provisions for majority voting on interior and justice policy as well as increased powers for the Commission, especially in the area of human rights, and an end to Britain's 'opt-out' over the Social Chapter. It also proposed more majority voting on foreign policy, and establishment of a common military policy.

The most controversial of the Commission's proposals, however, was an end to the power of veto over alterations to the EU's founding treaties. The Maastricht Treaty, for example, would not have come into force if any one of the 12 member states had failed to ratify it. As the membership expands, it will become harder and harder to achieve such unanimity. As the report says: "maintaining unanimity will lead to

A Global Parliament

paralysis. The European Union must not be condemned to progress at the rate of its slowest member. If the Treaties can only be changed by unanimity, the chance of real progress in European construction will be undermined."[19] Chancellor Kohl warned at one stage that if Britain continued to block further progress, the others might go on without her, forming a 'two-speed Europe'. In any case, the drive for further integration in Europe is clearly still going on.

Structure and Functions

The reader will now have become totally bewildered by the blizzard of acronyms passing under his (or her) nose. Let us pause to review the present structure of the European Union, and the functions of its various bodies.

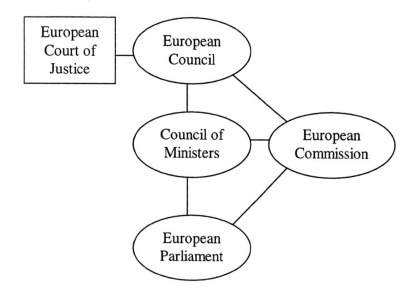

Figure 5. *Principal organs of the European Union*

The principal organs of the European Union consist of the following bodies.[20]

The European Council

This consists of the Heads of Government of the 15 member states, together with the President of the Commission, who hold a summit meeting two or three times a year. They are assisted by the Foreign Ministers of the member states, and by another member of the Commission. They make decisions on major issues confronting the Union, particularly those concerning changes to the structure and functions of the community, or progress towards further integration. Structural changes have hitherto required the unanimous assent of all members of the Council, as discussed above. The European Council was given formal status by the Single European Act.

The Council of the European Union (or Council of Ministers)

This is the main law-making body of the EU, and is composed of cabinet ministers, one from each member state. If the subject is agriculture, the agriculture ministers meet; if it is transport, the transport ministers meet, and so on. It is thus quite possible for two or more sittings of the Council to be going on simultaneously, concerning different subjects. The Presidency of the Council is held by each member state in turn for a period of six months. The Council has its own staff of some 2,500 officials in Brussels.

The proposals before the Council are generally prepared beforehand by the Commission, and the Council then decides whether to approve or disapprove the proposal. The Council may approve: a) regulations, binding on the member states; b) directives, which are binding but leave members free to choose how they will comply; c) decisions on specific actions; and d) recommendations and opinions, which are not binding. Unless there are provisions to the contrary, decisions are reached by a simple majority vote. More important matters require either unanimity, or a 'qualified' or weighted majority vote. Under the qualified voting rules, France, Germany, Italy and the UK receive 10 votes each; Spain 8; Belgium, Greece, the Netherlands and Portugal, 5 each; Austria and Sweden, 4 each; Ireland, Denmark and Finland, 3 each; and Luxembourg 2, for a total of 87 votes. A qualified majority requires the assent of 62 out of these 87 votes.

The Single European Act extended qualified majority voting to matters involving the single market, economic and social cohesion, and technological research and development. Unanimity is still required on matters involving taxation, common foreign and security policy (CFSP), and justice and home affairs. It is also required where the Council amends a proposal from the Commission, or overrides a rejection by the Parliament. In all these cases, a single member can thus veto a decision.

The European Commission

This is the executive branch of the EU. It consists of 20 Commissioners, who are appointed by agreement among the member states for a term of five years, renewable. They act as department heads for the EU bureaucracy, which consists of some 17,000 staff, located mainly in Brussels, with some in Luxembourg and other locations. The President and two Vice-Presidents are appointed from among the Commissioners. Decisions are taken by a simple majority of members.

The Commission is responsible for carrying out the decisions of the Council of Ministers. It prepares new proposals and legislation for the Council of Ministers and the European Council. It also represents the EU in negotiations with other countries or international organizations. It manages the EU funds and programs, and delivers aid to outside countries. The Commissioners undertake to remain completely independent of the national governments and the Council. They cannot be dismissed by the Council.

The right of the Commission to initiate and draft new proposals gives it a very powerful role in the union, which has been inherited from that of the High Authority in the ECSC. This role has been exploited to the full by strong Commission Presidents, such as Walter Hallstein and Jacques Delors.

The European Parliament

This consists of 626 members, directly elected every five years by the citizens of the member states according to their respective electoral systems. The number of seats in each state is based on population, with Germany having the largest representation at 99 seats.Turnout at the last elections in 1994 ranged from 90% in Belgium down to 36% in Holland and the UK. The members are grouped by political affiliation rather than nationality, with the largest group being the European Socialists with some 220 seats, and the next largest being the European

People's Party (or Christian Democrats). Other substantial groups include the Liberals, the Gaullists and Conservatives, the Greens and the Communists. The Parliament is headed by a President and 14 Vice-Presidents elected by the members. It meets in Strasbourg, France, and has its own staff of over 4,000 personnel.

The powers of the Parliament are limited mainly to consultation and review. The appointment of a new Commission is subject to a vote of approval by the Parliament. The assent of Parliament is required for the accession of new members, for all international agreements, and for sundry other matters. The Parliament works with the Council on the EU budget, and may reject a budget plan. If necessary, it can compel the Commission to resign, by adopting a censure motion with a two-thirds majority.

Committees of the Parliament review legislation before it goes to the Council of Ministers, and may propose amendments at that stage. After the Council has approved a proposal, a rather complicated decision-making process involving the Parliament comes into play. In cases where the Council adopts a decision by a qualified majority, a 'co-operation' procedure applies, by which the Parliament may decide to approve, amend, or reject the proposal. It then requires unanimous agreement for the Council to override the decision of the Parliament. In some limited areas, such as matters involving the internal market, a 'co-decision' rule applies, according to which the Council and Parliament attempt to settle any disagreements through a Conciliation Committee, where necessary. In these cases the Parliament acts on equal terms with the Council, and may finally decide to reject a proposal by a majority vote.

The Parliament has little power to initiate community legislation or determine policy for the community on its own account. It can ask for existing policies to be amended, or new ones initiated, as in the case of the Draft Treaty. It may, by a majority vote, ask the Commission to submit proposals in a certain limited number of less important fields.

The Court of Justice

This consists of 15 Judges and 9 Advocates-General, appointed for six-year terms by the member states. It is responsible for the interpretation and upholding of the Treaties, and for making sure that community law is observed. Cases may be brought either by member states or by individuals or organizations. A Court of First Instance was set up in 1989 to carry out initial hearings of cases brought by individuals. The Court sits in Luxembourg.

The decisions of the Court are binding on member states, and take precedence over national laws in areas of community responsibility. In the "Simmentha" case in 1978, the Court of Justice declared that "every national court must, in a case within its jurisdiction, apply Community law in its entirety and protect rights which the latter confers on individuals and must accordingly set aside any provision of national law which may conflict with it, whether prior or subsequent to the Community rule." Failure to comply may incur penalties, such as fines. Over 300 cases were settled one way or another by the Court in 1994. Individuals may also bring cases which involve Community law in their respective national courts.

In addition to the major organs listed above, there are also several lesser organs of the Union:

- The Court of Auditors, responsible for monitoring the accounts and expenditures of the community;
- The Economic and Social Committee, which has a consultative role on economic and social matters;
- The Committee of the Regions, which enables local and regional authorities to have a say in the work of the community;
- The ECSC Consultative Assembly still exists, as the last separate remaining organ of the original Coal and Steel Community;
- The European Investment Bank, established in 1958 to finance capital projects according to community policy;
- The European Monetary Institute was set up in 1994 to prepare the way for monetary union and for a European Central Bank, which is due to appear by 1999.

Budget [21]

The total revenue of the Union in 1995 amounted to 76.5 billion ecu, or approximately $100 billion, of which 50% came from value-added tax, 17% from customs duties, and 30% from a national levy based on each member's GDP. The total revenue amounted to 1.2% of the community's GDP.

Over half the total expenditure went to agriculture and fisheries, with the farm support program taking the lion's share. Another 32% went on structural funds, to encourage development in more backward regions of Europe. About 4% went to research and technology, and

2.2% to aid for ex-European colonies under the Lomé Convention. A further 6% was committed to external measures such as development finance and aid for countries of the former Soviet Union and Eastern Europe, and in other regions. Administration, carried out by a total of 28,500 officials, takes up 5% of the budget - quite an efficient operation.

Economically, Europe is the largest grouping in the world. Its population is 370 million, about 6.5% of the world total, but its GDP accounts for one-quarter of the entire world economy, and its trade is 22% of the world total. Its aid to Third World countries amounts to about 40% of the world total. All these exceed the corresponding figures for the United States.

Shortcomings and Future Prospects

From our comfortable position as armchair critics, how are we to assess the progress made towards a democratic European federation?

On the positive side, it is clear that the required pieces of the jigsaw are almost all in place. The European Union possesses:
- an executive, in the form of the European Commission;
- a democratically elected parliament to represent the people, in the European Parliament;
- an assembly to represent the member states, in the form of the Council of Ministers. The European Council can be considered as an extension of the Council of Ministers, corresponding to the case when the ministers happen to be Prime Ministers;
- a court to adjudicate community law, in the European Court of Justice.

The only missing item is a European security force to defend the federation and enforce the law, if necessary. So far, Europe has got on reasonably well without it.

Unlike the United Nations, the EU has gained the power to make legislation, and to make legal judgements which are binding on its members, based on that law. Economic union has been achieved, and monetary union is moving towards completion, although there may yet be some hiccups on the way. The Union also disposes of a budget commensurate with its obligations.

The major shortcomings of the Union arise from the fact that the pieces of the jigsaw do not quite fit together properly. They include the following.

The Parliament

The Parliament has not yet been given sufficient power or responsibility. As the democratically elected assembly, it should have the power to initiate legislation, and at least equal power with the Council to approve legislation. It should also have greater control over the executive, and ideally the executive should be elected from within its ranks. The battles over future policy and directions in Europe should be fought out primarily in debates within the Parliament, rather than outside it. Only then will true democratic accountability be achieved within the European government. Only then will European citizens develop any appreciable interest or loyalty towards the Union.

A number of these issues were addressed by the Parliament itself in the lead-up to the Maastricht Treaty. It produced a report entitled *1993: The New Treaties*, which contained its proposals for Maastricht.[22] The report refers to the "democratic deficit" within the community, and calls for "reform of the Community in the context of a federally-based European Union." It includes proposals whereby the Parliament:

- "Calls for Parliament and the Council to be given equal rights and equal weight in the legislative process";[23]
- "Calls for Parliament also to be given the right to initiate legislative proposals in cases where the Commission fails to respond within a specified deadline to a specific request adopted by a majority of Members"[24] (this would essentially give the Parliament the right to initiate legislation whenever it wanted);
- "Calls for Parliament to be given the right to elect the President of the Commission on a proposal from the European Council; the President should, with the agreement of the Council, choose the Members of the Commission; the debate and the vote of confidence in a new Commission, which Parliament has held since 1981, should be formalized in the Treaties"[24]; and later "a new Commission shall be appointed at the beginning of each parliamentary term." The Parliament did not go so far as to say that the Commission should be selected from within its ranks, but these proposals would certainly make it possible to do so in the future.

In the event the member states did make some concessions in the Maastricht Treaty. The Parliament was given a somewhat more equal say in the legislative process via the co-decision mechanism, while the Commission's term of office was changed to five years to match the Parliament, and the right to vote approval of a new Commission was formalized. The other points were not conceded.

The Parliament had also proposed that a single seat should be chosen for the Parliament, the Council and the Commission. This would put an end to the present absurd situation, where the Parliament sits in Strasbourg, but its committees meet in Brussels, while its secretariat is based in Luxembourg. As a result, much time is wasted while everyone perambulates around the countryside.

The Council

The Council functions effectively as an assembly representing the member states. It is not an elected body, like the Senate in the United States for instance, and thus does not conform to the classical pattern of a states' house. Instead, it has been set up to provide direct representation of the governments of the member states, and as such it arguably performs a more useful function than the classical 'senate'. The need for such an assembly has been felt in other federal systems: in America the state governors hold regular meetings, for instance, while in Australia the state premiers now hold periodic round-table meetings with the Federal government.

The difficulty with the Council of Ministers and with the European Council concerns the age-old problem of the veto. In cases where the unanimous voting rule holds, a single member state can frustrate the will of the majority, and paralyze the organization. But the Council has also shown the way out of the dilemma, in the form of the qualified majority rule. Once this has been extended to all the normal areas of business of the Council, the veto problem will be largely resolved. The Parliament, for instance, included in its 1991 proposals a declaration that it "believes that unanimity should no longer be required for decision-taking in Council, except for constitutional matters, accession of new Member States, and extension of the field of Community responsibilities." [25]

The Commission has made the radical proposal, as we saw previously, that the power of veto should be ended even for alterations to the EU's founding treaties, i.e. for constitutional alterations. [19] At present, Article N of the Maastricht Treaty talks about "determining by common accord the amendments to be made to those Treaties", and provides that "The amendments shall enter into force after being ratified by all the Member States in accordance with their respective constitutional requirements." [26]

Now a sovereign state cannot be forced to accede to a treaty against its will - that would only lead to disaffection and rebellion of some sort. But it might be possible to provide that amendments can proceed if some sort of qualified majority of member states agree to it, with the states opposed to them being allowed to 'opt out' of the amended sections. We have already seen how Britain opted out of the Social Chapter of the Maastricht Treaty, and Denmark opted out of the third stage of EMU. No doubt this would lead to a 'two-speed Europe' for a time, but it would remove a major impediment to further progress.

The Commission

The European Commission acts as the executive of the European government. It is a powerful body, and seems to have operated effectively hitherto. There are dangers, however, in having the executive and legislative branches of government separated. This can lead to disputes, and a budgetary or legislative deadlock between the two branches of government, as was shown recently in the United States in the stand-off between Bill Clinton and Newt Gingrich. Even American studies, such as that by Everett Millard's group CURE[27], have recognized the advantages of cabinet-style government. The Commission needs to be made more accountable to the Parliament, and ideally should be elected from within it, so as to provide leadership from the inside. This would also raise the status of parliament, and lead to higher quality among the parliamentarians themselves. The change involved would not be enormous: a number of people have already served both as MEP's and Commissioners, such as Altiero Spinelli, for example.

An alternative would be to move towards the American model, with the President of the Commission being directly elected by universal suffrage, and then appointing the remaining members of the Commission himself.

Common Foreign and Security Policy (CFSP)

Perhaps Europe's greatest shortcoming is its lack of a common foreign and security policy, which is one of the core areas of responsibility of any government. This problem was cruelly exposed by Europe's complete failure to resolve the recent crisis in Yugoslavia and Bosnia. It is often remarked that Europe at present is an economic giant, but a political dwarf.

The Maastricht Treaty declares that its members are "RESOLVED to implement a common foreign and security policy including the eventual framing of a common defence policy, which might in time lead to a common defence, thereby reinforcing the European identity and its independence in order to promote peace, security and progress in Europe and in the world."[28] It is a little vague about exactly how this is to be put into effect, but gives the major responsibility to the European Council and the Council of Ministers, which must act unanimously in these areas (meaning the veto applies). The Parliament is given only the right to be consulted.

The CFSP was one of the main topics of discussion at the recent inter-governmental conference, but the many contentious issues involved in areas of such vital importance are unlikely to be settled at one blow. Let us examine the two areas separately:

a) *Foreign policy*

The mechanisms for agreeing on common foreign policies are already in place. As part of the Council of Ministers organization, the Ministers for Foreign Affairs already meet regularly once a month, in what is dubbed the 'General Council', to deal with external relations and major political questions. If there was sufficient mutual confidence between the member states to allow qualified voting rules to apply in foreign affairs, then common policies could be arrived at in the General Council and the European Council.

On some matters, the union is already obliged to reach a common policy. Concerning foreign trade, for example, Europe must have a single policy because she forms a single market, and her policies are spoken for by the relevant Commissioner. In the same functional way, she is bound to develop over time a common policy in other areas of shared responsibility, such as research and technology, the environment, transport and foreign aid, to choose a few examples. The one major area where a coherent foreign policy is lacking is that of defence and security, where she has not put her own house in order.

The French have proposed that the Union should appoint a senior representative dubbed "Monsieur PESC" (Politique Ètrangère et de Sécurité Commune) to act as its official spokesperson in foreign affairs and defence, to help give the community more presence and stature in these areas.[18]

b) *Defence policy*

In the area of defence and security, Europe is faced with a choice between two basic options:

- To continue to rely on NATO for her collective defence, as she has done for almost 50 years since 1949;
- To establish her own joint forces for security and defence, possibly merging the old Western European Union with the EU to become her defence wing.

Some possible nuclei for a joint European force already exist. France and Germany have established a joint brigade-sized force called Eurocorps, based on Strasbourg; while France, Italy, Spain and Portugal have created a rapid intervention force called Euroforce, together with its aeronaval wing Eurmarforce. These are quite small at present, however.

There is strong opposition to any proposal to undermine NATO, as remarked previously.[18] President Chirac announced in 1995 that France would resume operational membership of NATO, after boycotting the alliance ever since the time of General de Gaulle. Discussions are likely to centre on ways of building a 'European pillar' to NATO, and indeed the North Atlantic Council met in June, 1996, to consider the creation of a European defence capability as part of the organization. One EU source has described the idea of a completely independent European army as "becoming ever more fanciful".[29] Objections to the NATO option, on the other hand, are likely to centre on the dominance of that organization by the United States.

Europe's present weakness in the area of security and defence can be illustrated by a hypothetical 'wargaming' example. Suppose that Spain were to announce that on historical and geographical grounds Gibraltar rightfully belonged to her, and began to mass troops on the border. Suppose that Britain rejected the claim, and began to reinforce the garrison by air, while sending aircraft carriers steaming towards the area. Suppose that both sides refused to negotiate, and rejected the jurisdiction of the World Court, so that fighting was imminent. What could the European Union do? Does she have the legal right to intervene, and demand that the Court of Justice adjudicate in the dispute? The answer is no, the Treaties give the Court of Justice no right of adjudication in territorial disputes. Does the EU have the military resources to intervene and prevent or halt any conflict? The answer is no, the EU has no substantial forces of her own. Her only recourse would be an appeal to NATO, which would also be highly embarrassed since Britain and Spain are both members of the alliance. Hopefully this example is highly unrealistic, but it does serve to highlight the present weakness of both the European and the world security systems.

Federalists versus Nationalists

The future shape of the European Union is clearly going to be determined by the outcome of the ongoing struggle between the 'supranationalists' or European federalists on the one hand, versus the 'nationalists' on the other hand. The federalists, represented in recent times by Delors, Kohl and Mitterand, have fought for a stronger union; while the nationalists, represented by de Gaulle and Thatcher, have fought against it.

The disagreement between the two camps is probably due largely to their different visions of the end-point of the federation process. Margaret Thatcher, for instance, has referred to the threat of a future "European super-state". She envisages a United States of Europe in which Great Britain has been reduced to the status of a mere province, like Massachusetts or Rhode Island in the USA, with her armed forces and her independent voice in world affairs gone, and her glorious history running from Drake through Marlborough, Trafalgar and Waterloo all forgotten. She would probably imagine England being run by squads of jack-booted inspectors from Brussels, and instinctively rejects any such frightful prospect.

The federalists, on the other hand, see a great vision of the nations of Europe living and working in harmony, with their citizens able to travel and do business in complete freedom anywhere in the union, bringing guaranteed peace and increased prosperity for all. If in the early days some of them may have envisaged the nation-states reduced to mere provinces, that has now changed. The events of the last fifty years have made it abundantly clear that the ancient nations of Europe will insist on keeping much more of their distinctive cultures and national identity than that. They may decide to contribute to a 'European pillar' of NATO, for instance, or to an independent joint security force, but they will also insist on preserving independent armed forces of their own, far into the foreseeable future. The Ministry of Defence and the Ministry of Foreign Affairs will remain in Whitehall, and may even have to be expanded to cope with the demands of European co-operation. Any European federation is going to be a much looser association than in the American model, and it is perhaps a mistake to keep on referring to the 'United States of Europe'. All the recent emphasis on the principle of subsidiarity is designed to reassure the member states that their national identities and cultures will indeed be preserved in the new Europe.

This raises the question: what actually defines a federation in the first place? Some useful comments have been made in a recent discussion paper prepared for the Fabian Society by Stephen Tindale and David Miliband.[30] They define the key features of a federation as:

- the existence of two or more tiers of government, with the powers and existence of lower tiers guaranteed and immune from arbitrary interference from the higher tier;
- an agreed division of competencies between tiers with, again, defences against arbitrary changes in the division;
- a written constitution enshrining the above, and a Constitutional Court to adjudicate between tiers.[31]

On this sort of definition, one could almost argue that the EU is a federation already. It has two tiers of government in the EU and the member states, both with legislative authority, and with an agreed division (temporarily, at least) of competencies between them; but the Maastricht Treaty does not really qualify as a formal written constitution guaranteeing the division of powers. That will have to await a more final determination of responsibilities between the two levels.

Tindale and Miliband discuss the concept of 'layered identity'. People may identify themselves simultaneously with a city, a county, a country, or a continent, and feel loyalty towards all of them. A man might be a Liverpudlean while watching his local football team on the television, but an Englishman while watching the national cricket team play the Pakistanis (he will probably not feel much loyalty towards the entity called 'Merseyside'). The federalists do not propose that he should lose or abate any of these feelings, but only that he should also consider himself a 'European' when watching the Ryder Cup team play the Americans at golf.

The European Union, like Merseyside, has not generated much loyalty amongst its citizens up till now. It has a flag, blue with gold stars on it, and it has an excellent anthem in Beethoven's 'Ode to Joy'. But it is hard to feel any loyalty towards a bunch of faceless bureaucrats in Brussels. That is one of the reasons why the EU needs to be made more democratic, in order to present a more human face to its citizens. It could probably also do more in the way of promoting sports festivals, sporting teams, and the like.

Theoretical Discussions

Many books have been written which have analyzed the process of European integration, and have attempted to produce a general theory of regional integration based upon the European example. I have neither the space nor the competence to do proper justice to these discussions here, but we may get some idea of the arguments from surveys by other authors.

The state of integration theory circa 1974 was surveyed by R.J. Harrison in *Europe in Question*. He classified the various approaches into three categories, namely 'functional', 'federal' and 'neo-functionalist'. Let us say a few words on each in turn.

The functionalist approach

The principal originator of this approach was David Mitrany in *A Working Peace System*. The idea is that a working international community will be built up piecemeal out of a network of functional agencies like the Postal Union, each one more or less autonomous and performing a specific technical or economic function, and each one involving the transfer of a small piece of national sovereignty to the international system. Eventually this functional network will become so extensive, and people will identify themselves so strongly as members of the international community, that no nation will be able to break the peace. Mitrany sees this as happening almost automatically, and sees no need for the construction of rigid constitutional structures: "No fixed rule is needed, and no rigid pattern is desirable for the organization of these working functional strata .. the function determines its appropriate *organs*. It also reveals through practice the nature of the action required under the given conditions, and in that way the *powers* needed by the respective authority .. Not only is there in all this no need for any fixed constitutional division of authority and power, prescribed in advance, but anything beyond the original formal definition of scope and purpose might embarrass the working of the practical arrangements .."[32]

The functionalists are generally not in favour of regional integration, particularly European integration, seeing it as a positive obstacle to world integration. Johan Galtung, for instance, wrote in *The European Community* a warning that Europe might become just another superpower, the greatest of them all, and thus produce new divisions between the peoples of the world. Europe might become involved in wars against the other superpowers, or engage in capitalist exploitation of the Third World. These fears would appear to be rather exaggerated at the moment, however. Europe currently possesses no forces of her own, and is no threat to anybody. She is also the single largest source of foreign aid to Third World countries.

Functionalists are generally distrustful of 'big government' in any form. They tend to ignore or discount political processes, and belong perhaps to the more left-wing or anarchist tradition of political theory. Harrison concludes as follows: "Functionalism, in other words, is virtually a mono-causal explanation of social activity, summed up in the dictum that a community may be regarded as the sum of the functions performed by its members. Like all mono-causal explanations of societal phenomena, it is inadequate."[33]

The federalist approach

The federalist viewpoint is of course the one taken in this book. It postulates that peace and order among men can only be secured by good government (recall William Penn's statement: "Peace is maintained by Justice, which is a Fruit of Government"), and that the natural form of government for a union of sovereign states is a federal one. One federal theorist of European integration was R.W.G. Mackay, a leader of the Federal Union group, who wrote: "We can hope for real economic and social progress in Europe only if there is a political authority with power to bring it about."[34] He envisages a federal authority, where federalism is defined as "a method of dividing powers of government so that the central and regional governments are within a limited sphere co-ordinate but independent. The test of the principle is: does it embody the division of powers between central and regional authorities, each being independent of the other?"[35] A similar definition was quoted in the preceding section. Other prominent federal theorists were Guy Héraud of France, and Professor Brugmans of the Netherlands, a leader of the European Union of Federalists.

Harrison draws a distinction between the 'moderate' federalists, who accept a gradual and incremental approach to federation like that adopted by Jean Monnet and Paul-Henri Spaak, as opposed to the 'radical' federalists, who demand that federation must be achieved in one revolutionary leap. An example of the latter was Alexandre Marc, who claimed that incrementalists had done more harm to integration in Europe than its declared opponents. They have been satisfied with "little nothings", he said in 1968.[36] But it is clearly only the moderates who have had any effect in practice. We have already recounted how the federalist movement has provided the driving force, step by step, towards European unification.

The neofunctionalist approach

The originator of this approach was Ernst Haas, who made a detailed study of European integration in *The Uniting of Europe* in 1958. Other prominent authors in this category include Leon Lindberg and Amitai Etzioni. Their position is somewhere between the functionalist and federalist positions, and David Mitrany has labelled it 'federalist-functionalist'.

Studying the extension of the Coal and Steel Community into the Common Market, Haas attempted to extract a general proposition: that integration in a particular sector can lead to broader integration by a "spillover" effect, provided certain conditions are met. The original integrative step must be inherently expansive, or advantageous, but not so far-reaching that it affects the vital interests of the state and threatens the power of ruling élites. The first step will then get organized groups and political parties involved in the integration process, and lead them to perceive a similar need for integration in other sectors. The demands and the loyalties of the interest groups will then shift gradually towards the central decision-making bodies.

Neofunctionalists do not ignore or write off the formal structure of government, but rather they recognize that central institutions with policy making powers have a critical role to play. Like the functionalists, however, they tend to argue that integration becomes an automatic process, driven by the self-interest of national interest groups who perceive advantages to themselves in further union. "Perhaps the most salient conclusion we can draw from the community building experience is the fact that major interest groups as well as politicians determine their support of or opposition to new central institutions and policies on the basis of a calculation of advantage. The "good Europeans" are not the main creators of the regional community that is growing up; the process of community formation is dominated by nationally constituted groups with specific interests and aims, willing and able to adjust their aspirations by turning to supra-national means when this course appears profitable."[37]

This thesis tends to ignore the human element in political affairs, and to predict that, once started, the integration process will roll on inevitably until complete integration is achieved. It denies the crucial role played by people like Monnet, Spaak and Spinelli in the integration process. As Harrison remarks: "The weak link then, in the chain of action and interaction of variables, as it is visualized in the neo-functionalist thesis, is that it is governments, and generally speaking the leaders of governments, who must, at least while unanimity procedures for community decision making obtain, make the next moves along the path to unity." [38] The check to further progress produced by General de Gaulle in the 1960s forced some degree of reappraisal of the thesis, and led Haas himself to admit: "Most neo-functionalists have not explicitly recognized .. the crucial question of whether .. this incremental style is not "foreseen" and manipulated by certain heroic actors (Jean Monnet, Sicco Mansholt, Walter Hallstein, Raoul Prebisch) - and eventually checked by certain equally prescient national actors (Charles de Gaulle)."[39]

The neofunctionalists were certainly correct, however, in identifying economic utility as a vital, if not essential, factor in generating community support for further integration. Business groups have recognized almost from the beginning the huge advantages offered by more open markets within Europe, and have been strong supporters of integration. An illustration was provided recently by one of Norway's largest engineering firms, which moved its headquarters from Oslo to London after the Norwegians rejected membership of the EU: the firm decided it could not afford to miss the advantages of the single market. Whether these groups will continue to support further moves towards political and defence co-operation remains to be seen. One prominent financier, Sir James Goldsmith, surfaced not long ago as a leader of the opposition to the EU in Britain.

Amitai Etzioni in his book *Political Unification* made a comparative study of four different regional associations. Two of them, the United Arab Republic and the Federation of the West Indies, were classed as unions that failed; one, the Nordic Association, was classified as stable; and the last one, the EEC, was classed as a successful, growing union. On this basis, he formed a ranking of different functional sectors as regards their potential for inducing further integration. Bottom of the list he puts service functions such as postal co-operation, radio frequency allocation, police co-operation, and so on. Next come organizations dealing with labour, health and cultural affairs; third are those dealing with tariff agreements and military organizations; and top of the heap come economic unions and common markets.

Neofunctionalism has remained the dominant academic theory of regional integration in subsequent years, in that it seems to offer a systematic explanation of the integration process.[40] One recent study by Milward et al.[41] has criticized the theory on the grounds that it has virtually ignored the nation-state as the central unit of political organization. In reality, they argue, virtually all power has remained with the nation-state in Europe, with only limited surrender of national sovereignty being made to central institutions for narrowly defined purposes. The authors contend that this limited integration has been driven mainly by the perceived self-interest of the nation-states themselves. They do not venture much in the way of future predictions, but the implication certainly is that national sovereignty is here to stay, and integration in Europe will not proceed much further.

Summary and Conclusions

Whereas the movement for world federation was defeated and stifled by the onset of the Cold War, the movement for European federation has flourished. Guided by men of extraordinary vision and enterprise, such as Monnet, Spaak, Adenauer and Spinelli, the Europeans have proceeded step by step to build the European Union. The process of integration has taken much longer than the founding fathers would have hoped, some fifty years already, and there is a long way still to go. It might easily be another fifty years or even more before the integration process is complete, and no-one can predict exactly what the end-point will be. But already it is possible to declare that some sort of European federation will be established. By some definitions, it is already here.

The European Union possesses an executive, a democratically elected parliament to represent the people, and a council to represent the member states. It has the power to make binding legislation in certain areas, and possesses a court with the power to make binding legal judgements. It has completed the formation of a single European market, and is moving towards complete economic and monetary union. It disposes of a substantial budget, in the neighbourhood of $100 billion.

Deficiencies which have been identified in the EU include its 'democratic deficit', or lack of democratic accountability, plus the perennial problem of the veto in the Council, and the lack of any substantial joint security forces. A major issue on the agenda at present is the question of how to achieve some sort of common foreign and security policy for the community.

A certain amount of disenchantment with Europe, or 'Euro-scepticism', is becoming evident, as the preparations for monetary union have been blamed for causing economic hardship and unemployment. But many proposals for reform and further integration have been raised, and remain on the public agenda. There is still a need for common foreign policies and common security mechanisms, as agreed under the Maastricht Treaty. This fact alone ensures that, after all the debates are over and some reasonable compromises are arrived at, Europe will continue to move towards a closer union - there can hardly be any going back now. The end-point is still unclear, but it will probably consist of a loosely-knit structure in which the member nations will retain most of their present autonomy.

English-speaking people, by the way, tend to get a slightly distorted view of public opinion in Europe, because their information usually comes by way of the British press. Support for European union has always been strongest and most consistent in the original Six, and that remains the case to this day. Public opinion has been more doubtful and less positive in the latecomers to the community, and most particularly in the UK and Denmark. The hot debates over Europe which go on in Britain are not a true reflection of the state of opinion across the Channel.

What are the lessons to be drawn from the European experience, which might help us in moving towards a world federation? There are a number of matters of principle, which will be taken up in the next chapter. But there are also some useful tactics which can be learnt from Jean Monnet and his friends, as follows.

- A federation between sovereign nation-states cannot be arrived at in a single revolutionary leap. The prospective member states will not accept any sudden and dramatic transfer of sovereignty. Instead, it is better to approach the federation in an incremental and evolutionary fashion, with a stage-by-stage transfer of functional authority. Judging by the European example, the process is likely to take many decades.

- It is not necessary to make the association universal from the outset, even if that is the ultimate aim. One can begin with a nucleus of the more progressive states, such as the Six in Europe. If the association is a success, other states will join in afterwards.

- The prototype association should be set up with all the necessary organs at the beginning, so that it forms a small but healthy embryo of the eventual federation. It will then be able to evolve and grow easily and naturally, even though it may look 'top-heavy' to begin with. It is important to get the structure right at the start, if possible, because political organizations show remarkable persistence once they are established. The idea of the league of great powers has persisted with little basic change from the Concert of Europe right through the League of Nations to the United Nations; and the structures adopted by Jean Monnet for the ECSC have persisted largely unchanged through to the European Union.

- The prototype association, according to neofunctionalist theory, should involve integration in an 'expansive' sector, which means an economic sector if possible, so that there are incentives for the organization to grow. A purely military organization, such as a military alliance for example, will simply remain static in most cases.

The European Union thus stands as a great beacon of hope and progress for the rest of the world. Whatever the outcome of the present arguments over further integration, it has already achieved the major aims of its founders. It has brought peace to Western Europe, and made war between the European powers virtually inconceivable (despite our wargaming exercise), although this does need to be cemented in place by a common security policy. One can confidently predict that there will never again be a major war between France and Germany. This is an astonishing achievement, when one recalls that only fifty years ago the nations of Western Europe were locked together in mortal combat. A huge transformation has occurred, by almost imperceptible degrees.

The single market has also brought unprecedented prosperity to the people of Europe, and allowed European firms to compete on equal terms with American and Japanese enterprises. Finally, Europe is making great efforts to lift living standards in its more deprived areas in the mountain uplands, the industrial rustbelts and the outlying regions. In all these ways Europe is providing an enormously hopeful and instructive example for the wider world to follow.

Chapter 5

Principles of World Federation

"We hold these truths to be self-evident, that all men are created equal, that they are endowed by their Creator with certain inalienable Rights, that among these are Life, Liberty, and the pursuit of Happiness. That to secure these rights, Governments are instituted among Men, deriving their just powers from the consent of the governed. That whenever any form of Government becomes destructive of these ends, it is the Right of the People to alter or to abolish it, and to institute new Government, laying its foundation on such principles and organizing its powers in such form, as to them should seem most likely to effect their Safety and Happiness."

Declaration of Independence, 1776

More than fifty detailed draft constitutions for a world federation have already appeared in the literature, each one different from the others.[1] It is an amusing game to build such castles in the air, and some interesting examples of a federal structure have been proposed; but in the end the details of the constitution can only be established by the founding commission or convention. There is little point in being too prescriptive at this stage, and it may even be counter-productive, because no two people will agree about the fine details. It is probably more useful to try and establish some common *principles* upon which the federation should be based, which might be able to win general agreement.

Let us first pause once more to recall the definition of the word 'federation'. According to K.C. Wheare,[2] a federation is "an association of states so organized that powers are divided between a general government which in certain matters .. is independent of the governments of the associated states, and, on the other hand, state governments which in certain matters are, in their turn, independent of the general government. This involves, as a necessary consequence, that general and regional governments both operate directly upon the people: each citizen is subject to two governments."

A simplified diagram of the association is given below.

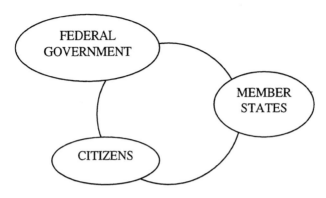

Figure 6. *Simplified diagram of a federal system.*

The "general government" in this case is the world federation, while the "regional governments" are the member nation-states (or possibly, in the future, regional associations or federations). Each of the two levels of government has separate spheres of responsibility: they "are not subordinate one to another, but co-ordinate with each other." Each of the three elements in the diagram has duties and responsibilities which it owes to the other two elements, and rights and benefits which it receives from them: these are represented by the lines in the diagram. Other elements could be added in, such as the transnational corporations, but for simplicity we shall leave them aside from this discussion.

Wheare's definition is a broad one, and could apply to many different systems. On the one hand, there are tight, unitary systems like the Commonwealth of Australia, where the states have very little revenue of their own, and are heavily dependent on the central government, and subordinate to it. On the other hand, there are loose and decentralized systems like the Swiss Confederation, where the cantons retain their independence in many respects, or the European Union, where the member states remain as independent nations. We would envisage a structure for the eventual world federation which lies at the looser end of the spectrum, somewhere between the current European "Union" and the Swiss "Confederation", as will shortly become apparent.

What are the principles upon which such a federation ought to be based? For these we will rely heavily on the lessons learned in the construction of the European Union. The preamble to the Maastricht Treaty mentions some important principles, although it gives no detailed exposition of them. According to the Treaty[3] the member states declare that:

"*CONFIRMING their attachment to the principles of liberty, democracy and respect for human rights and fundamental freedoms and of the rule of law,*

DESIRING to deepen the solidarity between their peoples while respecting their history, their culture and their traditions ..

RESOLVED to continue the process of creating an ever closer union among the peoples of Europe, in which decisions are taken as closely as possible to the citizen in accordance with the principle of subsidiarity ..

HAVE DECIDED to establish a European Union .."

Democracy

The first essential, to a Western mind at least, is that the government of the federation must be based upon the principle of democracy: "government of the people, by the people, and for the people". Our forefathers have fought and died for this principle on many historic occasions, including the revolution of Simon de Montfort, the English Civil War, the American War of Independence, and the French Revolution. The system may not be perfect, but as Winston Churchill once remarked: "No-one pretends that democracy is perfect or all-wise. Indeed, it has been said that democracy is the worst form of government except all those other forms that have been tried from time to time."[4]

To guard against autocracy and abuse of power, and to preserve the liberty and equality of all its citizens, the government must be chosen by means of free and fair elections, with guaranteed freedom of organized groups to stand in opposition to the government in power. The elements usually required of a democratic system of government include:

- free and open debate;
- mass media free of government control;
- access for citizens to office holders and bureaucrats;
- review of the executive by the legislature;
- an independent judiciary;
- multiple political parties competing at periodic elections, held by secret ballot on the basis of universal and equal adult suffrage.

These must be guaranteed by the founding treaty or constitution of the federation.

The fundamental advantages of a system of representative democracy are widely accepted. An elected government acquires legitimacy from the consent of the governed. It ensures representative, responsible and accountable administration, in that a governing party which is perceived as incompetent, corrupt or unjust can be replaced at the will of the people. The 'checks and balances' within the constitution and the separation of powers are designed to preserve the freedoms and rights of all citizens alike. Finally, the ability to replace or renew a government by constitutional means helps to assure peace and stability within the state.

While the Cold War was going on, it would clearly have been impractical to propose a universal world federation based on democratic principles, because it would have been rejected out of hand by the Communist countries of the Soviet bloc. But with the astonishing collapse of the Soviet Union that obstacle has disappeared, and democracy has been at least partially embraced by virtually all the countries of that bloc. No other principle of government retains any legitimacy, and even Third World military dictatorships like the one in Burma justify their rule as merely a "temporary expedient", necessary to "maintain law and order", before democracy is restored. The only remaining superpower with a non-democratic government is China.

This point of view has been put very forcefully by Francis Fukuyama in his book *The End of History and the Last Man.* He argues that a remarkable consensus concerning the legitimacy of liberal democracy as a system of government has emerged throughout the world over the past few years, as it conquered rival ideologies like hereditary monarchy, fascism, and more recently communism.

This does not mean that most national governments are fully democratic. The Freedom House group in the United States carries out a yearly rating of countries around the globe, based on a combination of political factors and civil liberties. They estimated in 1987 that 57 states and 34 'related territories' were "free", 57 states and 20 related territories were "partly free", and 53 states and 2 related territories were "not free."[5] By 1995, there had been some significant changes. After the Soviet collapse, the Baltic states and most of Eastern Europe had changed from "not free" to "free", and the former Soviet republics Russia, Belarus, Ukraine, Moldova and Georgia had become "partly free". South Africa and Namibia had become free, and Cambodia partly free. Elsewhere, there were mixed gains and losses to report. A number of Latin American states, including Peru, Colombia, Venezuela and Brazil, had slipped back from free to partly free, along with India; and other states, including Indonesia, Iran, Egypt, Sudan and Kenya, slipped back from partly free to not free. Many of the fledgling states in Asia and Africa are 'guided democracies', or in other words, autocracies in all but name. In these countries opposition leaders are likely to find themselves thrown in jail as soon as they provide any threat to the government in power, or a magazine may find itself closed down if it dares to criticize the government. Overall, however, there had undoubtedly been a significant increase in democracy world-wide over the period. In 1995, Freedom

House estimated that 76 states were free, comprising 20% of the world's population; 61 states were partly free, with 40% of the world's population; and 54 states were not free, with another 40% of the world's population.[6] A total of 114 states were rated as democracies, although 37 of these were only partly free.

What specific form should the democratic government of the federation take? Should it follow a parliamentary model, or a presidential model? There are many different examples to choose from. A long and detailed comparative study was made by the American Committee on United Europe as a contribution towards plans for the ECSC, which looked at the cases of Australia, Canada, Germany, Switzerland and the United States.[7] Nowadays the most obvious example to follow is perhaps the European Union itself; but the details hardly matter, since all these models of government have been reasonably stable and effective. The number of seats allotted to each member state must be determined on some equitable principle. The most obvious is "one man, one vote", which would allot seats strictly according to population. Other formulae have been suggested, such as seats allotted according to the square root of the population, which would give the smaller states somewhat more weight.[8] Only 12% of Everett Millard's group CURE were in favour of a strict "one man, one vote" rule.[9] A problem with both of the above formulae is that for instance they would give more seats in our hypothetical world parliament to India than to the USA, which would not be in accordance with the realities of world power. The likely consequence is that the US would simply refuse to join such a federation. Perhaps another rule of even greater antiquity should be taken into account, namely "he who pays the piper calls the tune". Thus seats might be allotted on the basis of the financial contributions made by each state, as well as its population.[10] The total number of representatives in the Assembly or Parliament (the 'House of the People') should not exceed something like six hundred - otherwise it becomes impossible to hold a true discussion or debate. Two sample distributions are given below.

Country	Population (m.)	Contribution to UN budget (%)	Seats (Scheme 1)	Seats (Scheme 2)
USA	254	25	29	89
China	1160	0.77	131	68
India	844	0.36	95	49
Russia	148	9.41	17	37
Japan	124	12.45	14	44
Germany	80	8.93	9	31
France	57	6	6	21
UK	57	5.02	6	21
Australia	17	1.51	2	5
Netherlands	15	1.5	2	5
Sweden	9	1.11	1	4

Table 1. *Selected examples of the distribution of parliamentary seats according to two sample schemes, normalized to a total of 600 seats worldwide.*
Scheme 1: proportional to population alone;
Scheme 2: based half on population, half on contributions to the UN budget.

Should the executive be elected from within the parliament as in the Westminster or German models, or should it be appointed by an elected president as in the American model, or should both systems be combined as in the French model, perhaps? We have expressed a preference for the cabinet or Westminster model, as did the CURE group,[11] on the grounds that it makes the executive more responsible to the parliament and the people, and avoids the possibility of deadlock between the executive and the parliament; but all the systems mentioned above have worked reasonably well in practice, so that there is no overwhelming reason to prefer one over another. It is not really satisfactory, however, to have an unelected executive which is totally separate from the parliament, as the European Union does at present.

Universality

Another fundamental objective is to create a federation which is "universal", that is one which includes every nation in the world. Only then will it be possible to arbitrate disputes between all nations, and to guarantee peace between them. Only then will it be possible to abolish nuclear weapons, and all other weapons of mass destruction. Only then will it be possible to formulate an effective global strategy to deal with other massive problems of the environment, and hunger and disease in the Third World. Only then will it be possible to extend the benefits of the association equally to all the peoples of the world. Universality was announced as the first principle of world federation at the great Montreux Congress of 1947.

Unfortunately, this immediately raises a most contentious issue, because in the present state of the world the two principles of universality and democracy are not mutually compatible. Should *all* states be eligible to join the proposed world federation; or should membership be restricted only to democratic states? In the long run, the aim is that all the world's states should be members. But in the long run, one would also hope that all the world's states will be democratic. In the shorter term, a little thought is enough to show that the federation ought to be *restricted* to democratic states. Otherwise the federation, in guaranteeing the security of its member states, could be put in the intolerable situation of propping up an autocracy or dictatorship. It would also be completely inconsistent to have a democratic government at the world level, mixed with a non-democratic one at a national level, and would be incompatible with the basic human rights that ought to be guaranteed by the federation, as discussed below.

For all these reasons, we would envisage a federation restricted to democratic states only, which would slowly be enlarged as more nation-states develop democratic institutions, until eventually it would become universal. As an added advantage, this would provide a strong incentive for each nation to make its government more democratic, in order that it might qualify for membership of the federation, and all the benefits and prestige thereof.

This is much the same scenario as was proposed by Henri de Saint-Simon in 1814, or Clarence Streit in 1939, who proposed an initial union of the North Atlantic democracies (actually a list of 15 democracies including South Africa, Australia and New Zealand), which would slowly spread to become universal. "This Union would be designed", said Streit,

"a) to provide effective common government in our democratic world in those fields where such common government will clearly serve man's freedom better than separate governments;

b) to maintain independent national governments in all other fields where such government will best serve man's freedom; and

c) to create by its constitution a nucleus world government capable of growing into universal world government peacefully and as rapidly as such growth will best serve man's freedom ...

Admission to the Union and to all its tremendous advantages for the individual man and woman would from the outset be open equally to every democracy, now or to come, which guarantees its citizens the Union's minimum Bill of Rights."[12]

This is the position adopted by the present-day Association to Unite the Democracies; and similar ideas were discussed by Karl Deutsch *et al* in their large-scale study *Political Community and the North Atlantic Area.* The existing European Union is also restricted to democratic states. The Draft Treaty of 1984, for instance, contained an explicit clause to this effect,[13] while Article F of the Maastricht Treaty states: "The Union shall respect the national identities of its Member States, whose systems of government are founded on the principles of democracy."

By way of contrast, the World Federalist Movement has always envisaged a system which was universal from the beginning, being based on a reformed United Nations. This was the position adopted at the Montreux Congress in 1947,[14] and further discussed by the CURE group,[15] along with many others. The difference clearly arises from the alternative paths by which a federation might be reached. If it begins with a small kernel of the more progressive states, like the ECSC, then it can be restricted to democratic states alone. If on the other hand the federation is achieved by a reform of the present UN, then it will be universal from the start, including both democratic and autocratic or totalitarian states. This would lead to problems and inconsistencies as outlined above, but the CURE group believed that these could be overcome.

Many people will find it unpalatable to demand democracy as a precondition for joining the federation, and some may regard it as a typical example of Western arrogance and cultural chauvinism. Samuel Huntington, for example, disputes the Fukuyama thesis in his book *The Clash of Civilizations and the Remaking of World Order.* He argues that the concept of democracy is unique to Western civilization, and is not necessarily shared by Asian and Islamic cultures, and that it would be immoral and dangerous to try and force it on other people. But what are the alternatives? Monarchy? Theocracy? Autocracy? Fascism or communism? All these forms of government can still be found in the world today; but none of them could be taken seriously for an instant as a basis for world federation. Democracy is the only form of government with a safety valve, whereby a bad government can be changed peacefully, at the will of the people.

Rule of law

In a federal association, both the central and the local governments (the member states, in this case) have separate and independent spheres of legislative responsibility. In its given sphere, the central association must have the right to make binding regulations and legislation. It must possess a court system empowered to make binding legal judgements based upon that law, and a "police force" or security force empowered to enforce that law if necessary.

The different spheres of responsibility of the central and local governments would be defined by the constitution or founding treaty of the federation. Anything involving international transactions which cannot be controlled by an individual nation would naturally become a federation responsibility. Thus the federation should control and regulate international trade, finance, communications and travel. It should of course be responsible for common security. It should control all matters concerning the 'global commons', consisting of the high seas, outer space, and (eventually) Antarctica. It should also be responsible for co-ordinating joint action on matters requiring a collective response, such as global environmental problems, disaster relief, and large transnational scientific, technological or industrial projects. Finally, it should be charged with co-ordinating joint action to promote development and better standards of living in the Third World. It may not be granted all these powers at once, but they clearly belong in the federal basket. Many of them are already undertaken, to some extent, by the United Nations.

Any disputes over the interpretation of the constitution or founding treaties, or over the spheres of legislative responsibility of the central and local governments, would be up to the federal court to settle. On matters within the central government sphere, the federal court would take precedence over the various national courts. These are normal practices in any federation.

The security forces would be charged with keeping the peace and maintaining the rule of law within the federation, and with protecting its members against any aggression from outside (if any "outside" remains!). These are also standard practices in any federation. Member states would probably demand to keep their own security forces for the immediately foreseeable future: they are likely to insist on retaining the "right to bear arms". But they would have to guarantee to use the processes of political negotiation and law to settle any disputes among themselves by peaceful means, and to come to the aid of the federation whenever called upon to do so.

It would fall upon the federal security forces to enforce the federation law when necessary. Many people have agonized over the difficulty of enforcing international law upon an independent nation state, pointing out that this could lead to a disastrous state of civil war. This is known as the "enforcement problem", which we shall discuss at more length in the next chapter. For the moment, let us simply point out that the existence of some twenty federal systems in the world today demonstrates that the problem is not insuperable.

Subsidiarity

There has been strong resistance in Europe, led by nationalist figures such as Charles de Gaulle and Margaret Thatcher, against any extension of the powers of the Community beyond those absolutely necessary. Ancient and well-established nation-states will not lightly give up their national sovereignty and cultural identity. To demonstrate that these will be protected, the EU has formulated the principle of "subsidiarity" or self-determination, which was recognized in the Maastricht Treaty.[16]

According to this principle, decisions should be taken as closely as possible to the individual citizen, so that whatever can be done locally, regionally or nationally should not be done at community level. Only those functions which absolutely require collective action, and cannot be performed by the member states independently, will become community responsibilities. Thus the member states will retain their sovereignty over internal affairs and most of their external functions as well.

The reasoning behind this principle is clear. To allow citizens to participate fully in the political process, and to avoid feelings of powerlessness and alienation among them, the government must be seated as closely as possible to the people governed. Local affairs should be managed at a local level, national affairs at a national level, and only those affairs which demand international agreement should be decided at the federal level.[17]

A similar rule was given long ago by James Bryce in his famous study *The American Commonwealth:* " the general principle, applicable in every part and branch of government, [is] that, where other things are equal, the more power is given to the units which compose the nation, be they large or small, and the less to the nation as a whole and to its central authority, so much the fuller will be the liberties and so much greater the energy of the individuals who compose the people."[18]

The United Nations declares in Article 7 of the Charter: "Nothing contained in the present Charter shall authorize the United Nations to intervene in matters which are essentially within the domestic jurisdiction of any state." In the Charter of Economic Rights and Duties of States adopted by the General Assembly in 1974, Article 1 also affirmed that "Every State has the sovereign and inalienable right to choose its economic system as well as its political, social and cultural systems in accordance with the will of its people, without outside interference, coercion and threat in any form whatsoever."[19]

The European Parliament in its Draft Treaty of 1984 defined the principle of subsidiarity slightly differently: "The union shall only act to carry out those tasks which may be undertaken more effectively in common than by member states acting separately, in particular those whose execution requires action by the union because their dimensions or effects extend beyond national frontiers."[20] This is a somewhat broader definition, and brings in the issue of "effectiveness". In any case, the principle is a rather elastic one, and many arguments are likely to take place before the respective competencies of the Union and the member states become permanently established.

The member states will certainly demand that the same principle of subsidiarity should also apply to any future world federation. Thus the federation will be a loose or 'minimalist' one. The member states must be guaranteed the right to preserve their national and cultural identities, and to manage their internal economic, social and political systems as they see fit, provided that the basic human rights are observed. Thus each nation will retain its own system of law, health, education, welfare, industry, local government, and so on:- the great bureaucratic fiefdoms of each national government would be preserved. We have already suggested that each country would continue to maintain its own ministries of foreign affairs and defence for the time being.

An example is provided by the electoral systems in Europe. Each nation has preserved its own electoral system, and uses that system to elect its representatives to the European Parliament. Some use proportional representation, while others have single-member constituencies, and use a first-past-the-post system. The basic democratic standards are observed in each case. This "pluralist democracy" offers an excellent example of *e pluribus unum* (or Unity in Diversity) in action.

In order to protect their autonomy and sovereignty, the member states have demanded a very direct voice in the running of the European Union, by way of the Council of Ministers and the European Council. One may expect that the governments of the member states will demand the same direct voice in any world federation. Thus the 'States House' in the federation is likely to consist of a Council on the European pattern, consisting of ministers or representatives directly appointed by the member state governments. To avoid the problem of the veto, the Council would have to adopt some sort of 'qualified majority' rule of voting for normal business, whereby each member receives a weighted vote roughly according to its population and/or financial contributions, and decisions are taken on a weighted majority of votes, without requiring unanimity.

Human Rights

Any world federation would have to guarantee a number of basic human rights to its citizens. This principle is logically not quite consistent with that of subsidiarity, because it overlaps with the internal sphere of responsibility of the member states, but it has already been recognized by the Council of Europe, the European Union, and the United Nations.

The principal conventions on human rights adopted by the UN are contained in the International Bill of Human Rights, in force since 1976. It includes two major conventions, the first one being the International Covenant on Economic, Social and Cultural Rights, which deals with conditions of work, trade unions, social security, protection of the family, standards of living and health, education and cultural life. The second convention is the International Covenant on Civil and Political Rights, which deals with such rights as freedom of movement, equality before the law, presumption of innocence, freedom of conscience and religion, freedom of opinion and expression, peaceful assembly, freedom of association, participation in public affairs and elections, and minority rights. It prohibits torture, cruel or degrading punishment, slavery, arbitrary arrest or imprisonment, war propaganda, and incitement to discrimination or violence.

The UN has no power to impose these obligations on the member states, but the covenants provide for these various rights to be progressively implemented over time by those states which ratify the conventions. By 1994, about two-thirds of the member states had done so. A United Nations High Commissioner of Human Rights was also appointed in that year, with responsibility for all UN Human Rights activities, under the authority of the Secretary-General.

The principal European agreement in this area is the European Convention for the Protection of Human Rights and Fundamental Freedoms, drawn up by the Council of Europe, which came into force in September 1953 after 10 ratifications had been received. The rights contained in this convention are legally binding, and are protected by the European Court of Human Rights, located in Strasbourg, which has precedence over the various national courts in this area. For instance, in one case it ruled that corporal punishment was no longer permissible in

Irish schools, because it contravened the Convention.

There are more than 1,000 private groups around the world monitoring and campaigning for human rights, the best known being Amnesty International. Amnesty has more than 1 million individual members, with subscribers from some 150 countries worldwide. They campaign on behalf of prisoners of conscience, and against violations of human rights such as torture, extrajudicial killings and so forth. An annual report is produced on the state of human rights in each country.

In spite of all this activity, the struggle for human rights still has a long way to go. Over the period 1980-85 Amnesty documented cases of torture in 50 different countries, about one-third of the membership of the UN.[21] In 1994, there were about 23 million refugees worldwide, and half a million civilians were killed in Rwanda. Amnesty also gave evidence before the Commission on Human Rights of "severe and systematic human rights violations" in Algeria, China, Peru, Turkey, Indonesia and East Timor.[22]

There has been great emphasis in recent years on the principles of *equal* rights. Civil rights groups all around the world have struggled and fought for racial equality, religious equality, equal rights for women, and equal rights for minority groups. These campaigns are continually extending the accepted boundaries of the human rights framework.

Solidarity

To maintain and increase mutual confidence and loyalty to the community amongst its citizens, it is axiomatic that equal rights and opportunities must be afforded to all the people of the federation. Everything possible must be done to eliminate economic and social disparities, and increase "cohesion" within the community. In particular, efforts must be made to alleviate poverty and foster development in the poorer regions of the federation, and bring them up to the same standard of living as the wealthier regions.

This principle was endorsed by the European Union in the Maastricht Treaty. The EU has set up various funds for "structural development", such as the European Development Fund (EDF), the European Social Fund (ESF), and the European Agricultural Guidance and Guarantee Fund (EAGGF). In 1988, it was agreed to double spending on these funds to 14 billion ecu per year over the period 1989 to 1993, and they now account for about a third of the entire community budget.[23] The money is used to promote development in backward regions, to create new jobs in declining industrial areas, to help the unemployed, and to modernize and restructure agricultural production in the poorer rural areas. The Social Fund, for instance, has been used to redeploy or compensate thousands of coal miners affected by pit closures within the community.

The United Nations has implicitly adopted a similar principle. Most of its efforts are directed towards helping the Third World. We have mentioned the work of the World Bank, the United Nations Development Programme and other agencies in Chapter 3.

Participation

It is important that private individuals and interest groups at a "grass-roots" level be closely and actively involved in the decisions taken by the federation, wherever possible. This helps to increase cohesion and loyalty within the community, and to prevent feelings of alienation and powerlessness among its citizens. The sinews which bind a community together are its civic associations - sporting clubs, parents and teachers associations, church groups, professional societies, labour unions, voluntary organizations, political parties and so forth. The federation must involve groups at this level if it is to receive the acceptance and loyalty of its people. This is closely allied with the principle of subsidiarity.

Participation was seen as the bedrock of democracy by Alexis de Tocqueville in his classic treatise on *Democracy in America.* "It is incontestably true", he says, "that the love and the habits of republican government in the United States were engendered in the townships and in the provincial assemblies. In a small State, like that of Connecticut for instance, where cutting a canal or laying down a road is a momentous political question, where the State has no army to pay and no wars to carry on, and where much wealth and much honour cannot be bestowed upon the chief citizens, no form of government can be more natural or more appropriate than that of a republic. But it is this same republican spirit, it is these manners and customs of a free people, which are engendered and nurtured in the different States to be afterwards applied in the country at large. The public spirit of the Union is, so to speak, nothing more than an abstract of the patriotic zeal of the provinces. Every citizen of the United States transfuses his attachment to his little republic into the common store of American patriotism. In defending the Union, he defends the increasing prosperity of his own district, the right of conducting its affairs, and the hope of carrying measures of improvement to be adopted which may be favourable to his own interests; and these are motives which are wont to stir men more readily than the general interests of the country and the glory of the nation."[24]

This principle has been recognized by the EU in its creation of the Economic and Social Committee, and the Committee of the Regions. These Committees have the right to be consulted, and to propose initiatives to the Commission and the Council, on appropriate community matters. The Economic and Social Committee is made up of representatives of employer groups, workers, small businesses, professionals, and consumers. The Committee of the Regions consists of representatives from local and regional authorities, and must be consulted on matters concerning education, public health, and structural expenditures.

The United Nations also involves many non-governmental organizations in the work of its functional agencies and committees. Some of the detailed schemes for world federation have included a separate house of assembly for non-governmental organizations and associations. A network of committees and agencies involving private interest groups and expert representatives would certainly be required to carry on the detailed work of any world federation.

Equity

Equity is the first principle of natural justice, and underlies all the other principles, but here it is meant in a more restricted sense. Each member state should contribute to the federation an amount proportional to its resources, and each state should get out of the federation something roughly equivalent to what it puts in. This is not something to be formally defined in a constitution, but more a practical rule of thumb, to be used as a guide in the day-to-day running of the association.

Perceived lack of equity, or unfairness, is the most common cause of resentment among member states of a community. In the United Nations, an obvious example is the United States, which feels (incorrectly) that it is being left to carry a disproportionate share of the UN budget. Within the European Union, the most prominent example is Britain, which has long felt that it contributes too much to the EU budget, while getting too little in return. Germany is also showing signs of impatience at being required to act as paymaster for the rest of the EU.

Equity is a principle which has to be carefully observed when funds are being allocated for new community projects. Industrial contracts in the EU have to be distributed roughly in proportion to the amount contributed by each member state, in pan-European ventures such as the Ariane space launcher programme, or the Airbus programme. Scientific and technological research facilities also have to be fairly distributed: thus the European particle accelerator laboratory CERN is located outside Geneva, while the plasma fusion laboratory JET is located at Culham in England, and so on.

Some redistribution of resources would still be necessary. Consistent with the principle of solidarity, a certain percentage of the community funds should be set aside for reconstruction and development in the poorer regions. But this principle has to be balanced with that of equity. The net redistribution of funds away from any given state cannot exceed, say, 1% of that state's GDP without producing severe effects on investment and economic well-being within that country, and thus arousing serious resentment.

Flexibility

If the association is going to be able to evolve and grow in a natural fashion, it needs to have some degree of constitutional flexibility. Whether this should be counted as a principle or a tactic is a matter of semantics, but it is an important point which is currently under discussion in Europe.

The European community has progressed through a series of treaties, each one overtaking or amending the other: the Treaty of Paris, the Rome Treaties, the Single European Act and finally the Maastricht Treaty. Each of these has required the unanimous consent of the member states. This procedure was feasible as long as the community remained small, but it becomes more and more difficult as the size of the community increases. The Maastricht Treaty, for instance, went perilously close to remaining unratified because of the reluctance of the Danes to approve it. As the number of member states increases, the dreaded problem of the veto becomes ever more serious.

The problem is illustrated in an extreme form by the United Nations, which has undergone no significant constitutional change in fifty years, and appears completely rigid and "pot-bound". In this case it is only the Permanent Members of the Security Council who have a veto, and a two-thirds majority of the General Assembly would be sufficient to approve a change. The number of members is so large, however, and the disparities between them are so great, that no consensus for change has ever emerged.

Some states in Europe, notably Germany, are beginning to discuss ideas whereby the more progressive states should be allowed to proceed towards closer integration, while others (such as Britain, Denmark, or prospective future members from Eastern Europe) should be allowed to opt out or "derogate" from the new provisions, forming a "two speed" European community.[25] This is one possible option for maintaining flexibility, and allowing for further progress and change. It would obviously lead to administrative difficulties, but no doubt these could be overcome. It is imperative that constitutional flexibility be somehow maintained in any prototype world federation.

Final remarks

These principles give a broad, qualitative guide to the scope of the rights and responsibilities which should be allotted to each of the three elements in our diagram at the beginning of the chapter. All except the last two have been explicitly mentioned in the preamble of the Maastricht Treaty, and most of them have been recognized, even if partially or implicitly, by the United Nations. They would form a natural basis for any new federal association.

A formal discussion of principles has not often been attempted before. A number of 'Principles of World Federal Government' were declared at the great Montreux Congress of World Federalists in 1947. The first of them was a requirement for universal membership. The rest consisted largely of a set of functional objectives, rather than principles of association such as we have outlined, although there are large areas of overlap. The list included the limitation of national sovereignty; enforcement of world law directly upon individuals; creation of supranational armed forces; control by the world federal government of weapons of mass destruction; and the power to raise revenue.[26]

More recently the World Federalist Movement has adopted a Statement of Purpose, which does include most of the principles we have discussed. The Statement declares that as citizens of the world, we must all join in achieving a new level of global co-operation to solve the problems of a planet in crisis. The ideals and principles of community life must be applied to international relations. *Democratic* world institutions of law must be developed, to assure a peaceful, just and ecologically sustainable world community. These institutions must have the power to *make and enforce law* in their given jurisdictions, subject to the basic federalist principle of *subsidiarity*. Individuals must be accountable under due process of world law for crimes against humanity; and the Movement promises to work for respect for *human rights* and freedoms, and equitable *participation* of all in the global economy and in global decisions which affect their lives.[27]

Guy Héraud in his book *Principes du fédéralisme* discusses six "keys to the Federal City" which appear at first sight quite different to ours. They are:

- Autonomy - the right of individuals and groups to autonomy within the community, which Héraud sees as an indispensable aspect of democracy. This would imply that ethnic groups like the Basques or the Bretons should have the right to declare themselves as independent and autonomous communities if they so desire;

- 'L'exacte adéquation' - or careful division of competencies between the different levels of government, determined on the basis of subsidiarity;
- Participation - the right of component groups to be actively involved in decisions taken by the general community;
- Co-operation - between the member states, as opposed to domination of one by another, or all of them by the central government;
- Complementarity - between the different levels of government, each performing separate functions, so that there should be no conflict between them;
- Guarantees - of the rights and powers of each level of government and of the individual citizen, which should be provided by the constitution, the courts, and the security forces. This corresponds roughly to our 'rule of law'.

In the end, both sets of principles cover similar ground. The major difference lies in Heraud's principle of autonomy. This deserves serious consideration; but it would certainly be a political hot potato, and would hardly command broad general agreement. Thus I would not propose it as a necessary starting principle for world federation.

David Held has proposed a different principle of autonomy in his recent book *Democracy and the Global Order*. By his definition, autonomy means that each person should be free and equal within the political framework, which perhaps corresponds to our principle of solidarity. He advocates a model of "cosmopolitan democracy", located somewhere between a federation and a confederation, which is quite close to our position.

The most contentious issue within the broader world federalist movement boils down to a single question: should the first principle of the association be democracy, or universality? The Association to Unite the Democracies lays primary stress on the idea of freedom and democracy, while the World Federalist Association has traditionally taken universality as its first criterion. The United Nations, for instance, has foregone democracy for the sake of universality. Its representatives are not democratically elected, nor is its membership restricted to democratic states. This is its greatest defect, and its greatest source of weakness. A better approach might be to do things the other way around, and to begin with a democratic association, foregoing universality instead. The ultimate aim of the association would certainly be to embrace all nations and become universal, but this could be achieved progressively over time, as the various nations advance politically and become democratic. The democratic system of government has been built up over many centuries of painful struggle, and has proved itself as the only means by which political stability, relatively efficient government, and the preservation of individual freedoms and human rights can be assured. Free citizens of the world community should not be afraid to reaffirm these facts from time to time.

Chapter 6

Problems and Objections

I happen to like war. It kills off a lot of rascals and clears the air.

Tonini, in *Don Camillo and the Prodigal Son,*
by Giovanni Guareschi

There have been many critics or opponents of the idea of world federation over the years. The 'realists' dismiss the idea as naive and impractical, while others see world government as downright dangerous, and liable to lead to an Orwellian super-state.

The arguments raised by these commentators need to be addressed.. It has to be shown that there are satisfactory and logical answers to their criticisms, or else the whole case for world federation falls to the ground. Furthermore, their analyses are extremely valuable in pinpointing the obstacles to be overcome on the way to federation.

Luckily, there is always the crucial example of the European Union to show that a federation between sovereign states is feasible. The principles which have been adopted by the EU have been expressly designed to answer the objections of the critics and allay their fears.

The Problem of National Sovereignty

Members of the realist school of political science, led by men such as Professor Hans Morgenthau of the University of Chicago, have tended to regard world federalists as naive and Utopian dreamers, ignorant of the realities of world politics. International politics is all about the struggle for power, they claim. National leaders and national governments guard their sovereignty and independence jealously, and will never agree to give them up to a supranational authority.

The views of Morgenthau himself are not quite so negative as this would suggest. He actually agrees, in theory at least, that world government is the correct answer to the problem of warfare. "The argument of the advocates of the world state is unanswerable", he says. "There can be no permanent international peace without a state extensive with the confines of the political world."[1] He argues, however, that such a world state is simply not practicable or feasible at the present time. "No society exists coextensive with the presumed range of a world state. The nation is the recipient of man's highest secular loyalties. Beyond it there are other nations, but no community for which man would be willing to act regardless of what he understands the interests of his own nation to be. In other words, the peoples of the world are not ready to accept world government, and their overriding loyalty to the nation erects an insurmountable obstacle to its establishment."[2] A little later he concludes that "a world state cannot be established under the present moral, social, and political conditions of the world. In no period of modern history was civilization more in need of permanent peace and hence, of a world state, and in no period of modern history were the moral, social, and political conditions less favourable for the establishment of a world state. There can be no world state without a world community willing and able to support it."[3]

Thus Morgenthau's primary conclusion is that a world community must precede a world state. He goes on to discuss ways in which such a world community might be built up, through the functional approach, and by international organizations like UNESCO, NATO, and the European Communities. For the time being, he concludes, we must content ourselves with the amelioration of conflict by means of diplomacy.

The problem of national sovereignty was already noted three hundred years ago by William Penn, who examined the proposition: *"That Soveraign Princes and States will hereby become not Soveraign: a Thing they will never endure"*. He answers that this is a Mistake: *"they remain as Soveraign at Home as ever they were. Neither their Power over their People, nor the usual Revenue they pay them is diminished. So that the Soveraignties are as they were, for none of them have now any Soveraignty over one another: And if this be called a lessening of their Power, it must be only because the great Fish can no longer eat up the little ones, and that each Soveraignty is equally defended from Injuries, and disabled from committing them."* [4] Under a federal system, the internal sovereignty of national governments over their own people would remain essentially the same, guaranteed by the principle of *subsidiarity*.

It must be admitted, however, that the nation-states would lose much of their individual freedom of action in external relations. There is no blinking the fact that any national government would be making a very large commitment by joining a world federation. As Inis Claude has said: "The leaders of nations and their constituents must be prepared to subordinate to the requirements of the collective security system their apparent and immediate national interest - to incur economic loss and run the risk of war, even in situations where the national interest does not seem to be involved, or when this policy seems to conflict with the national interest or to undermine established national policies. This means that states must renounce both pacifism and the right to use war as an instrument of national policy, while standing to resort to force for the fulfillment of their international obligations."[5] In return for this sacrifice, of course, the states would receive a guarantee of their own security, along with other great benefits from the federation.

This loss of sovereignty over external relations is perhaps more apparent than real. It has often been pointed out that states are not free to do exactly as they please in foreign affairs. They are constrained by international treaties and conventions. They cannot dictate policies to other states, but must sit down and negotiate new agreements with them by diplomatic means. A world federation would merely provide more formal mechanisms for arriving at these agreements and regulating them. Even the security commitments mentioned above are not very different to those made by a nation entering an alliance, for example. The only difference is that a nation may find it easier to evade its obligations under an alliance agreement.

If the realist critique was intended to prove that nations will never voluntarily abridge or diminish their sovereignty under any circumstances, then it was clearly wrong. Two notable counter-examples have occurred since World War II. One was when the Soviet Union voluntarily withdrew its forces from Eastern Europe under Mikhail Gorbachev. The second and much more important example has been the gradual integration of the nations of Western Europe to form the European Union. This has demonstrated that national statesmen and their constituents can, very occasionally, show enough vision and foresight to give up part of their national sovereignty for the common good. Politics does not always consist solely of a naked struggle for power.

It is certainly true, however, that national sovereignty forms a major obstacle to world federation. Under normal circumstances, national leaders *are* very reluctant to give up any of their power, and they will take a great deal of convincing before they will admit it is necessary. The resistance of nationalist leaders like Charles de Gaulle and Margaret Thatcher in Europe has demonstrated the powerful hold of national sovereignty on the popular imagination. This has been the factor primarily responsible for the slow pace of European integration. The battle between the federalists and the nationalists still continues to this day, and the balance between the two camps will ultimately determine the shape of the European federation. This is no more than a normal and healthy political process. A similar process of 'punctuated evolution' may be expected to occur as the eventual world federation takes shape. For a long time nothing will happen, and then every so often a shift will occur, and a step forward will be taken.

The Problem of Diverse Values

We come now to an even more fundamental question. Is the sense of community and solidarity between the peoples of the world yet strong enough to form the basis for a world federation? Are the values which are shared between them sufficient? It is difficult to assess the answers to these questions, but they are crucial to the viability of the whole idea.

Many writers in the past have given a negative answer. "For a machinery of central justice to work satisfactorily, its judgments would have to be based upon a worldwide community of values", said W.T.R. Fox, for instance. "That community of values does not exist today."[6] The theologian Rienhold Niebuhr wrote an essay in 1949 on *The Illusions of World Government,* in which he argued very forcefully that no world government can be created without the prior existence of a world community, which in turn requires the gradual growth of what he calls "social tissue". "The fallacy of world government can be stated in two simple propositions", he claims. "The first is that governments are not created by fiat (though sometimes they can be imposed by tyranny). The second is that governments have only limited efficacy in integrating a community ... Governments cannot create communities for the simple reason that the authority of government is not primarily the authority of law nor the authority of force, but the authority of the community itself. Laws are obeyed because the community accepts them as corresponding, on the whole, to its conception of justice."[7]

Niebuhr admitted that the international community is not totally lacking in social tissue, noting for instance the increasing economic interdependence among nations, their fear of mutual annihilation, and the moral sense of obligation to their fellow-men. The primary differences in the conception of justice in the world do not spring from religious and cultural differences between east and west, he argued. "The primary differences arise from a civil war in the heart of western civilization, in which a fanatical equalitarian creed has been pitted against a libertarian one .. Russia has become the national center of the equalitarian creed, while America has become the outstanding proponent of the libertarian one."[8]

Finally, Niebuhr concluded that "the forces which are operating to integrate the world community are limited. To call attention to this fact does not mean that all striving for a higher and wider integration of the world community is vain. That task must and will engage the conscience of mankind for ages to come. But the edifice of government which we build will be sound and useful if its height is proportionate to the strength of the materials from which it is constructed."[9]

During the period of the Cold War, it was perfectly clear that the sceptics were right. The East and West had different economic systems, Communist versus capitalist, as well as different political systems, totalitarian versus democratic. The two systems were competing in a bitter struggle for world power and influence. There was never more than a forlorn hope that they would recognize sufficient community of interest to join together in a world federation. As David Mitrany remarked, "if a federal house cannot be half free or half slave, neither can it be half capitalist and half communist."[10]

The picture has changed dramatically since the fall of the Soviet Union. The Communist system was unable to meet the aspirations of the people. Russians became fed up with the inconvenience of having to queue for hours to purchase a loaf of bread, for example, and in the end the system collapsed like a house of cards, to the great surprise of the rest of the world. The remaining Communist superpower in China has meanwhile embraced capitalism in practice, while nominally remaining Communist in theory, and has so far escaped the fate of the Soviets. The Western doctrines of free enterprise and capitalism in the economic sphere, and liberty and democracy in the political sphere, rule virtually unchallenged in the theoretical arena. Socialism remains a living ideal, but even the socialist parties in the West seem to be falling over themselves to embrace 'economic rationalism'. Thus the great civil war in the heart of western civilization has been resolved, and there has been a major convergence of values between the two sides. That is the argument of Francis Fukuyama.

More recently, Samuel Huntington has challenged the Fukuyama thesis on behalf of the realists. He sees major fault-lines remaining between the "declining" civilization of the West and the growing civilizations of Asia and Islam, which adhere to different values. The concepts of individual liberty and political democracy are unique to Western civilization. Huntington rejects the ideas of multiculturalism and "universalism". Claims that Western values are universally relevant are false, immoral and dangerous: - immoral, because they are imposing Western values on other societies, and dangerous, because they lead to undue interference by the West in other people's affairs, which could even lead to war between the civilizations. He argues that the West should pull up the drawbridge, and mind its own business. My viewpoint here is very much closer to Fukuyama's than Huntington's.

What exactly *are* the common values which would be sufficient to form the basis for a world federation? Of course there is no necessity for *all* values to be held in common: the watchword is "unity in diversity". The federation should be able to embrace different religions, different social systems and different political and economic systems. The basic requirements consist of an agreed set of common goals, based on common interests, and an agreed set of principles of association, upon which a loose federal structure could be built.

The common goals were discussed in Chapter 1, and can be summarized in terms of the five great world order values: peace, economic well-being, social justice, ecological stability, and positive identity for all. There is unlikely to be much dispute about these general aims. The World Order Models Project team, which includes participants from all over the world, has spent a good deal of effort ensuring that they express universal aspirations.[11] The mere existence of the United Nations already testifies to the fact that the nations of the world recognize a number of common interests, and are willing in some degree to associate to meet these aims.

In the previous chapter we have tried to identify the basic principles of association upon which a world federation could be founded: the major ones are democracy, the rule of law, subsidiarity, human rights and solidarity. They have already been endorsed by the countries of the European Union (i.e. the West); and the United Nations has also recognized them through its Charter and Conventions, with the single exception of the principle of democracy. Democracy has not yet been universally adopted, but it offers advantages which are universally applicable - whether it originated in the West or not is irrelevant. The prime examples of India and Japan show that a democratic system can take root and flourish in a non-Western context.

It all comes back again, perhaps, to the problem of transition. Morgenthau and Niebuhr are perfectly correct in saying that a world government cannot be created in a single giant leap, by means of a grand constitutional convention, unless a sufficient sense of world community already exists. A worldwide consensus for change would be needed, which has certainly not existed up to the present time. The sense of international community is growing stronger year by year, as exemplified by festivals like the Olympic Games, where the whole world can admire the endurance of distance runners from Ethiopia or South Africa, say, or the grace of springboard divers from China. Nevertheless, the world still does not appear ready for complete political integration, achieved in one fell swoop.

The more relevant question is whether the world might be ready to begin the integration process in a more gradual and evolutionary fashion, following the European example. After all, the sense of community cannot have been very strong when the European Coal and Steel Community was founded in 1950, only five years after the battles and massacres of World War II. The loyalty of European citizens towards the EU is still not very strong, even today. Yet the Europeans were able to recognize some common needs and common purposes, which were sufficient to allow the association to establish itself and grow. The political superstructures of Europe have been built in a stepwise fashion, in tandem with various slowly growing "social tissues". Can we now begin to duplicate this process on the world stage?

The Problem of Enforcement

Within its sphere of responsibility, the federation must have the right to make binding regulations and legislation, with a 'police force' or security force empowered if necessary to enforce that law. Many people have agonized over the difficulty of enforcing laws upon an autonomous member state. A nation obviously cannot be treated like an individual criminal malefactor, and clapped up in a prison cell. If a serious disagreement were to arise between the federation and a member state, and the federation attempted to impose a solution by force, the result could be an outbreak of civil war, which would be catastrophic for all parties.

This problem has been discussed by Inis Claude in his book *Power*

and International Relations. He makes an analogy with the problem of
dissident groups within an individual nation. If a disagreement arises
between the national government and a dissident group, such as a trade
union for instance, then the best way of settling the problem is by a
process of political adjustment, rather than coercion. The dissident
group will in general have legitimate interests or grievances, which
need to be accommodated by means of discussions and political
compromises. The use of force only hardens attitudes on both sides, and
makes things worse; it should be considered very much as a last resort.

The best analogy of all is that of the relationship between the states
and the federal government in one of the existing federal systems, such
as the USA. The state governments, by and large, are made up of
practical and responsible men and women. If a disagreement arises with
the national government, it will either be settled by political means, or
referred to a court for adjudication. The judgement of the court, after
any appeals process has been gone through, will generally be
automatically accepted. Thus the problem of enforcement hardly ever
arises. The modern, democratic federal systems of Canada, Australia
and Germany, for example, have never experienced the final calamity of
a civil war during their entire existence.

One great exception to this rule was of course the American Civil
War, fought out over the issues of abolition of slavery and states' rights,
which was indeed very destructive. One can never guarantee that such
disasters will not occur; but at least they are very rare within democratic
states. As Inis Claude remarks, "Americans today regard civil war as
unthinkable; the threat and reality of such internal disorder has become
a historical memory. This fundamental change of outlook seems to me
to be based upon confidence in the adequacy of our political process for
working out compromises and promoting accommodations of interest
among the diverse and overlapping groups which constitute American
society. We expect to be able to cope with disaffected or recalcitrant
groups not by imprisoning their leaders but by negotiating with them."[12]

Thus one expects that a serious problem of law enforcement upon
member states will seldom if ever arise; and if it does arise, it will
usually be settled by some process of political adjustment. A remarkable
example is provided by the European Union. The EU at the present time
has no security force of its own, and no way of physically enforcing
community law; yet it has hardly even noticed the lack. The member
states usually obey their legal obligations under the treaties in an
essentially automatic fashion.

There are several different ways in which the federation could penalize a member state without resorting to force, including fines, forfeitures, embargoes and sanctions. The European Commission was given the right to fine member states under the Maastricht Treaty. Just recently the Commission has announced that it will impose fines in a number of relatively minor cases in which a state, despite being condemned in the European Court of Justice, has still not acted on Union law. One case concerned some professional teachers who were prevented from opening a language school in Greece, despite having valid qualifications from the UK.[13] It is already routine for the Commission to fine companies for taking part in unlawful cartels or other restrictive trade practices. Thus we have some concrete examples of how federal law would work in practice.

The enforcement problem does, however, provide another reason for restricting membership of the federation to democratic states. Non-democratic states are often run by a single autocrat rather than a democratic group, and are thus much less responsible and more prone to conflict.[14] Hence the enforcement problem would be likely to arise much more frequently, and in more serious forms, if non-democratic states were admitted to the federation.

Another aspect of the problem concerns what are called 'non-justiciable' disputes. The war in Vietnam, for instance, began as an anti-colonial revolt, and then developed into a struggle between two different ideological systems, capitalist and Communist. There was never any possibility that the issues could be settled in a court of law, or that both sides would even recognize the jurisdiction and legitimacy of the same court. Similarly, the continuing outbreaks of violence between the Catholics and Protestants in Northern Ireland, or the Muslims and Hindus in Kashmir, or the Croats, the Serbs and the Muslims in Yugoslavia, are not disputes which can be settled in a court of law. The antagonism between these communities has deep historical roots, which cannot be removed at the stroke of a judge's gavel.

Grant Gilmore has commented that "there are some issues which it is not healthy to bring before an international court because they escape or transcend judicial competence. 'Adjudication' of such issues will be fruitless and inconclusive at best, and at worst prejudicial to peace."[15] He states that "the function of courts is essentially conservative - to maintain, or to settle incidental disputes within the framework of, a status quo satisfactory to the [community]. When the existing order is radically altered, courts go out of business for a time. Revolution and war are not justiciable .."[16]

How would a world federation cope with issues like these? There is no easy answer to this question, and it is idle to suggest otherwise. The settlement of major conflicts and adjustments to the status quo are political questions rather than legal ones. Ethnic and religious conflicts are liable to break out periodically under any system, and the only real answer is for the different communities themselves to learn to accept each other and live in peace together. Many of these conflicts occur within national boundaries in any case, and would remain the responsibility of the national governments.

A world federation would nevertheless play a vital role in reducing and eventually eliminating these disputes. First of all, it would limit and control any international outbursts of violence, in the same way that the United Nations does now, but much more effectively. Secondly, it would provide new political and legal avenues for the settlement of grievances and disputes, thus removing the original causes of conflict. Disputes over territory or individual rights could be settled in the courts, while ideological and political contests could be settled at the ballot-box. Thus the causes and occasions for violence would be progressively reduced, and new armed disputes would be less likely to arise in the first place. The second phase of the Vietnam war might have been avoided, for instance, if South Vietnam had kept its promise to hold elections after the departure of the French from Indo-China.

Despite this hopeful scenario, there can be no guarantee that organized violence would ever be eliminated entirely. Once a conflict between two different communities has begun, and fear and hatred have developed between them, it seems very hard to stop the violence. The Catholics and Protestants in Northern Ireland have had all the resources of liberal and democratic government at their disposal, and yet they have still found it difficult to live at peace. Infinite patience and time seem to be the only answers for deep-seated problems like these. We cannot hope to wave a magic wand and eliminate all wars and all violence overnight; but we can aim to progressively reduce their occurrence by providing other avenues for resolving tensions and settling disputes.

A detailed and exhaustive documentary history and analysis of the enforcement problem has been given by Benjamin Ferencz, formerly prosecutor at the Nuremberg war crimes tribunal, in a series of six volumes entitled *An International Criminal Court - A Step Toward World Peace; Defining International Aggression - The Search for World*

Peace; and *Enforcing International Law - A Way to World Peace*. These works cover the issues in much greater depth than we can do here.

The Fear of Tyranny

There are many people who instinctively reject the whole idea of world federation. The phrase "world government" evokes for them a nightmare picture of a tyrannical world super-state, with all individual liberties crushed out under the jackbooted heels of a world police force resembling Hitler's SS squads. Their immediate reaction is to oppose any federalist proposals.

Much of the blame for this unfortunate state of affairs can be laid at the feet of authors such as Aldous Huxley and George Orwell. Their horrifying visions of the future seem to have become part of the global consciousness. All we can do here is to analyze these fears rationally, and show that the dangers are actually quite remote.

In *Brave New World*, Huxley satirized the visions of progress put forward by scientists and philosophers (such as his own relations, no doubt). He pictured a world in which humans were bred into different castes by eugenic techniques, and fed drugs to keep them happy and compliant. "A life-span without war, violence and the dread of cruel disease - is it not worth the silly slogans, the scent organ, the Feelies and the lack of an unknown freedom?" asks one of the supervisors.[17] Ironically enough, Huxley himself was actually sympathetic to the idea of world federation. Although his main interest was the decentralization of power, he remarks in passing while discussing the problem of atomic weapons that "Enlightened self-interest will unquestioningly vote for world government, international inspection, and the pooling of information."[18]

George Orwell created even more powerful images in *Animal Farm* and especially in *Nineteen Eighty-Four*. He pictured the state as 'Big Brother', controlling the population by the power of the Thought Police and the propaganda of the Ministry of Truth. "War is Peace. Freedom is Slavery. Ignorance is Strength" ran the slogans of the Ministry. "Big Brother is watching you." The hero Winston Smith is eventually broken by the interrogators under the threat of having his face being eaten by rats. Many people now seem to associate these images with the idea of world government!

Orwell's real intention was to satirize the totalitarian régimes of the time, such as Fascist Italy, Spain and Germany, and Stalinist Russia. He was certainly afraid that they might represent the future, and that the confrontation between East and West might end up with two or three monolithic and totalitarian super-states facing up against each other; but fortunately no such dreadful scenario has eventuated.

Many members of the peace movement seem to share these fears of tyranny. They reject the Big Brother image of world government, and hold instead to the credo "Small is Beautiful". Jonathan Schell, in a book on the elimination of nuclear weapons entitled *The Abolition,* writes as follows. "The heart sinks at the thought of world government not because it is "unrealistic" but because it is all too real. We want relief from the nuclear peril, but if we sign up for world government as the means of getting it we find that global institution after global institution is inexorably delivered on our doorstep thereafter, each one equipped to meddle in some area of our lives."[19] Later he remarks " if a lawless government were to assume control of the world .. the horror of the situation would be beyond all imagining. Even if one regards these worst-case nightmares of world government run amok as unlikely, the prospect of a supreme political power ruling over the whole world remains chilling. Anarchy is not liberty, yet it could be that in anarchy, with all its violence, the human spirit has greater latitude to live and grow than it would have in the uniform shadow of a global state."[20] Unfortunately, this leaves him with no very credible alternative proposal for eliminating nuclear weapons.

Schell appears to be contemplating the old simplistic and unrealistic idea in which the sovereign nation-state is entirely superseded by a world government of universal extent and powers. But world federalists nowadays conceive a world in which the nation-state still exists, and regulates most aspects of national life just as it does now. Individual rights and freedoms would receive even firmer guarantees than they do at present, under the principle of human rights, according to conventions such as those recognized by the UN and the EU. Political freedoms would be guaranteed under the principles of democracy and the rule of law, as they are in Europe. International travel, trade and finance would certainly be regulated by the world federation, but these activities would be virtually transparent to the ordinary citizen, being overseen by expert international committees much as they are at present. How many of us can claim to have had a global institution "delivered on our doorstep", or "meddling in our daily lives"?

Another example of this viewpoint is the book *The New World Order,* by the right-wing American broadcaster and evangelist Pat

Robertson. Robertson claims to have uncovered a conspiracy between millionaire capitalists, the liberal Establishment, New Agers and Communists to foist world government upon us, and to extinguish the liberty and sovereignty of the American people. He apparently believes that this plot is inspired by the Devil! The theory is nonsensical, as most conspiracy theories are; but it is interesting to note that Robertson himself proposes the establishment of a Community of Democratic Nations, which leaves him not very far from our final position.

In the end, a world federation should actually *enhance* world freedom, and remove the threat of tyranny. In the present semi-anarchy of world affairs, there are still many states run by cruel and autocratic régimes, which regularly engage in arbitrary arrest, torture, and all sorts of horrible violations of human rights and dignity. Within a world federation, on the other hand, all such abuses would be forbidden under enforceable international law.

The only danger that could possibly arise would be the overthrow of the democratic government by some sort of coup. It would certainly be a catastrophe if any future world federation was subverted to become an autocracy or dictatorship, and every precaution would have to be taken to ensure that no such disaster could happen. All the usual 'checks and balances' would have to be built into the Constitution, including an independent judiciary and parliament, and a security force which is pledged to uphold the Constitution at all times. Perhaps even a ceremonial head of state might be necessary, charged with ensuring that the Constitution was upheld.

Experience has shown that the democratic form of government is very stable, once it is well established. The United States government has existed now for over two hundred years, and the idea of its being overthrown by a totalitarian group is virtually inconceivable, except in the fevered minds of pulp fiction writers. It is over three hundred years since the last revolution in Britain, although the government has evolved substantially over that time. Many other examples might be quoted: the Nordic countries, Switzerland, Holland, Canada, Australia and New Zealand all have long traditions of peaceful democratic government. Japan and India are thriving examples of democracy in Asia.

There are some counter-examples which might be raised. Democracies have sometimes been supplanted by military juntas in South America, for example, where overthrowing the government has seemed at times to be a national sport. One can only plead that these countries were relatively undeveloped, both economically and politically, with a very small governing class and no strong democratic traditions. Another example is that of Germany in the 1930s, where Hitler was voted into power, and then overthrew the Weimar Republic. The circumstances there were very special, however. The Weimar Republic was newly established after World War I, and was tainted by association with the hated Versailles Peace Treaty, while the economy of Germany had been savagely battered first by war reparations and then by the onset of the Great Depression. These factors are more than enough to account for the fatal weakness of the fledgling Republic.

The stability question does provide a further reason for limiting membership of the world federation to democratic states. If the member states all have a strong and well-established democratic tradition, so that their citizens would never dream of attempting to subvert the government, then the federation itself will be stable and secure.

The final, clinching factor which would provide a virtually iron-clad guarantee of the federation's stability would be the support of the member states. The United States, for instance, would never stand idly by and allow the federation to be subverted by a non-democratic group. The other member states would likewise take action, and thus any attempt at subversion would be doomed to fail.

All this is illustrated once again by the European Union. The EU is often accused of bureaucratic meddling and officiousness, and the European Parliament needs to be given more power to restrain these annoyances; but that is a far cry from actual tyranny. No-one has ever seriously suggested that the Union is liable to be taken over by a totalitarian group, as far as I am aware. Such an idea is simply not within the bounds of practical possibility.

Thus the fear of world tyranny is really little more than a chimaera or fantasy. If a democratic world federation was once securely established, its overthrow or subversion would become virtually inconceivable. The present danger lies all in the opposite direction. The world security system today is far too *weak*, and needs to be strengthened - it seems perverse to worry about whether it might one day become too *strong*. The issue is essentially that of government versus anarchy. World federalists argue that we need a democratic world government to achieve peace and order in the international arena; whereas their opponents prefer to have no government at all, because of their fear of world tyranny. Yet on the domestic scene, they would mostly accept the necessity for a national government without question.

The Fear of Loss of Identity

Another objection sometimes raised by opponents of world federation is that it would lead to a loss of national and cultural identity for the member states. They fear a "homogenization" of world culture. It would certainly be a tragedy if all the fascinating and diverse societies of the world were to be replaced by a single bland and homogeneous world culture. But the principle of subsidiarity adopted by the EU is intended to prevent this: it declares that each nation and each region must be left free to manage its own affairs, whenever possible. We have already discussed how national sovereignty would be preserved, for the most part, under this principle. Cultural independence would be protected in a similar way. The preservation of cultural diversity is also a major aim of UNESCO and the United Nations. The watchword is 'Unity in Diversity', once again.

The major threat to cultural diversity has nothing to do with government, in fact, but arises from the power of the global media. The worldwide reach of the American film and television industries means that we are all in danger of being submerged by the culture of Walt Disney and Hollywood. Perhaps this is the price we pay for belonging to the global village; but it has nothing to do with the question of world government. Each different culture will have to find its own way of withstanding the onslaught from the global media barons.

'War is Good'

Coming now to the less serious objections, there may be some people who would oppose common security and world federation on the grounds that war is a natural and useful aspect of human society. War is part of human nature, they might say, and will never be eradicated. War allows a stronger society to replace a weaker one, and thus leads to social progress and evolution. The law of "survival of the fittest" should continue to operate, for the good of human society. Even at the individual level, they might argue, war eliminates the weaker members of society in favour of the fitter and stronger ones, leading to improvement of the human race. It may even help to solve the problem of overpopulation!

Such savage arguments can hardly be taken seriously in this day and age. They would certainly be regarded as 'politically incorrect', and one can only expect to find them in the writings of a Nietzsche or an Adolf Schicklgruber. Let us only make a few brief remarks. Firstly, in the era of mass destruction, war is liable to kill both weak and strong without distinction. Bravery and strength are of no value against atomic bombs, or high-tech weapons guided by remote control. Secondly, there are more humane ways of dealing with the population problem. And finally, war has already been largely eliminated within the boundaries of the more advanced nation-states, and more peaceful and democratic means of political evolution have been developed. Surely it is time to try the same experiment on the world stage.

Want of Employment

There is one final objection which was raised by William Penn, namely: *"That there will be a great Want of Employment for younger Brothers of Families; and that the Poor must either turn Soldiers or Thieves."* The answers to this will be left as an exercise for the reader.

Summary and Conclusions

Even during the first flush of popular enthusiasm for world federalism, in the years immediately following the Second World War, there were plenty of critics to inject a more sober and realistic note into the discussion, such as Hans Morgenthau, Inis Claude, and the theologian Rienhold Niebuhr. Significantly, none of these commentators disagreed with the concept of world federation as the ultimate means of securing world peace; but they argued that it was an impractical and unrealistic aim at that point in time. Instead, they maintained, it was better to concentrate for the time being on more mundane and achievable targets, such as establishing functional co-operation between nations, strengthening international organizations like the UN, and establishing better diplomatic procedures for avoiding or settling international disputes.

Some enormous hurdles which must be surmounted on the way to world federation were identified. The strong attachment of each people to their own national sovereignty, the absence of any strong feeling of international community, and the lack of common values and social fabric make it very difficult to achieve the target. A large segment of popular opinion is actually opposed to the idea of world federation, for fear that it might lead to worldwide tyranny. But the greatest of all obstacles in the early days was the deepening chasm between East and West. The onset of the Cold War and the increasing tension between the United States and the Soviet Union stifled all hopes of further integration between the nations for the time being, and led to a prolonged decline in the world federalist movement.

Almost fifty years have now passed since those early days, and some momentous changes have occurred. Gradually and imperceptibly, the "social tissue" of the world community has been strengthened. The old divisive forces of colonialism and apartheid have been vanquished. The structure of international law has been reinforced with a network of new treaties and conventions covering arms control and disarmament, human rights, the law of the sea, trade and development, and many other areas. There is a spreading consensus of international opinion on all these issues. Environmental problems have been recognized as another vital issue confronting the whole world in common. Joint peacekeeping operations have become a major focus of the United Nations. Most important of all, the Cold War has ended, the divisive symbol of the Berlin Wall has been torn down, and the nuclear arms race between the superpowers has been halted and reversed.

Meanwhile, the development of the European Union has provided a crucial example to show that the objections raised by the critics are not insuperable. National statesmen can occasionally be persuaded to cede a little of their sovereignty for the common good. The process of European integration was successfully begun, in pursuit of a well-defined common purpose, despite the fact that France and Germany had only recently been wartime adversaries, so that there was little sense of community between them. By now, the EU forms a loose and decentralized federation in all but name. It has encountered no significant problems in the enforcement of Union law. It has a stable and well-established political structure, providing secure guarantees of liberty to its citizens; and its overthrow by some sort of anti-democratic coup is virtually inconceivable.

The principles which have been adopted by the European Union have been designed to satisfy the doubts of the critics. The principles of democracy and human rights ensure that individual freedoms are protected, while the principles of subsidiarity, solidarity and participation ensure that national and regional identities and cultural diversity are preserved as far as possible. Experience has shown that a democratic federal structure is a very stable form of government, and that the member states may be expected to obey the federal laws in an almost automatic fashion.

One might question, perhaps, whether Europe really provides a good model for the rest of the world. The mutual understanding and common values shared within Europe are obviously much greater than those shared at a global level, and the impediments to federation are correspondingly much less. Nevertheless, the same *principles* should apply equally well in both cases.

Finally, our discussions have reinforced two of the tactical lessons drawn from the European experiment. The first is that integration is most likely to be achieved in a gradual and evolutionary fashion, starting from a smaller association of progressive states with limited aims and scope, and building upwards from there, as Jean Monnet and company did with the European Coal and Steel Community. The popular support and sense of community are still not strong enough in our global village to allow world federation to be established in one grand constitutional leap. It is better and safer to proceed in stages as the Europeans have done, pausing to consolidate and reinforce the cohesion within the association after each stage.

The second lesson to be drawn is that membership of the prototype association should be restricted to democratic states only. There are a number of compelling reasons for this, which can be recapitulated as follows. Firstly, it would violate the key principle of democracy to include a non-democratic state in the association, and would lead to impossible constitutional and legal anomalies. Inclusion of a non-democratic state would violate many of the civil rights that ought to be guaranteed by the association; and the association could not tolerate a situation where, in guaranteeing the security and integrity of its members, it found itself propping up an autocracy or dictatorship. Secondly, democratic states are much less prone to conflict and to violations of international law than non-democratic ones. Given the huge difficulty and costs, both human and material, of enforcing international law against a recalcitrant nation-state, it is best to avoid such problems as far as possible by excluding non-democratic states from the outset. Furthermore, democratic states are much more stable politically, so that restricting membership to democracies would minimize the likelihood of internal instability in a member state, when the association might be forced to intervene to settle a domestic conflict. Finally, the restriction to democratic member states would ensure that the federal association itself remains stable and free from tyranny.

Many people will object that this would leave the non-democratic states out in the cold, including many of the poorer states of Africa and the Third World, thus violating many of the original aims of world federation. The answer to this is that the association would grow over time until eventually it would become universal, and embrace all the nations of the earth. Each nation, as it advanced politically and acquired a stable and democratic form of government, would 'graduate' as a member of the association. Over half the nations of the world already have democratic governments, although a number of them are democratic in name only, and are rated only 'partly free' by Freedom House. In concept, there is hardly any serious challenge to the principle of democracy in the world today; and the benefits flowing from membership of the association could provide an important incentive for nations to modernize their forms of government in order to qualify. In the meantime, the needs of the non-democratic states would be partly catered for through the United Nations, which is already universal.

Chapter 7

How Do We Get There From Here?

"Then let us pray that come it may,
As come it will for a' that,
That sense and worth, o'er a' the earth,
May bear the gree and a' that;
For a' that and a' that,
It's coming yet for a' that,
That man to man the warld o'er,
Shall brothers be for a' that. "

Robert Burns

If the final objective is world federation, by what path can we reach it? This is known in the trade as the "transition problem", and it is an extremely difficult one to solve. Some of the hurdles to be overcome were discussed in the last chapter. It is impossible to predict exactly how the federation will eventually come about, but at least we can discuss some of the options which seem to be available at the present time.

Reform of the United Nations

The most obvious path would be a constitutional reform of the United Nations, to transform it into a genuine, democratic world federation of nations. This has been the primary aim of the World Federalists Association in the United States for many years. Proposal after proposal has been made, as outlined at the end of Chapter 3, but so far none of these efforts has had any success. The UN has never even convened a conference to review the Charter.

Many reasons might be found for this failure. One excuse commonly given is that the UN performs a useful though limited function as it stands, and that any attempt to amend the Charter might destroy the organization entirely. The Charter is extremely rigid and difficult to amend in any case. It requires the approval of all five permanent members of the Security Council, and a virtual consensus among the remaining 190-odd states in the General Assembly, to achieve any change. The UN is a huge and unwieldy organization, made up of nations of many disparate cultures and stages of development. As Morgenthau and Niebuhr pointed out long ago, the sense of community between them is weak, and the will to unite is not there. One cannot realistically expect all the member states to agree simultaneously on a revolutionary leap into an unknown, federal future - the hurdle is just too high, and no serious attempt has ever been made at the diplomatic level to overcome it. It might be better to look for some more gradual and evolutionary way forward, bypassing the UN for the moment, just as Jean Monnet bypassed the Council of Europe in setting up the ECSC.

In recent years, the federalists have fallen back on less ambitious proposals, such as the CAMDUN movement to set up a democratic Second Assembly of the UN, which could be introduced without requiring any formal amendment of the UN Charter. This is a useful and worthwhile proposal, which deserves to be supported. As a subsidiary organ of the General Assembly, however, the new Assembly would have very little power or influence, and would be in danger of becoming just another talkshop. It seems unlikely to provide the answer to our problem.

Enlargement of the European Union

Another possible avenue might be the gradual enlargement of the European Union to become a world federation. The economic success of the community has already led to its expansion from the original six members to the present fifteen, with a long queue of prospective future members knocking on the door. A number of Mediterranean states are applying for membership, along with virtually all the former members of the Warsaw Pact in Eastern Europe. It is conceivable that Russia and other members of the CIS might also join in future years: Russia has always considered herself as a European power, and has already been admitted to the Council of Europe. In that case, the EU would already form a huge organization, embracing almost all of Europe and Northern Asia. Might it not then continue to expand in a gradual and peaceful fashion, until it embraced the entire world?

A little thought shows that this is an unlikely scenario, and probably unsuitable as well. The EU was never intended or designed to be a world organization. It has already rejected a membership application from Morocco, for example, on the grounds that Morocco is not a European nation; and the European Commission is actively encouraging the development of other regional organizations, among the Arab states, or in Africa. Furthermore, integration among the European nations has already proceeded further than would be possible or desirable in a world organization at present. It would hardly seem feasible to form a single market covering the entire globe, for instance, or to decree common citizenship with the right to work, live and study anywhere in the world. These might be worthy aims for the distant future, but at present the social and economic disparities are just too great. Europe might find itself swamped with millions of Chinese peasants looking for work, for example. It would probably be better to aim for a wider but shallower degree of integration at the world level for the time being.

The Functional Approach

The functionalists such as David Mitrany would argue for what might be called the "look, no hands!" approach. The functional needs of the world community will demand their own solutions. Agencies and committees will be set up to handle these common problems, and little by little the various national sovereignties will be whittled away and transferred to the growing network of international agencies. There is no need to set up any formal political structures to achieve integration.

This functional integration has indeed been occurring at an ever-increasing pace over a period of some two centuries. The number and scope of international agencies and commissions has increased enormously since World War II, particularly in areas involving economic and technical co-operation, but also in the fields of international law, arms control and disarmament, and security matters. In 1989, there were nearly 300 international government organizations (IGOs) in existence, and 4624 international non-government organizations (INGOs).[1] These developments provide an indispensable underpinning for deeper political integration.

It was pointed out by neofunctionalists such as Ernst Haas, however, that the establishment of a true community, whether it be an economic, political or security community, does require a conscious act of political will. The deeper issues of national security and national sovereignty cannot be settled by default, or by stealth. "Functionalism and functional arrangements have little effect by themselves upon the eventual success or failure of efforts to establish amalgamated security communities", argued Karl Deutsch. "The outcome in each case is most likely to depend on other conditions and processes, particularly on how rewarding or unrewarding were the experiences associated with functional arrangements. The most that can be said for functionalism is that it avoids the perils of premature overall amalgamation, and that it gives the participating governments, élites, and peoples more time gradually to learn the habits and skills of more far-reaching, stable, and rewarding integration."[2] Functional co-operation is helping to build the "social tissue" of the world community, and laying the groundwork for an eventual world federation, but is not sufficient in itself to complete the process.

The Regional Approach

Following the economic success of the European Common Market, organizations to promote economic integration and free trade have sprung up in many other regions of the globe. Recent examples have been the formation of the North American Free Trade Association (NAFTA) and the group for Asia-Pacific Economic Cooperation (APEC). Some other well-known associations are the Organization of American States (OAS), the Organization of African Unity (OAU), the Association of South-East Asian Nations (ASEAN), the Nordic Council, and the League of Arab States. Economic integration is proceeding apace, although none of these other organizations has a political superstructure as powerful and well-developed as that of the European Union, and most remain as rather loose consultative groupings.

An interesting exception to this rule is the Andean Group, consisting of Bolivia, Colombia, Ecuador, Peru and Venezuela. In deliberate imitation of the European Community, they have aimed at both economic and political co-operation, and have established joint supranational bodies including an Andean Council, a Commission, a Parliament, a Court of Justice, and a "Junta", which is a technical body to facilitate the fulfilment of the Cartagena Agreement which established the organization in 1969. The Parliament is directly elected, and comprises five members from each country. A common market has been established within the group, although some tariffs still remain, and trade within the group has been increasing by leaps and bounds.

These developments in regional integration represent important steps in the right direction, just as they did in the European case. Besides promoting economic development, each step in the integrative process makes the possibility of war between the member states more remote. Thus the association helps to bring peace and prosperity to the region.

The question at issue, however, is whether the process of regional integration will help to bring about world integration as well. Theorists of regional integration such as Ernst Haas, Amitai Etzioni and Joseph Nye believe that it will. Amitai Etzioni, for example, states that "the rise of regional communities may provide a stepping-stone on the way from a world of a hundred odd states to a world of stable and just peace. Such an achievement seems to require the establishment of a world political community. The rise of a world community is by no means assured; at best it will be a long and difficult process. Nor does the evolution of every regional community serve to advance the cause of world community. And one must note that, so far, for every regional association that has succeeded, several have failed. But the increase in the number of regional communities and their growing success seems to indicate that the one avenue by which a world community - and not a world empire - might rise is the growth of regionalism."[3] Later, he writes: "Few observers believe that a global state can be the next step in the development of political institutions. Many, however, view regional unions as a way of augmenting and eventually replacing the nation-state. Others have warned that the region-states might serve as a barrier on the way to one global state."[4]

A spokesman for this latter viewpoint is Johan Galtung, who has warned that Europe might develop into another superpower to rival the United States and the Soviet Union. He feared that a world divided into vast regional power-blocs might be subjected to even more destructive wars and oppression than we have seen in the past, just as George Orwell depicted in *Nineteen Eighty-Four*. This would certainly be a disastrous state of affairs; but its likelihood seems to be extremely remote at the present time. None of the regional groupings, Europe included, has anywhere near the strength or the political cohesion which could make them the slightest threat to their neighbours.

Bruce Russett of Yale University imagined a debate on the issue in 1967 between a World Federalist and an Atlantic Unionist. "The Federalist emphasizes the need for over-arching worldwide institutions .. only a global organization can prevent war and promote a co-operative effort for the good of all mankind. The advocate of Atlantic Union may accept much of this argument as the statement of a long-term goal, but for now he dwells on the divisions and heterogeneity so manifest among nations. For the present, he says, we must take whatever islands of relative similarity we find, and integrate them as units which can solve their own internal problems and contribute to the stability of the larger international system, without transforming it drastically. In the long run a world community may well be built by aggregating these units at a yet higher level of organization, in which they, not the existing nation-states, might be the basic building-blocks in a global federal hierarchy."[5] In connection with the problem of regional power-blocs, he then warns that: "Regional integration without concurrent pressures, and probably deliberate effort, toward integrating the entire international system would be at best a short-term and at worst a highly volatile "solution". If we take the Atlantic Unionist seriously, we must also take the World Federalist seriously. These are not yet mutually exclusive roads. The world is not now ready for amalgamation in the style of the Federalist; the basic ecological under-pinnings do not exist. Maybe we will want to work in that direction in the long run. At this stage, however, a central choice of strategy is not forced upon us. We can lay a multi-purpose foundation without now choosing the eventual form of the structure to be built, leaving room for the ingenuity and learning of later architects to devise a stronger habitation than we now know how to construct."[6]

The fact is that the process of regional integration is now well under way in several different areas of the globe, and is bound to continue onwards, by fits and starts. The benefits of economic integration are obvious, and are now universally accepted, and some degree of political integration is likely to follow at a later stage. These processes should be encouraged, because of the increased stability and prosperity which they will bring to each region. They also pave the way for integration at a higher level, by providing positive examples, and shaping public attitudes in favour of integration in general. But it is also a fact that regional integration and world integration are not at all the same thing. To achieve the final goal, a further level of integration will be required between either the different regional associations, or the individual nation-states. Ideally one would like these processes to occur in parallel, so that world integration should be well under way before the different regional associations have time to crystallize into powerful blocs, which might come into conflict with each other.

The Evolutionary Approach

The best and most feasible way of achieving a world federation would seem to be an evolutionary approach, following the example set by Jean Monnet and the European federalists. The strategy is to begin with an association of a few of the more progressive states, with a specific and limited set of aims, and then let it evolve in a natural, stage-by-stage fashion towards a more deeply integrated community with wider membership. Several reasons have already been given why the membership should be restricted to democratic states.

This strategy has a number of advantages. It means that the barrier to be overcome in starting the association is enormously reduced, because only a small number of relatively homogeneous and like-minded states will be involved, and the initial aims of the association are more limited and sharply defined. Secondly, each further stage of the integration process can be considered and appraised over a period of time, and will only proceed in accordance with the political equilibrium at the time: thus it should be possible to avoid any disastrous mistakes, and the member states will be able to choose how far and how fast they want to take the integration process as they go. And finally, as a fall-back position, much less harm is done if the association should turn out to be a failure. The crucial question then remains: how can we make a start? How can the first seed be planted?

A World Peace-Keeping Association

One possibility which comes to mind is to set up an association which would complement the present United Nations, and remedy some of its shortcomings. Now the most important shortcomings of the UN are its "missing organs": it has no democratically elected representative assembly, and no standing military or peace-keeping forces of its own. A very substantial international security force was proposed for the UN in its early days, but was abandoned because the United States and the Soviet Union could not agree on the conditions. Boutros Boutros-Ghali and Brian Urquhart have recently renewed calls for a standing peace-keeping force to be set up, which could be used in a "preventive" fashion, to try and prevent conflicts before they occur.[7,8]

This leads us to propose the establishment of what might be called a World Peace-Keeping Association. Its aims would include:

- To ensure the security of all its member states;

- To fulfill the external peace-keeping obligations of its member-states towards the UN, and to establish a joint, standing peace-keeping force which might be used, at the discretion of the Association and at the request of the UN, for "preventive" peacekeeping purposes;
- To promote economic and political co-operation among its members;
- To provide avenues for peaceful settlement of any dispute among its members;
- To provide a basis for further integration among its members in the future, in whatever ways seem appropriate at the time.

The most obvious model for such an Association would be the pattern established in Europe, consisting of:

- · A Council of Ministers from the member states to approve policy, under a 'weighted majority' voting formula. Heads of government would meet periodically to formulate general policy, while regular meetings would consist of Foreign Ministers, Defence Ministers, or others as appropriate to the subject under discussion. Thus the member states collectively would maintain a controlling voice in the Association;
- A democratic Assembly to represent the people of the member states, with an equal voice along with the Council in proposing and approving policy and the laws and regulations of the Association. This would provide the democratic heart of the organization, giving it a collective will and purpose of its own. To begin with, the Assembly might consist of representatives from the Parliaments of the member states. At a later stage, once the Association is well established, the representatives should be directly elected by the people of the member states;
- A Commission to oversee the day-to-day administration of the Association, and to formulate new policy initiatives and laws and regulations, for approval by the Council and the Assembly. The Commission would act as Cabinet for the Association. Ideally it should sit within the Assembly, and be responsible to it; and eventually its members should be elected from within the Assembly, even if at first they were appointed by the member states;
- A Court of Justice, to see that the laws and regulations of the Association are observed, and to adjudicate on disputes between member states where necessary;
- A joint Military Force to carry out the peace-keeping duties of the

Association. This might consist partly of a permanent 'core' organization composed of volunteers from the citizens of the member states, plus rotating contingents from the armed forces of the member states. The permanent core force need not be very big: its main purposes would be to provide training for the national contingents in co-operative international action, to provide a rapid-reaction force in case of need, and to provide a basis for expansion in times of emergency. Its operations would be overseen by a Military Council or Staff Committee consisting of the Chiefs of Staff of the member states, or their representatives;

• A Secretariat to carry out the administrative duties of the Association.

The Budget of the Association would presumably consist initially of agreed levies or contributions from the member states, but eventually the Association should be given its own independent sources of funds, made up perhaps from levies or taxes on international trade and financial transactions between the member states.

Membership of the Association should be open to any stable and democratic state, subject to approval by the existing members, with the aim of eventually achieving universal membership. This would demonstrate that the Association is not directed against any particular state or group of states, and that its aim is global security for all.

Such an association would form what Karl Deutsch calls a "security community". It would fill an obvious current need, by reinforcing the peace-keeping capacity of the UN, which is far too weak at present. It would provide a powerful new guarantee of the security of its member states. It would also allow the United States to share the burden of acting as 'global policeman', which is a role that does not properly belong to any single nation in any case. And finally, it would lay a suitable foundation for further integration at a later stage.

There is one drawback to this idea, according to neofunctionalist theory. Such an association would be based on military rather than economic co-operation, and thus the 'spillover' effect leading to further integration in other sectors would not be so strong. I have not proposed to begin with an economic association, because there seems to be no such obvious need for it at the present time. One could hardly propose to begin with a global community of coal and steel producers in this day and age; and under agreements such as GATT the trade barriers between the nations are rapidly being whittled away in any case. The association should by all means include an economic aspect, and the promotion of economic and political integration would undoubtedly be its most important and fruitful function, in the long run. The Assembly and the Commission might also be expected to provide an impetus towards further integration, as they have done in Europe.

Who might be prospective members of such an association? First on the list would be those middle-ranking powers which have been the most loyal and consistent supporters of UN peacekeeping efforts over the years, such as the Scandinavian countries Sweden, Norway, Denmark and Finland, together with British Commonwealth countries such as Canada, Australia and New Zealand. Next would come the members of the European Union, and of course the United States. Japan is an obvious candidate, having shown herself to be a model citizen of the world community since World War II. Many other states would also merit consideration.

There is an obvious question which arises at this point, namely: - where does NATO fit in? NATO is a powerful security organization which already exists, and involves many of the states we have mentioned. As a matter of fact, it could provide an ideal basis for the proposed Peace-Keeping Association. Let us explore this option a little more closely.

The NATO option

The North Atlantic Treaty Organization (NATO) was established by the North Atlantic Treaty in 1949, largely at the instigation of Ernest Bevin, Foreign Secretary in the British Labour government after World War II. Its purpose was to act as a defensive political and military alliance to protect Western Europe against the Soviet Union. Its original members consisted of the US and Canada, together with 10 European members. There are now 14 European members, consisting of Belgium, Denmark, France, Germany, Greece, Iceland, Italy, Luxembourg, the Netherlands, Norway, Portugal, Spain, Turkey, and the United Kingdom.The neutral countries of Sweden, Austria, Ireland and Finland are not members. France withdrew from the integrated military structure of NATO in 1966 under Charles De Gaulle, but rejoined in 1995.

The organizational structure of NATO includes the following elements:

- The North Atlantic Council, consisting of heads of state, foreign ministers, or their permanent representatives, which determines the policy of the organization by consensus;

- A number of committees have been established under the Council, to oversee various aspects of the organization's work. They include a Military Committee, consisting of the allied Chiefs-of Staff or their representatives, as well as a Defence Planning Committee and others;
- The Secretary-General is the operational head of the organization, and acts as Chairman of the Council and head of the international secretariat;
- The military commands of NATO include an Allied Command Europe and an Allied Command Atlantic, as well as an Allied Command Europe Rapid Reaction Corps. The first Supreme Allied Commander Europe was none other than Dwight D. Eisenhower;
- Finally, there is the North Atlantic Assembly, founded in 1955, which consists of an inter-parliamentary assembly formed to encourage Atlantic solidarity and provide a link between NATO and the member parliaments. It contains 188 members, with representation weighted according to population, so that the USA has 36 members, while Iceland and Luxembourg have 3 each. The Assembly is not formally part of the NATO structure, but maintains close relations with it. It addresses recommendations to the Secretary-General, and the Secretary-General presents a review of major alliance problems at annual plenary sessions of the Assembly.

The dominant member of the NATO alliance has traditionally been the United States, which has promised to protect its European allies with nuclear weapons if necessary, and fills the chief office of Supreme Allied Commander Europe. The early years of the organization involved a tense period of confrontation between East and West at the height of the Cold War. Then in 1967 a landmark was reached with the publication of the Harmel Report, which called for a shift in NATO policy to one of "deterrence with dialogue". Members undertook to pursue simultaneously a policy of maintaining adequate military forces for defence and deterrence, while also engaging the East in a dialogue designed to bring about realistic solutions to existing problems, and eventually the removal of the underlying causes of tension between East and West. This farsighted policy led to the establishment of the Conference on Security and Co-operation in Europe, and to long-running talks on "Mutual and Balanced Force Reductions" (MBFR).[9] It contributed substantially to the lessening of tensions in Europe, and culminated after many years in the INF Treaty and the Conventional Forces in Europe (CFE) Treaty of 1991, which provided for major reductions in the numbers of tanks, aircraft, and other conventional weapons on both sides of the former Iron Curtain. At the same time, NATO's nuclear arsenal in Europe has been reduced by 80%.

With the disbandment of the Warsaw Pact and the collapse of the Soviet Union in 1991, the original purpose of NATO was lost. An extensive review was begun in 1990, which resulted in a new 'Strategic Concept' for the organization. It reaffirmed NATO's role in ensuring the security of Europe, and called for further reductions of military forces within Europe, together with active involvement in international peace-keeping operations, increased co-operation with other international institutions, and close co-operation with Russia and the countries of Eastern Europe, the former adversaries of NATO.[10]

In recent years, NATO has been engaged in discussions with the European Union on the establishment of a common foreign and security policy (CFSP) for Europe, and a "European pillar" of the NATO force structure. The concept of Combined Joint Task Forces has been endorsed. In 1991, a new North Atlantic Co-operation Council (NACC) was set up to provide a forum for consultation with the countries of Eastern Europe, including the former Soviet republics. In 1993, a program of "Partnership for Peace" was inaugurated, and the first joint military exercises with former members of the Warsaw Pact were held in 1995. Some 27 countries are now participating in this programme. It is envisaged that NATO will eventually be enlarged by the admission of many of these countries, although strong opposition from Russia has delayed the process.

NATO has also been engaged in a peace keeping operation for the first time in Yugoslavia and Bosnia. The Dayton peace accord provided for a NATO-led implementation force (IFOR) to ensure compliance with the treaty, under the authority of a Security Council mandate from the UN. This mission involved approximately 60,000 troops from 32 NATO and non-NATO countries. There were various setbacks and shortcomings in the operations on the ground, as one might very well expect, but this important new role which NATO has taken on represents a new landmark in the history of the organization.

In view of these developments, it would not take an impossibly large step to transform NATO further into a world peace-keeping association such as we have discussed above. The organization would need to be opened for progressive enlargement by the accession of stable and democratic states, not only from Eastern Europe, but also from other regions of the world. The security guarantees of the organization would then be extended to these new members, as well as to the North Atlantic states. Prime candidates for membership would include countries such as Japan, Australia, New Zealand, and others. In time, once stable democracy has become established there, even Russia would become a candidate. This would demonstrate that the organization is no longer directed against any particular country or group, but is dedicated to peace and security for all. Russia's objections to enlargement should then be removed.

The charter of the organization would need to be expanded to allow it to act as the principal peace-keeping organ of its members, under the aegis of the UN. This would represent no more than a continuation of current trends, and would release the USA from its self-imposed role as 'global policeman', which it has no right to assume anyway.

The administrative superstructure of the organization would need re-organizing to allow for greater co-operation and possible closer integration in the future. According to the European model, this would require the establishment of a Court, an independent Commission to replace the Secretary-General, and a democratic Assembly. The last feature could be achieved, in the first instance, by incorporating the North Atlantic Assembly as a formal part of the organization.

The economic and technical aspects of the organization would also need to be expanded. NATO already funds a strong program of scientific and technical collaboration, by means of fellowships, workshops and schools. One option for strengthening the economic side might be to fold in the OECD with the new association. The OECD already includes all the members of NATO, plus many prospective members of the enlarged organization, and it already comprises a powerful economic organization.

This would imply a major revision of the North Atlantic Treaty, but would represent no more than a natural extension of current trends. It would give NATO a very powerful, important, and positive new role, to replace that which disappeared when the Soviet Union collapsed and the only realistic threat to Europe's security evaporated. It would allow the USA to share the burden of major peace-keeping operations around the globe, and give these operations the added legitimacy and authority of a common security organization. Finally, it would provide a ready-made and very substantial basis for further co-operation and integration between the democratic member states.

Many of the aims of the proposed peace-keeping association are already enshrined in the North Atlantic Treaty. Under the treaty, the parties undertook "to settle any international dispute in which they may be involved by peaceful means" (Article 1); declared that they "will encourage economic collaboration between any or all of them" (Article 2); and that they "agree that an armed attack against one or more of them ... shall be considered an attack against them all" (Article 4).

The major obstacle lies in the fact that NATO is presently a mere *alliance* of sovereign states. NATO publications emphasize very heavily that "NATO is composed of sovereign states which retain their independence in all fields including foreign policy."[11] To allow for deeper integration, the members would have to agree to change the nature of the organization, in order to give it an independent voice of its own in the form of a Commission and an Assembly. They would also have to cede some of their sovereignty, and give the association the power to make binding regulations or laws in at least some of the areas for which it is responsible. These changes would involve some momentous changes in principle. The natural conservatism and inertia of the member states will make it difficult to reach an agreement for change, and one is likely to confront the old argument: "if it ain't broke, don't fix it." The organization performs some useful functions as it stands, so why meddle with it?

The answer to this question is that there are some far more useful functions which it could perform, as outlined above. Given that the original primary purpose of the alliance has recently been lost, a golden opportunity now exists to refocus NATO as the nucleus of a great new organization of common security for the world.

One would hope that the European members of NATO would be sympathetic to these ideas, which follow the established European pattern. The major question is whether the United States, as the dominant partner in the present alliance, could be persuaded to agree. It would mean that the US would have to accept a less dominant position, and resign a certain amount of its power and influence over international events to the new association, agreeing to a closer degree of co-operation and integration with its partners in the security field. Although this would clearly be for the greater common good, it would require a great deal of political foresight and courage in the White House to recognize that fact, and to persuade two-thirds of the Senate to agree to it, especially considering the long-term tendency in America towards isolationism and suspicion of entangling foreign alliances.

On the other hand, America has traditionally been a stronghold of the World Federalist and Atlantic Union movements. The ideas outlined above are actually quite close to those of the Atlantic Union movement founded by Clarence Streit, except that he proposed a radical leap straight to a federal union of all the Atlantic democracies, whereas we are advocating a much more modest toe in the water, in the shape of a loose peace-keeping association. This would also be in accordance with the Declaration of Paris, adopted by the Atlantic Convention of 1962, which called for "the creation of a true Atlantic Community", which would receive "a measure of delegated sovereignty" from its member states.[12]

An earlier call for the further development of NATO was made by Karl Deutsch and his collaborators in their interdisciplinary study, *Political Community and the North Atlantic Area* in 1957. They argued that "The most progressive steps would seem to be more and more towards the economic and social potentialities of this unique organization, and toward the greater political possibilities that might come from new organs of consultation and decision which could be built into it. There may well be an opportunity in the near future to make NATO much more than a military alliance and, without alienating any nonmembers within the area, to move at least some of its member countries closer toward integration. This may be one of the most effective ways to advance the development of political community in the North Atlantic area, and to contribute to the eventual abolition of war."[13]

In the event, closer integration was achieved within the European Community rather than via NATO. The majority of world federalists were not in favour of Atlantic Union at that time in any case. Everett Millard's study group CURE, for instance, feared that an Atlantic Union would perpetuate the East-West divide and intensify the arms race, and would also be seen as exclusive by those countries left out.[14] They preferred to work towards reform of the UN Charter.

The intervening years have seen some dramatic changes. The Soviet Union has now collapsed, and the divide between East and West is rapidly disappearing, so that the main objection of the federalists has lost its force. An association based upon NATO might even be joined by most of the countries of the former Soviet bloc within a short period of time. Just recently, the former Secretary of State Henry Kissinger has suggested that "the Atlantic Alliance must deepen its political dimension", and that "the time has come to move the project of a North Atlantic Free Trade area from study committees to the action phase."[15]

Polls show that public opinion remains very positive upon these

issues: for instance, a poll in the US on "The Emerging World Order" in 1991 showed that:
- 68% recognized the importance of an enlarged US peacekeeping role;
- 78% approved of the job being done by the UN;
- 90% thought the US should promote action on world environmental problems;
- 88% favoured standby peacekeeping forces for the UN;
- 67% favoured elections for the UN Secretary-General;
- 59% believed that "UN resolutions should rule over the actions and laws of individual countries, including the US."[16]

So there is reason to hope that a proposal such as ours might now be deemed acceptable by the American public.

Summary and Conclusions

Several alternative routes to world federation have been discussed. It could happen by means of a reform of the United Nations; but that has proved extremely hard to achieve. Another possibility is that the European Union could expand over time to become a global organization; but that is probably an unsuitable path, and would be ruled out by the Europeans themselves. The functionalists would argue that it will all happen almost automatically, as functional organizations spread and international agencies proliferate; but in the last analysis it does require an act of political will to create a political community with a life and purpose of its own. Functional co-operation can lay the foundations, but eventually something more is needed.

The growth of regional organizations as a stepping-stone to world federation is a more likely option. Organizations for economic co-operation are already springing up rapidly in all quarters of the globe. These all help to provide examples of international collaboration, and lay the groundwork for worldwide integration; but they do not solve the problem in themselves. Unless worldwide institutions begin to develop in parallel, there is a real possibility (though hopefully a slight one) that the regional organizations could develop into warring power-blocs.

The most likely path seems to be an evolutionary one, starting from a small association of stable and democratic states, and then expanding its membership and functions, after the European model. Some of the major deficiencies of the present UN could be repaired, for instance, by setting up a World Peace-Keeping Association of democratic states. This would provide a standing peace-keeping force, something the UN lacks, which could be used in a "preventative" peace-keeping role. The association should also include a democratic assembly, to give an independent voice to the organization, which the UN again does not have. It would provide a virtually cast-iron guarantee of the security of its member states; and it would relieve the United States from the burden of acting as global policeman on its own.

NATO could be transformed into the nucleus of such an association. A golden opportunity now exists, because the primary purpose of NATO in defending Western Europe against Soviet attack has now evaporated, and NATO has been searching for a new role. It has already begun to act as a peace-keeper in the European region, and to build new bridges with the countries of the former Warsaw Pact. Why not go further, and turn it into a democratic, world-wide peacekeeping association? An economic aspect might also be added, perhaps, by folding in the OECD with the new organization. This would be the quickest and most effective way to proceed; but the crucial question is whether the United States would agree to such a transformation. As the dominant member of the present NATO alliance, nothing could be done without the leadership and agreement of the US.

These are only examples of what might be done to begin the process of global integration. If these opportunities are not taken, no doubt some other avenue will be found eventually. The construction of a world federation is an enormous task, which might well take centuries of evolution to complete; and popular enthusiasm for the idea is not very high just now. The battle will be fought out in the hearts and minds of our global villagers, as they slowly become convinced of the need for a village council. But given the present climate of peace and co-operation between the superpowers, there has never been a better time to make a start. There is a need for some statesman on the international stage to assume the mantle of Jean Monnet, and show us the way forwards - a place in history awaits the one who can do it. A sensible and carefully limited proposal should generate substantial public support. The start of the new millennium, which is now close upon us, would be an ideal and auspicious date to begin some sort of new association, although the time available may already be too short.

The direction we want to go is clear. Increased international co-operation, leading to an eventual world federation, will bring peace and prosperity for all. In time it will allow the abolition of nuclear weapons, and even the eradication of war itself. It will allow a joint attack on the problems of environmental degradation, over-population, disease and poverty. It will establish new standards of human rights and democracy worldwide, and it will open a great new era of progress and harmony in human affairs, as energies are released from the unprofitable business of preparing for war.

The principles of association are also fairly clear. Democracy, human rights and the rule of law would be taken for granted as founding principles. Important principles established by the European experiment include subsidiarity, to preserve national autonomy wherever possible, and solidarity, to promote economic and social cohesion within the community. The ideas of participation, flexibility and equity have also been discussed.

The route by which we shall achieve these goals is much less clear, but the important thing to recognize is that everyone is pulling in the same direction. World federalists, UN reformers, functionalists, neofunctionalists, regionalists or Atlantic Unionists, all are working towards increased international collaboration and integration as the answer to the world's problems. We can see the new Jerusalem shining on the hill, and though it may take decades or even centuries to arrive there, the struggle will be well worthwhile in the end. This vision was beautifully expressed in a speech that Arthur Sweetser gave to his colleagues of the United Nations staff when he retired after thirty-four years with the organization: [17]

"You were born out of the labor and travail of these older days [of the League of Nations]; you are the successors of those who tried to build before you, got swept temporarily away, but still left foundations to which you could anchor. You have built prodigiously upon them; I would not, in those first days of 1920, have dared dream you would get so far so fast. Don't underestimate this progress.

The great lesson of all this effort and suffering, even frequent disappointment, is that you are right, eternally right, in the fight you are making. You have got hold of all the big things of life; you are on the road to the future; you are working for all the ends that make life worthwhile on this planet - for peace, for the eradication of war, for human advancement, for human rights and decencies, for better living standards, better education, better travel and communications - in short, for the world as it ought to be.

This is the highest secular cause on earth. You deserve to be immensely proud of what you are doing, especially that you are privileged to be part of the permanent staff. During your low and grim moments, lift your eyes, I beg you, to those vaster horizons beyond: rise up out of the irritations and anxieties of the moment and realize that you have opportunities permitted to very few indeed.

You cannot feel too strongly that right is on your side and that your cause will win in the long run; it is your opponents who are wrong and on the losing side."

References

Entries mostly refer to works listed in the bibliography. Those works referred to explicitly in the text are not repeated here.

Chapter 1. The Need for World Federation

1. Levi1983
2. SIPRI1995
3. Nathan1968, p. 336
4. Houghton1996
5. *Sydney Morning Herald,* 8 May, 1996
6. *Sydney Morning Herald,* 23 February, 1996
7. Brown1989, pp. 16-17
8. *New Scientist,* 16 December 1995, p. 14
9. *The Australian,* 27 May, 1996
10. *Sydney Morning Herald,* 6 February 1996
11. Wells1922, Vol. II, p. 754

Chapter 2. Some Snippets of History

1. Bartlett1968, p. 87
2. Millard1959, p. 111
3. Grotius1625, p. 35
4. Penn1692, p. 4
5. Hemleben1943, p. 79
6. Quoted in Millard1969, p. 112
7. Kant1795
8. UHJ1986, pp. 25 & 38
9. Walker1993, p. 823
10. Woolf1916, p. 167
11. Woolf1916, p. 75
12. Dupuy1973, p. 78
13. Walters1952, v. 1, p. 27
14. Northedge1986, p. 83
15. Churchill1948
16. Nathan1968, p. 4
17. Lecture at MIT, 25 Nov. 1947; see Bartlett1968
18. Nathan1968, p. 376
19. Reves1945, p. 121
20. *ibid,* p. 122
21. *ibid,* p. 150
22. Quoted in Wittner1993, p. 307
23. *ibid,* p.307
24. *ibid,* p. 144
25. *ibid,* p. 321

26. *ibid,* p. 321
27. Nathan1968, p. 634
28. Crutzen1982
29. Sagan1990
30. Baratta1989, p. 380
31. SIPRI1995
32. Morgenthau1973

33. Quoted in Wagar1963,
    p. 15
34. Mitrany1943, p. 31
35. Suter1986
36. Mendlovitz1975, Falk1975,
    Galtung1980, Falk1982
37. Beres1974, p. v
38. WCPA1977

Chapter 3. The United Nations

1. UNDPI1989, p.1
2. UNDPI1995, p. 308
3. *ibid*, p. 253
4. *ibid*, p. 17
5. *ibid*, p. 19
6. *ibid*, p. 21
7. UNDPI1989, p. 4
8. *ibid*, p. 3
9. Luard1982, p. 101
10. Simons1994, p. 112
11. SIPRI1995, and companion
    volumes
12. UNDPI1995, p. 21
13. Simons1994, p. 205
14. UNDPI1989, p. 3
15. *ibid*, p. 3
16. *ibid*, p. 10
17. UNDDA1988, p. 2

18. *Sydney Morning Herald,*
    May 13, 1995
19. UNDPI1992, p. 124
20. Hazzard1973, p. 218
21. Urquhart1990
22. Simons1994, p. 239
23. *Sydney Morning Herald,*
    April 25 and May 1, 1996
24. Walters1952, Vol. I, p.134
25. Baratta1987, p. 38
26. Suter1981, p. 45
27. Heinrich 1992
28. Quoted by Hanna
    Newcombe, in
    Barnaby1991, p. 89
29. Barnaby1991
30. Segall1992
31. Boutros-Ghali1994, p. 281

Chapter 4. Europe

1. Zurcher1958, p. 19
2. *ibid,* p. 20
3. R. Mayne, in Bond1996,
    p. 33
4. *ibid,* p. 39
5. T. Jansen, in Bond1996,

    p. 98
6. Mayne1970, p. 173
7. J. Pinder, in Bond1996, p. 9
8. Wright1965, p. 1542
9. Mayne1970, p. 169
10. *ibid,* p. 178

13. *ibid*, p. 258
14. *ibid*, p. 272
15. Wistrich1989, p. 39
16. Eurostat1995, p. 12
17. *The European*, 2-8 May, 1996
18. *ibid*, 11-17 April, 1996
19. *The Sydney Morning Herald*, 22 February, 1996
20. Eurostat1995, pp. 32-57
21. *ibid*
22. EPDGR1991
23. *ibid*, p. 30
24. *ibid*, p. 31
25. EPDGR1991, p. 27
26. Council1992, p. 138
27. Millard1969
28. Council1992, p. 4
29. *The European*, 16-22 May, 1996
30. Tindale1991
31. *ibid*, p. 11
32. Mitrany1943, p. 72-3
33. Harrison1974, p. 39
34. Mackay1969, p. 140
35. *ibid*, p. 81
36. A. Marc, *L'Europe en formation*, 100, July 1968, p. 2
37. Haas1958, p. xiv
38. Harrison1974, p. 90
39. E.B. Haas, *International Organization*, XXIV, 4, 1970, p. 627
40. e.g. George1991
41. Milward1993

Chapter 5. Principles of World Federation

1. Baratta1987
2. Wheare1964, p. 2
3. Council1992, p. 3
4. Sir Winston Churchill, House of Commons, 11 Nov. 1947
5. Gastil1987
6. Karatnycky1995
7. Bowie1954
8. Millard1969, p. 61
9. *ibid*, p. 58
10. For a detailed discussion, see Newcombe1983
11. *ibid*, p. 91
12. Streit1939, pp. 18-19
13. Capotorti1986, p. 17
14. Walker1993, p. 174
15. Millard1969
16. Council1992
17. See Newcombe1992, pp. 92-96
18. Bryce1888, v. I, p.467
19. General Assembly, Twenty-Ninth Session; quoted in Ferencz1983, Vol. II, p.868
20. Capotorti1986, p. 73
21. Amnesty1985
22. Amnesty1995
23. Fontaine1992, p. 15
24. Tocqueville, v. 1, p. 181
25. *Sydney Morning Herald*, 22 Feb. 1996
26. Walters1993, p. 174
27. *ibid*, p. 350

Chapter 6. Problems and Objections

1. Morgenthau1973, p. 487
2. *ibid,* p. 489, abridged
3. *ibid,* p.491, abridged
4. Penn1692, p. 13, abridged
5. Claude1956, p. 258
6. quoted in Schell1984, p. 39
7. Niebuhr1949, pp. 225-228, abridged
8. *ibid,* p. 231, abridged
9. *ibid,* pp. 231-232, abridged
10. Mitrany1943, p. 155
11. Mendlovitz1975
12. Claude1962, p. 265ff, abridged
13. *The European,* 18-24 July, 1996
14. For evidence of the peacefulness of liberal democracies see Doyle1983, or Rummel1991
15. Gilmore1946, p. 209, abridged
16. *ibid,* p. 212
17. Huxley1946
18. Huxley1950
19. Schell1984, p. 87
20. *ibid,* p. 96, abridged

Chapter 7. How Do We Get There From Here?

1. Zacher1993
2. Deutsch1988, p. 277, abridged
3. Etzioni1965, pp. x-xi
4. *ibid,* p. xvii
5. Russett1967, p. 227
6. *ibid,* p. 233, abridged
7. Boutros-Ghali1994
8. Urquhart1995
9. NATO1989
10. Europa1996
11. NATO1989, p. 185
12. Wooley1988, p. 131
13. Deutsch1957, p. 103
14. Millard1967, pp. 184-5
15. *Newsweek,* June 18, 1996
16. Survey by the Americans Talk Issues Foundation, *The Christian Science Monitor,* July 31, 1991
17. This quotation was previously used by Inis Claude: Claude1956, p. 449

Suggestions for Further Reading

Chapter 1. The Need for World Federation

Arguments for world federation can be found in any of the writings on world federalism to be discussed in the following chapter. The World Order Models Project team have attempted a systematic formulation in terms of four or five 'world order values', outlined in *A Study of Future Worlds,* by Richard Falk, or *On the Creation of a Just World Order,* edited by Saul Mendlovitz. The arguments were reviewed more recently by Ronald Glossop in *World Federation?* Areas which cry out for international regulation were also discussed in the final chapter of the textbook by Walter Jones on *The Logic of International Relations.* A useful discussion from a European perspective is given by Christopher Layton in his paper *One Europe, One World.*

The issues of peace and disarmament are central to all works on world federalism. The United Nations has commissioned a report in this area known as the Palme Report, *Common Security.* Ecological issues are likewise discussed in the Brundtland Report, *Our Common Future.* The population issue is vividly argued in Paul Ehrlich's well-known book, *The Population Explosion,* and he and his wife have also discussed the environmental crisis in *Healing the Planet.* A well-known early discussion of global problems is the Report to the Club of Rome, *Reshaping the International Order,* co-ordinated by Jan Tinbergen.

Chapter 2. Some Snippets of History

A detailed history of peace projects and schemes for world federation up until the First World War is *Plans for World Peace through Six Centuries,* by S.J. Hemleben. Some of the early projects are reprinted, with commentaries, in the series *Peace Projects of the Seventeenth Century, Eighteenth Century,* etc., from the Garland Library of War and Peace, edited by B.W. Cook, S.E. Cooper and C.

Chatfield. An extensive commentary from a sceptic's viewpoint is given by F.H. Hinsley, *Power and the Pursuit of Peace*. The texts of many peace treaties, peace plans, and arms control agreements (or extracts therefrom) are given together with a few introductory remarks in *A Documentary History of Arms Control and Disarmament* by T.N. Dupuy and G.M. Hammermann. The book *A History of Peace* by A.C.F. Beales gives a history of the organized peace movement from 1815 up to 1930. *Swords into Plowshares* by Inis Claude is a classic study of the growth of international organizations.

The story of the foundation of the Baha'i faith is told in *The Baha'i Faith* by W.M. Miller, and *The Baha'i Religion*, by Peter Smith. Their current attitudes to world government are outlined in the booklet *The Promise of World Peace* from the Universal House of Justice, and *World Peace and World Government* by J. Tyson.

The history of the League of Nations is recounted in detail by a former Deputy Secretary-General in *A History of the League of Nations* by F.P. Walters. An academic history, analyzing the reasons for the failure of the League, is F.S. Northedge, *The League of Nations*. A lively and brief account is given by J.A. Joyce in *Broken Star*.

Works on the life and times of Aristide Briand are mostly written in French or German. An American work, with references, is *Briand's Locarno Policy*, by E.D. Keeton.

A Pulitzer-Prize-winning account of the atomic scientists' involvement with the Bomb is Richard Rhodes, *The Making of the Atomic Bomb*, and its sequel *Dark Sun: The Making of the Hydrogen Bomb*. The argument over the H-bomb is recounted in H.F. York, *The Advisors: Oppenheimer, Teller and the Superbomb*.

The history of the peace, nuclear disarmament, and world federalist movements after World War II is being written by L.S. Wittner in a three-volume work entitled *The Struggle Against The Bomb*, which is likely to become a standard reference in the field. Unfortunately, only the first volume, *One World or None*, was available at the time of writing, which carries the story up to 1953. I have relied on it heavily in my account of this period. Two other useful references in this area are Wesley T. Wooley, *Alternatives to Anarchy*, which covers the American scene, and Hanna Newcombe, *World Unification Plans and Analyses*. Joseph Baratta has compiled a bibliography on U.N. reform and world federalism in *Strengthening the United Nations*, and has written a journal article on *The International History of the World Federalist Movement*. Keith Suter's *A New International Order* is an excellent little book on these same themes. Barbara Walker's recent collection of extracts *Uniting the Peoples and Nations* provides an excellent overview of the history of the world federalist movement.

Descriptions of the nuclear arsenals built up by the superpowers are given in K. Tsipis, *Understanding Nuclear Weapons,* and a journal article by B.G. Levi, *The nuclear arsenals of the US and USSR.* Up-to-date figures are given in the SIPRI Yearbook, *World Armaments and Disarmament.* An authoritative source giving texts and commentaries on *Arms Control and Disarmament Agreements* has been published by the US Arms Control and Disarmament Agency, and an independent viewpoint is given by Jozef Goldblat, *Agreements for Arms Control: A Critical Survey.*

An excellent survey of the various academic viewpoints in this area is given by L.R. Beres and H.R. Targ in *Reordering the Planet.* A more recent political science textbook which contains an extensive and valuable discussion is *The Logic of International Relations,* by Walter Jones.

A useful reference source, with a bibliography but also with many gaps, is the *World Encyclopedia of Peace*, edited by E. Laszlo and J.Y. You.

Chapter 3. The United Nations

A great deal of information about the United Nations is contained in the organization's own publications, such as *Basic Facts about the United Nations,* from the UN Department of Public Information. The Secretary-General produces an annual report, for instance *Building Peace and Development* by Boutros Boutros-Ghali (1994).

A history of the UN has been written in two volumes by Evan Luard, *A History of the United Nations,* and a more recent account, marred by a distinctly anti-American bias, is *The United Nations,* by Geoff Simons. A review of UN peacekeeping efforts is given in *The Blue Helmets,* from UNDPI.

A very useful earlier work, discussing many of the issues of interest here, is *Toward World Order* by A. Vandenbosch and W.N. Hogan. A vivid account of the problems in the UN Secretariat up to 1970, as mentioned in the text, is Shirley Hazzard's *Defeat of an Ideal.*

A bibliography of proposals for UN reform is given in *Strengthening the United Nations* by Joseph Baratta, and a brief earlier account appears in Keith Suter, *A New International Order.* A more recent review has been given by Daniele Archibugi (1993). Barbara Walker gives extracts from a number of schemes in *Uniting the Peoples and Nations.*

Chapter 4. Europe

The European Union also produces a great deal of information about itself, principally through the Office for Official Publications of the European Communities. I have referred particularly to *Europe in Figures* from the statistical office Eurostat. A very useful introductory booklet is *Europe in Ten Lessons* by Pascal Fontaine.

A history of the early years of European integration from an insider's point of view is *The Recovery of Europe* by Richard Mayne, and another from an American point of view is *The Struggle to Unite Europe 1940-58* by Arnold Zurcher. Jean Monnet's own account is given in his *Memoirs.* Later works are *Cautious Revolution* by Clifford Hackett, and *The Politics of European Integration in the Twentieth Century* by D. Arter. An excellent history, containing a comprehensive survey of the literature, is *The Community of Europe,* by Derek Urwin. Very recently, a book profiling the major actors in the drama has appeared in *Eminent Europeans,* edited by Martyn Bond, Julie Smith and William Wallace.

A review of academic theories of European integration circa 1974 was given in *Europe in Question* by R.J. Harrison, as mentioned in the text. *The Logic of International Relations* by Walter Jones is again very useful in this area. A more recent discussion is S. George, *Politics and Policy in the European Community.* An alternative viewpoint is presented in Alan Milward *et al* in *The Frontier of National Sovereignty,* also mentioned in the text.

A useful little book analyzing the present deficiencies of the European Union, and arguing the need for further integration cogently and in detail is *After 1992: The United States of Europe* , by Ernest Wistrich, who was Director for seventeen years of the British section of the European Movement. New discussions of these topics are appearing all the time: we have mentioned for example the discussion paper called *Beyond Economics: European government after Maastricht* prepared for the Fabian Society by Stephen Tindale and David Miliband.

Chapter 5. Principles of World Federation

Very few works on world federalism have attempted to identify principles as we have done here. Guy Héraud has done so in *Les Principes du Fédéralisme et la Fédération Européenne* discussed at the end of the chapter. *Federal Government* by K.C. Wheare is a standard reference. The classic account of the American system is James Bryce, *The American Commonwealth*. A detailed comparative study of five different federations was compiled by the American Committee on United Europe in *Studies in Federalism,* edited by Robert R. Bowie and Carl J. Friedrich.

Some of these principles were anticipated in a famous treatise by the great liberal economist Friedrich von Hayek, *The Road to Serfdom*, in 1944. Every word of his last chapter on 'The Prospects of International Order' still rings true today.

The concept of democratic government has been explored in detail by David Held in his recent book *Democracy and the Global Order*. The current state of democracy and civil rights around the world is surveyed each year by the Freedom House group in *Freedom in the World*. Human rights are also surveyed in *The Amnesty International Report* each year.

Chapter 6. Problems and Objections

Some important critiques of the early proposals for world government are referred to in the text. Hans Morgenthau discusses the problem of national sovereignty in his classic textbook *Politics Among Nations*. Reinhold Niebuhr emphasizes the lack of community feeling and "social tissue" in his essay *Illusions of World Government*. The problem of enforcement of international law is extensively treated in another classic textbook by Inis Claude, *Power and International Relations,* and a further sceptical discussion appears in his book on international organization, *Swords into Plowshares*.

Most advocates of world federation attempt to counter the anticipated arguments from the sceptics. Two examples have been quoted from William Penn three hundred years ago. A more recent example is J. Tyson's little book *World Peace and World Government*, which addresses various arguments "To the Skeptics" and "To the Fearful".A very extensive discussion of the arguments on both sides is given by Ronald Glossop in *World Federation? A Critical Analysis of Federal World Government*.

Chapter 7. How Do We Get There From Here?

The transition problem has been discussed by the study group CURE in Everett Millard's book *Freedom in a Federal World*, and various options were considered there, including UN reform and Atlantic Union. A WOMP perspective has been given by Richard Falk in *A Study of Future Worlds*, as mentioned briefly in Chapter 2. Ronald Glossop prefers the route of UN reform, rather than a union of the democracies. Textbooks on international relations do not generally go so far as to discuss the transition problem in any detail.

Works on UN reform have already been quoted in Chapter 3. Important works on regional integration include the seminal book by Ernst Haas, *The Uniting of Europe*, and the case studies in *Political Unification*, by Amitai Etzioni. Another early work is *International Regions and the International System* by Bruce Russett. Treatments of the subject may be found in many recent textbooks on international relations, such as Karl Deutsch, *The Analysis of International Relations*. Other works relating specifically to the European case have already been referred to in Chapter 4.

Information on NATO may be obtained from the NATO Information Service, such as *The North Atlantic Treaty Organization. Facts and Figures*, or the *NATO Handbook*. An early multi-disciplinary study which advocated further integration based on NATO is K.W. Deutsch et al, *Political Community and the North Atlantic Area*. The history of the Atlantic Union movement is recounted in *Alternatives to Anarchy*, by Wesley T. Wooley.

Bibliography

Amnesty1995: *The Amnesty International Report* (Amnesty
International Publications, London, 1995)

Angell1911: Norman Angell, *The Great Illusion* (Heinemann, London,
1911)

Archibugi1993: D. Archibugi, *The Reform of the UN and Cosmopolitan
Democracy: A Critical Review,* Journal of Peace Research, No. 3,
301 (1993)

Arter1993: David Arter, *The Politics of European Integration in the
Twentieth Century* (Dartmouth, Aldershot, 1993)

Baratta1987: J.P. Baratta, *Strengthening the United Nations: A
Bibliography on U.N. Reform and World Federalism* (Greenwood,
Westport, 1987)

Baratta1989: J.P. Baratta, *The International History of the World
Federalist Movement* , Peace and Change **14,** 372 (1989)

Barnaby1991: Frank Barnaby (ed.), *Building a More Democratic United
Nations; Proceedings of the 1st. International Conference on a More
Democratic U.N.* (Frank Cass, London, 1991)

Bartlett1968: *Bartlett's Familiar Quotations, 14th. ed.,* (Macmillan,
London, 1968)

Beales1931: A.F.C. Beales, *The History of Peace* (G.Bell, London,
1931)

Bentham1789: Jeremy Bentham, *Plan for an Universal and Perpetual
Peace* (1789), see Cooper1974

Beres1974: Louis Beres and Harry Targ, *Reordering the Planet* (Allyn
and Bacon, Boston, 1974)

Bond1996: M. Bond, J. Smith and W. Wallace (eds.), *Eminent
Europeans* (Greycoat Press, London, 1996)

Boutros-Ghali1994: Boutros Boutros-Ghali, *Building Peace and
Development* (UNDPI, New York, 1994)

Bowie1954: R.R. Bowie and C.J. Friedrich, *Studies in Federalism*
(Little, Brown; Boston, 1954)

Brown1989: Lester R. Brown (ed.), *State of the World 1989* (W.W.

A Global Parliament

Norton, New York, 1989)

Brundtland1987: *Our Common Future*, Report of the World
Commission on Environment and Development, chaired by Gro
Harlem Brundtland (Oxford University Press, Oxford, 1990)

Bryce1888: James Bryce, *The American Commonwealth*, 3 vols.
(Macmillan, London, 1888)

Capotorti1986: F. Capotorti, M. Hilf, F.G. Jacobs and J-P. Jacqué, *The
European Union Treaty* (Clarendon, Oxford, 1986)

Carlsson1995: Ingvar Carlsson and Sridath Ramphal (chairs), *Our
Global Neighbourhood; Report of the Commission on Global
Governance* (Oxford University Press, Oxford, 1995)

Carson1963: Rachel Carson, *The Silent Spring,* (Hamish Hamilton,
London, 1963)

Carter1978: President Jimmy Carter, *Report on the Reform and
Restructuring of the U.N. System* (1978)

Childers1994: E. Childers and B. Urquhart, *Renewing the United
Nations* (Dag Hammarskjöld Foundation, Uppsala, 1994)

Churchill1948: W.S. Churchill, *The Second World War* (Cassell,
London, 1948)

Clark1966: Grenville Clark and Louis Sohn, *World Peace through
World Law* (Harvard University Press, Cambridge, 1966)

Claude1956: Inis L. Claude, Jr., *Swords into Plowshares* (Random
House, New York, 1956)

Claude1962: Inis L. Claude, Jr., *Power and International Relations*
(Random House, New York, 1962)

Cook1972: B.W. Cook, S.E. Cooper and C. Chatfield (eds.), *Peace
Projects of the Seventeenth Century* (Garland, New York, 1972)

Cook1989: *Forging the Alliance: NATO, 1945-1950* (Martin Secker and
Warburg, London, 1989)

Cooper1974: S. Cooper (ed.), *Peace Projects of the Eighteenth Century*
(Garland, New York, 1974)

Coudenhove1923: Richard N. Coudenhove-Kalergi, *Pan-Europa* (Pan
Europa Verlag, Vienna, 1923)

Council1992: Council of the European Communities, *Treaty on
European Union* (Office for Official Publications of the European
Communities, Brussels, 1992)

Cousins1961: Norman Cousins, *In Place of Folly* (Harper, NewYork,
1961)

Crucé1623: Emeric Crucé, *The New Cyneas* (1623) (reprinted Garland,
New York, 1972)

Crutzen1982: P.J. Crutzen and J.W. Birks, Ambio **11,** no. 2-3 (1982)

Dante1312: Dante Alighieri, *De Monarchia,* transl. F.J. Church (Macmillan, London, 1879)

Davis1961: Garry Davis, *The World is my Country* (Putnam, New York, 1961)

Deutsch1957: K.W. Deutsch et al., *Political Community and the North Atlantic Area* (Princeton University Press, Princeton, 1957)

Deutsch1988: K.W. Deutsch, *The Analysis of International Relations, 3rd. edition,* (Prentice-Hall, Englewood Cliffs, 1968)

Doyle1983: Michael Doyle, *Kant, liberal legacies and foreign affairs,* Philosophy and Public Affairs **12**, pp. 205-235 and 323-353 (1983)

VanDoren1987: Carl Van Doren, *The Great Rehearsal* (Viking Penguin, New York, 1987)

Dubois1306: Pierre Dubois, *De Recuperatione Terre Sancte* (reprinted Columbia University Press, New York, 1956)

Dupuy1973: T.N. Dupuy and G.M. Hammermann, *A Documentary History of Arms Control and Disarmament* (Bowker, New York, 1973)

Ehrlich1990: Paul R. Ehrlich and Anne H. Ehrlich, *The Population Explosion* (Simon & Schuster, New York, 1990)

Ehrlich1991: Paul R. Ehrlich and Anne H. Ehrlich, *Healing the Planet* (Surrey Beatty & Sons, NSW, 1991)

EPDGR1991: European Parliament's Directorate-General for Research, *1993: The New Treaties: European Parliament Proposals* (Office for Official Publications of the European Communities, Brussels, 1991)

Eurostat1995: Statistical Office of the European Communities, *Europe in Figures* (Office for Official Publications of the European Communities, Brussels, 1995)

Europa1996: *The Europa World Yearbook 1996* (Europa Publications, London, 1996)

Etzioni1965: A. Etzioni, *Political Unification* (Holt, Rinehart and Winston, New York, 1965)

Evatt1948: H.V. Evatt, *The United Nations* (Harvard University Press, Cambridge, 1948)

Falk1975: Richard Falk, *A Study of Future Worlds* (Free Press, New York, 1982)

Falk1982: R.A. Falk, S.S. Kim and S.H. Mendlovitz (eds.), *Towards a Just World Order* (Westview Press, Boulder, 1982)

Ferencz1988: Benjamin B. Ferencz and Ken Keyes, Jr., *Planethood* (Vision Books, Coos Bay, 1988)

Ferencz1983: Benjamin B. Ferencz, *Enforcing International Law*, 2 volumes (Oceana Publications, New York, 1983)

Fontaine1992: Pascal Fontaine, *Europe in Ten Lessons* (Office for Official Puiblications of the European Communities, Brussels, 1992)

Fukuyama1992: Francis Fukuyama, *The End of History and the Last Man* (Penguin, London, 1992)

Galtung1973: Johan Galtung, *The European Community: A Superpower in the Making* (George Allen & Unwin, London, 1973)

Galtung1980: Johan Galtung, *The True Worlds* (Free Press, New York, 1980)

Gasset1960: Ortega y Gasset, *The Revolt of the Masses* (Norton, New York, 1960)

Gastil1987: R.D. Gastil (ed.), *Freedom in the World*, Freedom House Yearbook (Greenwood Press, New York, 1987)

George1991: S. George, *Politics and Policy in the European Community* (Oxford University Press, Oxford, 1991)

Gilmore1946: Grant Gilmore, *The Feasibility of Compulsory Legal Settlement*, Yale Law Journal **55**, 1049 (1946); reprinted in Hartmann1952.

Glossop1993: Ronald J. Glossop, *World Federation? A Critical Analysis of Federal World Government* (McFarland & Co., Jefferson NC, 1993)

Goldblat1982: Jozef Goldblat, *Agreements for Arms Control* (Taylor and Francis, London, 1982)

Gorbachev1987: Mikhail Gorbachev, *Perestroika* (Fontana, London, 1987)

Grotius1625: Hugo Grotius, *De Jure Belli ac Pacis* (selections reprinted in Cook1972)

Haas1958: Ernst B. Haas, *The Uniting of Europe* (Stanford University Press, Stanford, 1958)

Haas1964: Ernst B. Haas, *Beyond the Nation-State* (Stanford University Press, Stanford, 1964)

Hackett1990: Clifford Hackett, *Cautious Revolution: the European Community arrives* (Greenwood, New York, 1990)

Hallstein1962: Walter Hallstein, *United Europe - Challenge and Opportunity* (Harvard University Press, Cambridge, 1962)

Harrison1974: R.J. Harrison, *Europe in Question: Theories of Regional International Integration* (George Allen & Unwin, London, 1974)

Hartmann1952: Frederick H. Hartmann (ed.), *Readings in International Relations* (McGraw-Hill, New York, 1952)

Hayek1944: F.A. von Hayek, *The Road to Serfdom* (Dymock's, Sydney, 1944)

Hazzard1973: Shirley Hazzard, *Defeat of an Ideal: A Study of the Self-Destruction of theUnited Nations* (Macmillan, London, 1973)

Heilbroner1961: Robert L. Heilbroner, *Forging a United Europe* (New York, 1961)

Heinrich1992: Dieter Heinrich, *The Case for a United Nations Parliamentary Assembly (World Federalist Movement, New York, 1992)*

Held1995: David Held, *Democracy and the Global Order* (Polity Press, Cambridge, 1995)

Hemleben1943: S.J. Hemleben, *Plans for World Peace through Six Centuries* (Chicago University Press, Chicago, 1943)

Héraud1968: Guy Héraud, *Les principes du fédéralisme et la fédération Européenne* (Presses d'Europe, Paris, 1968)

Hinsley1968: F.H. Hinsley, *Power and the Pursuit of Peace* (Oxford University Press, London, 1968)

Houghton1996: J.T. Houghton et al. (eds.), *Climate Change 1995: The Science of Climate Change*, Second Assessment Report of the Intergovernmental Panel on Climate Change (Cambridge University Press, Cambridge, 1996)

Hudson1976: Richard Hudson, *Time for Mutations in the United Nations,* Bulletin of the Atomic Scientists, Vol. 32, # 9, pp. 39-43 (1976)

Huntington1996: Samuel P. Huntington, *The clash of civilizations and the remaking of world order* (Simon & Schuster, New York, 1996)

Huxley1946: Aldous Huxley, *Brave New World* (Harper, New York, 1946)

Huxley1950: Aldous Huxley, *Science, Liberty and Peace* (Chatto & Windus, London, 1950)

Johansen1979: R. Johansen, *The National Interest and the Human Interest* (Princeton University Press, Princeton, 1979)

Jones1985: Walter S. Jones, *The Logic of International Relations* (Little,Brown; Boston, 1985)

Joyce1978: James Avery Joyce, *Broken Star: The Story of the League of Nations* (Christopher Davis, Swansea, 1978)

Jungk1958: Robert Jungk, *Brighter than a Thousand Suns* (Harcourt, Brace, New York, 1958)

Kant1795: Immanuel Kant, *Perpetual Peace: A Philosophic Essay* (1795) (reprinted Garland, New York, 1977)

Karatnycky1995: Adrian Karatnycky et al., *Freedom in the World,* The Annual Survey of Political Rights and Civil Liberties 1994-1995 (Freedom House, New York, 1995)

Keeton1987: E.D. Keeton, *Briand's Locarno Policy* (Garland, New York, 1987)

Keynes1919: John Maynard Keynes, *The Economic Consequences of the Peace* (Macmillan, London, 1919)

Laszlo1986: E. Laszlo and J.Y. You (eds.), *World Encyclopedia of Peace* (Pergamon, London, 1986)

Layton1986: Christopher Layton, *One Europe, One World* (Federal Trust for Education and Research, London, 1986)

Levi1983: B.G. Levi, *The Nuclear Arsenals of the US and USSR,* Physics Today, March 1983, p.43.

Lindberg1963: Leon N. Lindberg, *The Political Dynamics of European Economic Integration* (Stanford University Press, Stanford, 1963)

Lipgens1982: Walter Lipgens, *A History of European Integration 1945-1947* (Clarendon Press, Oxford, 1982)

Luard1982: Evan Luard, *A History of the United Nations,* Vol I (Macmillan, London, 1982), Vol. II (St. Martin's Press, New York, 1989)

Mackay1969: R.W.G. Mackay, *Toward a United States of Europe* (Hutchinson, London, 1969)

Mayne1970: R. Mayne, *The Recovery of Europe, 1945-1973* (Weidenfeld & Nicolson, London, 1970)

Mendlowitz1975: S. Mendlowitz (ed.), *On the Creation of a Just World Order: Preferred Worlds for the 1990s* (Free Press, New York, 1975)

Meyer1947: Cord Meyer, Jr., *Peace or Anarchy* (Little, Brown: Boston, 1947)

Millard1969: Everett Lee Millard, *Freedom in a Federal World, 5th. edition* (Oceana, New York, 1959)

Miller1974: W.M. Miller, *The Baha'i Faith* (William Carey Library, Pasadena, 1974)

Milward1984: A.S. Milward, *The Reconstruction of Western Europe, 1945-51* (Methuen, London, 1984)

Milward1993: A.S. Milward, F.M.B. Lynch, R. Ranieri, F. Romero & V. Sørenson, *The Frontier of National Sovereignty: History and Theory 1945-1992* (Routledge, London, 1993)

Mitrany1943: David Mitrany, *A Working Peace System* (reprinted Quadrangle Books, Chicago, 1966)

Mitrany1975: David Mitrany, *The Functional Theory of Politics*

(Martin Robertson, London, 1975)

Monnet1978: Jean Monnet, *Memoirs* , transl. R. Mayne (Collins, London, 1978)

Morgenthau1973: Hans Morgenthau, *Politics among Nations, 5th. edition* (Alfred A. Knopf, New York, 1973)

McCain1989: Morriss McCain, *Understanding Arms Control* (Norton, New York, 1989)

Nathan1968: Otto Nathan and Heinz Nordern, *Einstein on Peace* (Schocken Books, New York, 1968)

NATO1980: *NATO Handbook* (NATO Information Service, Brussels, 1980)

NATO1989: *The North Atlantic Treaty Organization. Facts and Figures.* (NATO Information Service, Brussels, 1989)

Newcombe1980: Hanna Newcombe, *World Unification Plans and Analyses* (Peace Research Institute, Dundas, Ontario, 1980)

Newcombe1983: Hanna Newcombe, *Design for a Better World* (University Press of America, Lanham MD, 1983)

Newcombe1992: Hanna Newcombe (ed.), *Hopes and Fears: The Human Future* (University of Toronto, 1992)

Niebuhr1949: Rienhold Niebuhr, *Illusions of World Government,* Foreign Affairs **27,** 379 (1949), reprinted in Hartmann1952.

Northedge1986: F.S. Northedge, *The League of Nations, its Life and Times 1920-1946* (Holmes and Meier, New York, 1986)

Orwell1954: George Orwell, *Nineteen Eighty-Four* (Penguin, London, 1954)

Palme1982: *Common Security,* The Report of the Independent Commission on Disarmament and Security Issues under the Chairmanship of Olof Palme (Pan, London, 1982)

Penn1692: William Penn, *Essay Towards the Present and Future Peace of Europe* (reprinted in Cook1972)

PopeJohn1963: Pope John XXIII, *Pacem in Terris* (Vatican Press, 1963)

Reves1945: Emery Reves, *The Anatomy of Peace* (Harper, New York, 1945)

Rhodes1986: Richard Rhodes, *The Making of the Atomic Bomb* (Penguin, London, 1986)

Rhodes1995: Richard Rhodes, *Dark Sun: The Making of the Hydrogen Bomb* (Simon and Schuster, New York,1995)

Robertson1991: Pat Robertson, *The New World Order* (Word Publishing, Dallas, 1991)

Rousseau: Jean-Jacques Rousseau, *A Project of Perpetual Peace*

(reprinted Cooper1974)

Rummel1991: R.J. Rummel, *Political Systems, Violence and War,* in *Approaches to Peace: An Intellectual Map,* ed. W. Scott Thompson and K.M. Jensen (U.S. Institute of Peace, Washington, 1991)

Russett1967: Bruce M. Russett, *International Regions and the International System* (Rand McNally, Chicago, 1967)

Sagan1990: Carl Sagan and Richard Turco, *A Path Where No Man Thought* (Random House, New York, 1990)

Sakharov1968: Andrei D. Sakharov, *Progress, Coexistence and Intellectual Freedom* (André Deutsch, London, 1968)

Schell1982: Jonathan Schell, *The Fate of the Earth* (Alfred A. Knopf, New York, 1982)

Schell1984: Jonathan Schell, *The Abolition* (Alfred A. Knopf, New York, 1984)

Segall1992: Jeffrey J. Segall and Harry H. Lerner (eds.), *CAMDUN-2, The United Nations and a New World Order for Peace and Justice,* Report of the 2nd. International Conference on a More Democratic UN, Vienna 1991 (CAMDUN Project, London, 1992)

Simons1994: Geoff Simons, *The United Nations: A Chronology of Conflict* (Macmillan, London, 1994)

SIPRI1995: Stockholm International Peace Research Institute Yearbook, *World Armaments and Disarmament* (Oxford University Press, New York, 1995)

Smith1988: Peter Smith, *The Baha'i Religion* (George Ronald, Oxford, 1988)

Smuts(1918): Jan Christian Smuts, *The League of Nations: A Practical Suggestion* (Hodder & Stoughton, London, 1918)

StPierre1713: Abbé Charles Irénée Castel de Saint Pierre, *Plan for Perpetual Peace* (1713), reprinted Cooper1974.

Streit1939: Clarence K. Streit, *Union Now* (Harper & Brothers, New York, 1939)

Sully1617: Maximilien de Béthune, Duc de Sully, *The Grand Design of Henry IV* , reprinted in Cook1972.

Suter1981: Keith Suter, *A New International Order: Proposals for Making a Better World* (WAWF Australia, North Ryde, 1981)

Suter1986: Keith Suter, *Reshaping the Global Agenda: The UN at 40* (UNAA, Sydney, 1986)

Tinbergen1976: Jan Tinbergen, *Reshaping the International Order; A Report to the Club of Rome* (Dutton, New York, 1976)

Tindale1991: Stephen Tindale and David Miliband, *Beyond Economics:*

European Government after Maastricht (Fabian Society, London, 1991)

Tocqueville: Alexis de Tocqueville, *Democracy in America,* 2 vols. (Schocken Books, New York, 1964)

Toynbee1948: Arnold Toynbee, *Civilization on Trial* (Oxford University Press, New York, 1948)

Tsipis1983: Kosta Tsipis, *Arsenal: Understanding Weapons in the Nuclear Age* (Simon and Schuster, New York, 1983)

Tyson1986: J. Tyson, *World Peace and World Government* (George Ronald, Oxford, 1986)

UHJ1986: The Universal House of Justice, *The Promise of World Peace* (Baha'i Publications, Canberra, 1986)

UNDDA1988: UN Department for Disarmament Affairs, *The United Nations and Disarmament: a Short History* (United Nations, New York, 1988)

UNDPI1989: UN Department of Public Information, *Charter of the United Nations and Statute of the International Court of Justice* (United Nations, New York, 1989)

UNDPI1990: UN Department of Public Information, *The Blue Helmets: A Review of UN Peace-Keeping, 2nd. edition* (UN, New York, 1990)

UNDPI1992: UN Department of Public Information, *Basic Facts about the United Nations* (United Nations, New York, 1992)

UNDPI1995: UN Department of Public Information, *Basic Facts about the United Nations* (United Nations, New York, 1995)

Urwin1995: Derek W. Urwin, *The Community of Europe: A History of European Integration, 2nd. edition* (Longman, London, 1995)

Urquhart1990: Brian Urquhart and Erskine Childers, *A World in Need of Leadership: Tomorrow's United Nations* (Dag Hammarskjöld Foundation, Uppsala, 1990)

Urquhart1995: Brian Urquhart, *Towards a new United Nations,* in SIPRI1995, p. 13

USACDA1982: US Arms Control and Disarmament Agency, *Arms Control and Disarmament Agreements (Govt. Printing Office, Washington, 1982)*

Vandenbosch1963: A. Vandenbosch and W.N. Hogan, *Toward World Order* (McGraw-Hill, 1963)

Wagar1963: W. Warren Wagar, *Building the City of Man: Outlines of a World Civilization*

Walker1987: Barbara M. Walker (ed), *World Federalist Bicentennial Reader* (World Federalist Association, Washington, 1987)

Walker1993: Barbara M. Walker (ed), *Uniting the Peoples and Nations* (World Federalist Movement, New York, 1993)

Walters1952: F.P. Walters, *A History of the League of Nations* (Oxford University Press, London, 1952)

Wells1927: H.G. Wells, *The World Set Free* (Benn, London, 1927)

Wells1922: H.G. Wells, *The Outline of History* (George Newnes, London, 1922)

Wells1974: H.G. Wells, *The Shape of Things to Come* (Corgi, London, 1974)

Wheare1964: K.C. Wheare, *Federal Government, 4th. edition* (Galaxy, New York, 1964)

Willkie1943: Wendell L. Willkie, *One World* (Simon and Schuster, New York, 1943)

Wistrich1989: Ernest Wistrich, *After 1992: The United States of Europe* (Routledge, London, 1989)

Wittner1993: L.S. Wittner, *One World or None* (Stanford University Press, Stanford, 1993)

Wittner1984: Laurence Wittner, *Rebels Against War* (Temple University Press, Philadelphia, 1984)

Wooley1988: Wesley T. Wooley, *Alternatives to Anarchy* (Indiana University Press, Bloomington, 1988)

Woolf1916: L.S. Woolf, *International Government* (George Allen and Unwin, London, 1916)

WCPA1977: World Constitution and Parliament Association, *Constitution for the Federation of Earth* (1977)

Wright1965: Quincy Wright, *A Study of War* (University of Chicago Press, Chicago, 1965)

York1976: H.F. York, *The Advisors: Oppenheimer, Teller and the superbomb* (W.H. Freeman, San Francisco, 1976)

Zacher1993: M.W. Zacher, *International Organizations,* in J.Krieger (ed.), *The Oxford Companion to Politics in the World* (Oxford University Press, Oxford, 1993)

Zurcher1958: A.J. Zurcher, *The Struggle to Unite Europe, 1940-58* (New York University Press, Washington Square, 1958)

Current Organizations

(for a much more complete list, see Baratta1987, or Laszlo1986, or web addresses below)

Association to Unite the
  Democracies
1506 Pennsylvania Avenue SE
Washington DC 20003, USA
http://msx4.pha.jhu.edu
/aud.html

Baha'i World Center
Haifa , Israel

Campaign for UN Reform
713 D Street SE
Washington, DC 20003, USA

Planetary Citizens
PO Box 1045
Mt Shasta, CA 96067, USA

International Registry of World
  Citizens
66 Bd. Vincent Auriol
F-75013 Paris, France

Union of European Federalists,
  & The European Movement
Rue de Treves 66
B-1040 Bruxelles, Belgium

United Nations Association
  see telephone directory in
  your capital city, or
United Nations, DC1-1177
One United Nations Plaza
New York, NY 10017, USA

World Association of World
  Federalists (WAWF)
Leliegracht 21
1016 GR Amsterdam, The
Netherlands

World Constitution and
  Parliament Association
1480 Hoyt Street, Suite 31
Lakewood, CO 80215, USA

World Federalist Association
418 7th Street, SE
Washington, DC 20003, USA
wfa@igc.apc.org
http://www.getnet.com/wfa

World Federalist Movement
United Nations Office,
777 UN Plaza, 12th Floor,
New York, NY 10017, USA

Index